Cardinal Bea Buried

Cardinal Augustin Bea, president of the Vatican Secretariat for Promoting Christian Unity, was buried in his native village in Germany Nov. 22. The 87-year-old Cardinal, the Church's best known figure in the ecumenical movement, died Nov. 16. Cardinal Bea had been a priest more than 50 years before an appointment by Pope John XXIII launched his career at the head of the quest for Christian unity at the age of 79.

UNITY IN FREEDOM

Reflections on the Human Family

RELIGIOUS PERSPECTIVES

Planned and Edited by

RUTH NANDA ANSHEN

BOARD OF EDITORS

RELIGIOUS PERSPECTIVES · VOLUME ELEVEN

UNITY IN FREEDOM

Reflections on the Human Family

by

Augustin Cardinal Bea

HARPER & ROW, PUBLISHERS

NEW YORK AND EVANSTON

LIBRARY OF CONGRESS CATALOG CARD NUMBER: 64-20199

CONTENTS

v

Religious Perspectives

UNITY IN FREEDOM

Reflections on the Human Family

I

Encounters of Free Men

SPACE EXPLORATION ROUSES ALMOST UNIVER-
sal human interest. The enterprises of brave astronauts like
Major Gagarin and Major Gordon Cooper were both novel
and dangerous. There was the drama of suspense, with hope
and fear, and the ultimate relief of achievement. But in addition
to this sense of drama there was, among great multitudes of
people, an instinctive feeling that their flights into unknown
space at once brought to a focus the long labours of many of
the most intelligent men on earth and were making real for
mankind possibilities which hitherto had existed only in the
dreams of poets or the imagination of story-tellers. Hence it was
that the flights were followed not only with intense hope and
fear but also with a vague but real feeling that mankind was
meeting the challenge of the unknown and lifting its aspirations
and its powers beyond the confines of this earth. The universe
was being opened to man.

This common interest and common feeling recall the biblical
days, before the building of the tower of Babel, when "the whole
earth was of one language and of one speech" (Genesis 11 : 1);
that is to say, was as one in aspirations, purposes and intents.
But whatever may have been the mind of the author of Genesis,
space exploration is one fact among many which attracts attention to an increasing human awareness of being one single
family on this earth; an awareness, too, that the modern world
provides better means and resources than ever before to make

mankind a family in the fullest sense, that is, a family not merely in sharing the same human nature, but also in sharing the physical, intellectual and spiritual resources of the world; and, lastly, an awareness that there is a duty to make right use of these resources, so that the solidarity of the human family may not remain merely an ideal but may become effective and real.

Unhappily, a multitude of harsh yet undeniable facts bear witness to the stark difference between the ideal and the real. There is no need to speak of politico-economic estrangements with the consequent armament race. Long discussions have not yet succeeded in suspending all nuclear tests (though, thank God, there are some gleams of light in this sky). The complete banning of nuclear weapons, much more general disarmament, seems outside the range of practical possibilities. Consider the prejudices and antagonisms which spoil or ruin human relations between different races and nations, between different classes of society and between economic groupings. Even in the domain of religion, which should be sacrosanct and unifying, there are divisions, ignorance, prejudices, suspicions, resentments and aversions, the practical consequences of which are endlessly ramifying. It might be imagined that the modern wonders by which news is rapidly transmitted—newspapers, cinema, radio, television—could tend to mitigate or correct this deplorable state of affairs; but rapid dissemination of "news" may even aggravate the evil, since closer contact is made between people of differing cultures, differing standards of living and differing political, social and religious outlooks, and the closeness and vividness of the contact increase the frequency and violence of the contrasts, even the clash, between them.

Such developments, to which others could be added, afflict the hearts of everyone of good will, of everyone who loves men and mankind and leads them to ask: "Where is all this going to end? What can be done to remove ignorance, to dispel prejudice, to lessen inequalities, to assuage antagonisms? What can be done to draw men together, to foster brotherhood, to make the human family really one?" In answer, I venture to refer to the wide and warm welcome given to Pope John XXIII's Encyclical entitled *Peace on Earth*, which dealt with the fundamental requirements for peace and with the unity of the human race. This welcome showed how widespread and deep is human concern about peace, and this very fact is an encouraging sign. Twenty or thirty years ago concern about peace may have been widespread, but on the whole it was, as serious students of the political scene at national and international levels will agree, more superficial and less aware of the interconnection of the various factors involved. But the reception given to the insights of Pope John showed a very general willingness to reflect seriously on things spiritual and showed a recognition that human existence itself is in peril, and that its future can only be secured by the emergence of stronger and deeper spiritual forces. This is a sign of the greater depth of thinking achieved by men in our day and age.

Here, I shall give a preliminary outline of the problem and of some solutions : what spiritual foundations are capable of bearing the weight of a humanity really built into solidarity ? What general means and initiatives are there which can win general acceptance and so help to achieve peace and unity among men ?

THE FOUNDATIONS OF PEACE

In the modern world there are a number of factors, and of causes, which have tended and continue to tend to produce a certain unity among the inhabitants of the world : quick and easy travel, and so contacts with many people; mass communication which informs about events in every part of the world; an increasing interdependence caused by political and economic necessity; cultural and scientific developments which directly or indirectly affect all peoples. All this draws the world together into a certain conscious world community, and does so almost by force of circumstances, or almost automatically. The rush-hour in a large city illustrates a certain kind of unity, and the tension involved in it. Everyone hurries, by bus, or car, or railway (above or below ground), and in one sense is closely united with many others. But he is united with the others merely externally, for each has his own purpose and his own interests. There is close contact but no real unity.

The illustration, rough as it is, serves to show that mere external, or even physical, unity does not necessarily create a deep and authentic unity. A certain kind of unity may be induced by fear of an atomic war, with its threat to destroy all that man holds dear, and, indeed, to destroy the human race itself. But a unity induced by fear and by merely external factors rests on precarious foundations. Men are not machines which work automatically through well-oiled wheels and complicated interdependent cogs and connections. Real unity among men must be a human work. It must spring from the conscious encounter of free men.

Here is revealed, beneath all sand and clay and rubble, the solid rock which alone can bear the weight of the immense building of human unity. This bed-rock is human nature with unalterable characteristics implanted in it, man's high dignity and nobility. Man is a being endowed with intelligence and free will, who, in a genuine sense which I shall determine later, is the real, and, in a true though limited way, the autonomous master of his own destiny. This is the foundation on which the whole building must rest, and the principle to which we must reduce all the complicated problems encountered in the construction of human unity. In this light, unity is perceived as a conscious and responsible encounter of free men, and consists in the reciprocal giving and receiving not only of material goods but, above all, of spiritual possessions. This exchange is a symbol of the mutual surrender of free persons themselves such as happens both between man and woman, and in authentic friendship.

THE NEED OF RECIPROCITY

This conception affirms above all the need for unity, both because the encountering of other free persons is the fulfilment of a deep and invincible tendency in man, and because man is able to find the full development of his personality only in such meeting. Indeed, nature itself inserts man, from the moment of his birth, not only into the family and into various forms of religious and civil society, but also into the great family of nations, or rather, into the whole of mankind. And man is able to achieve his development only in such conscious encounters with other individuals and groups in society. These encounters do not signify merely receiving help, support and other things which man needs, but also—and no less fundamentally—the giving and the communicating of his possessions and his help to other men. In this reciprocal action of giving and receiving, with other persons who are as free and autonomous as himself, man enriches himself, develops his own personality, and contributes towards the complete development and full manifestation of the immense potentialities latent in himself as in humanity. What is true of individuals is true, in the broad, of groups in society, of nations and of races—all nations and races with their specific characteristics, their distinctive cultures and the varied creations they make by human intelligence. Art, music, building, agriculture, science, adaptation to environment, social and political institutions, even manners and dress—all can work together, inserting thread after thread in that magnificent variegated texture which makes up the human family, on its way towards its proper development and its proper destinies.

The conception given above of the unity of mankind indicates, moreover, the manner in which the encounter takes place, and the manner of giving and receiving. It is essential for this that it shall occur in freedom. Any unity which does not respect freedom is a unity which is unworthy of beings endowed with intelligence and freedom, of free and responsible men, but is a unity of machines or of slaves. What is this freedom? It is man's capacity and right to be himself and to decide his own destiny freely, with no compulsion on the part of others, in accordance with the dictates of his own intelligence, especially in the sphere of specifically human, and therefore free, actions; that is, man must be free to follow the guidance of what is called an upright conscience. The term "conscience" immediately excludes anarchy and establishes the existence of a whole world of moral relations and hence also of duties for man towards his neighbour. In the last analysis, man fulfils these obligations in order to follow his own conscience.

TENSION BETWEEN UNITY AND FREEDOM

Pause for a moment and reflect on these two matters, the need for human unity, that is, the encounter of man with other men, and the equal need for freedom. They touch upon two of the deepest instincts or tendencies, and of the deepest anxieties, of modern man : the impulse and effort to attain reasonable unity and the equally deep and pervasive desire for liberty. There is a polarity in these two concepts that makes for a constant tension between them. In a certain sense, a large part of the problems of mankind today can be reduced to the difficulty of harmonizing in practice these tendencies towards unity and towards freedom, without harming the one or sacrificing the other. From this then springs the problem, whether there is a principle which can guide man's conduct in such a manner as to guarantee both the unity of man with other men, and the freedom of every person. The answer to this question must be found in man's own nature; and the principle we are seeking is none other than the rule which is written in man's heart, prompting him to do what is good and to avoid what is evil. Each of us, in fact, experiences daily that inner tension pithily summed up by the ancient poet, Ovid : "video meliora proboque, deteriora sequor"—"I see the better and approve it, yet often I follow the worse". This is a confession of awareness that some things, from the specifically human point of view of the conscience, are good, and other things evil; and that the obligation lies upon us to opt for the good things and to perform them, and, on the other hand, to avoid what is evil. Any freedom that does not conform to this law is no true freedom; it undermines unity, creates anarchy and leads to mutual destruction. On the other hand, a unity that does not respect the principle of freedom may eventually create a certain form of unity, but not a human one; it is not a unity of free and responsible men, but of slaves.

Need I stress the fact that every man has a conscience and that every man must follow it? A man's conscience may be misguided, but he still must follow it. A man can muffle up his conscience, and in various odd ways distort or almost silence it; to the extent that he does so, he is the less a man, and it may be doubted whether a man can ever succeed in extirpating all conscience, for the most degraded of men still generally retain some remnants of decency and say there are some things which they would not do. Many men may rebel against the moral standards conventional in the society in which they live; yet they generally do so claiming the sanction of a more enlightened conscience. As long as men are men, they will praise or blame one another, which is an implicit acknowledgement of freedom and of conscience. If it is really proved that someone has absolutely no conscience, he is regarded as deranged, not subject to law and as unfit to live in human society.

THE TRINITY OF TRUTH, JUSTICE AND CHARITY

Are there more detailed applications which may be deduced from this general principle of the supremacy of conscience in freedom? Pope John XXIII once said that in his own life, he always tried to pay most attention to what tends to unite men, and to go along with every man as far as possible without betraying the demands of justice and truth. In other circumstances, especially in his *Encyclical* on Peace, the same Pope John added charity to the truth and justice which he could not betray, thus creating the trinity of truth, justice and charity. These are directives which derive from man's noble human nature itself, as endowed with intelligence and with freedom; and as such they are to be explained in the light of this their origin.

Truth is the correlative of the almost divine gift of intelligence. It affirms man's capacity, and obligation, to adapt himself, primarily in his awareness, consciousness and judgements, to the reality of things, and this especially regarding his relations with other people. This means a diligent and conscious search for the truth, which is of vital importance not merely for the intellect but for the whole man. It is the man, and not any sole faculty of man, who possesses the truth. But it is not only abstract truth for which man must seek, but truth as the basis for specifically human, and therefore free, decisions. This involves, in particular, the truth regarding a man's personal integrity and regarding his obligations to others, so that he may form his conscience honestly and justly, and make his decisions in honesty and justice. Further, what I say about truth includes what may be called the practice of truth, that is, following the known truth and being guided by it in one's actions.

Search for truth and the following of it can contribute greatly towards unity among men. They lead to eradication of the prejudices and suspicions which eat like cancer at the union of free persons; they foster the exchange of those precious possessions, ideas and knowledge; they encourage that serene yet vigorous emulation in the search for deeper insights and wider outlooks which is characteristic of lofty minds; and they bring to simple people a certain equity of judgement akin to wisdom. All these are things which unite, just as love of high ideals unites, and in a most splendid way. To love and follow the truth is the first requirement in overcoming hostilities and in achieving the real unity of the human family.

Justice renders everyone his due. It is both a personal virtue and a social virtue, for societies have their rights no less than individuals. The rights of men are at once the expression of freedom and autonomy and the safeguard of these precious prerogatives.

The sphere of justice is wide, for it touches human relationships at almost every point. To be convinced of this, read the famous Universal Declaration of Human Rights, approved by the General Assembly of the United Nations on December 10, 1948.[1] Pope John XXIII, in his *Encyclical* on Peace, like-

---

[1] Cf. Appendix I, pp. 233-238.

wise shows the wide range and the supreme importance of justice, and I shall be quoting him in chapter 4.

Yet, even where the law of truth and the law of justice are respected, the encounters between persons endowed with intelligence and freedom would be lacking in their most noble, delicate and profound aspect, if there were no *charity*. Mankind has instinctively recognized that in human relationships truth and justice are not enough. Though cynics and misanthropes may scoff, the witness of humanity stands firm : "man is naturally a friend to man". "Do to others as you would be done by" has been accepted by the sages and wise men of all peoples, and is enshrined in the heart of humanity. "Despise not your own flesh" is the condemnation of cruelty and of hardheartedness towards the afflictions of others. Hard conditions of life may induce selfishness and self-seeking and may blind men to the sufferings and needs of their fellow-men. Perverted philosophies may elevate self-seeking into a virtue. Yet the truth stands : pity, mercy, forgiveness, benevolence, kindness are universally recognized as virtues becoming man as man, becoming the strong especially, and "compassion" and "common human charity" are acknowledged as at once a need and a demand falling upon all men.

MUTUAL PERSONAL SURRENDER

The word "charity" has sometimes been misunderstood, as if it meant a dole of some kind administered by superior affluence to inferior indigence. This is a woeful misconception. Charity is a mutual surrender of free persons, such as occurs in all genuine love; and this over and above the mutual surrendering of material goods, or even ideas, and over and above due respect. It is thus important to note that it is not enough to have some exchange of goods, if this is not accompanied by the giving of oneself to one's neighbour. The goods given derive their special value from their being the symbol of a giving of the person. *Vice versa*, the mere affective giving of the person can hardly be authentic if it is not accompanied by the giving of whatever one has or is able to give or do for one's neighbour. There is a reciprocal influence in both these factors: the inner giving of the person, as it is the source and the reason for the giving of goods, is itself reinforced by brotherly help and by exchange of that which one has or can do.

Charity gives a motive both for the search for truth and for the fulfilment of justice; it is a corrective to the bloodlessness of intellectualism and the harshness of legalism. There must be truth and there must be justice, but there must, also, be forgiveness and human compassion for human frailty. Charity is the best guarantee of justice, and enables justice to be fulfilled in a wider spirit, as it springs not only from respect for the freedom of others and for their rights, but also by kindly concern for them as persons.

But let me insist upon the reciprocal influence of the affective giving of oneself and of the mutual exchange of possessions. This has important practical consequences. The giving to others of possessions helps the inner giving of oneself, and as this is known to others, a certain mutuality is encouraged. On the other hand, where exchange, or the giving of possessions is not possible, a certain charity in the sense of an inner giving and an inner good will is still possible, and thus one may have genuine charity towards the whole of mankind, and this, too, when known, as it can come to be known, is a mutual encouragement.

THE FULL DIMENSION OF HUMAN LIFE

Is there still more to be said about the spiritual foundations on which human unity depends? There is, indeed. Man's relations with other free beings are not limited to this earthly world of ours. When man retains and develops his spontaneous reflections about the full dimension of human life, unimpeded by distortions allegedly philosophic or "scientific", then he has an almost instinctive sense and awareness that his personal relations reach beyond and above merely human society. Progress in the sciences of anthropology and ethnology has strengthened the evidence that the whole known history of mankind bears witness to a very widespread and deep-rooted belief among all peoples that man's personal relations reach beyond and above the level of merely human society. In spite of degraded customs, superstitious practices and perverted notions, belief in "the High God", the one true God, has persisted.

There are, of course, agnostics, atheists, dialectical materialists. Is it not possible that in rejecting "God" they are rejecting in fact a false concept or image of God and not God himself? In their acknowledgement of absolute moral obligations, is there not contained, perhaps unrealized, a true reference to the God who is Justice unqualified? In the primacy of the ideal of love and service of humanity, in heart-felt concern for the underprivileged and the wretched, is it not possible to find some confused idea of the universal and transcendent Good, which is God? Certainly what Tertullian said in the third century remains undeniable : " 'Good God', 'Great God' and 'May God grant it' are expressions used by all. That he is also a judge is attested by the words, 'God sees', 'I commend to God', 'God make it up to me', and 'God will judge between you and me'." Since the far-off days of Tertullian, countless multitudes of men have used similar language. If God does not exist, it is strange indeed that belief in him is so widespread, so deep-rooted and so effective in its influence upon the lives of men.

In acknowledging God as the one to whom he owes his existence, man perceives that God must be supremely intelligent and supremely free. Hence it is that man has come to regard himself as in some way made like to God in intelligence and freedom. And as he thinks this of himself, so too he thinks the same of other men, who likewise are made in the likeness and image of God's primordial intelligence and freedom. Consequently, in view of the fact that both he himself and all other men owe their existence and life to the Supreme Being, he comes to regard this Being as in some way his own Father and the Father of the great human family. "We are indeed his offspring" wrote the

Greek poet Aratus, who lived about 270 B.C., whom Paul quoted to the Athenians.[1]

If all men are the offspring, or children, of a common Father, then there is another reason why all men can and should feel that they are brothers, members of a single human family. Their special endowment of intelligence and freedom comes to them not from a series of accidental causes, but as a personal communication of his own nature by the supreme Intelligence and Freedom, which is God.

TRUST IN GOD'S HELP

Between God and man can there be that reciprocal exchange of giving and receiving, similar to that which exists between himself and other men? Certainly man, in believing in God, believes also in God's fatherly care of himself and the whole human family. Therefore, on solemn occasions, in times of crisis, affliction and danger, man has recourse to this Being, and trusts in the help of this all-powerful guide of human events and of man's destiny. Can man, however, give anything to God? Can there be a real exchange, such as true friendship and love require? God indeed needs nothing of man's, for all man has is God's gift. And yet man can give to God: "what does the Lord require of you but to do justice, and to love kindness (or mercy), and to walk humbly before thy God" (Micheas 6 :8). Christ said "as you did it to the least of these my brethren, you did it to me", thus showing that service to our fellow-men is service to God himself. Love of God and love of the neighbour cannot be separated.

Inherent in belief in God is belief that the supreme Being is an ever-present witness to man's actions, approving the good, condemning the bad; and this belief can be a powerful curb upon arrogance, tyranny and the exploitation of the weak, and can be an even more powerful spur to justice, mercy and

---

[1] Cf. *Phaenomena*, quoted in Eusebius, *Praeparatio Evangelica*, XIII, 26-27, P.G. 21, 1101. The same was also said by Cleanthes, *Hymn to Zeus*, ed. J. von Arnim, *Stoicorum Veterum Fragmenta*, I, (1938), Frag. 537.

unselfish love. Man, made in the image of God, can rise in thought above the limitations of space and of time, and thus his destiny cannot be limited to the merely terrestrial, fleeting and transitory. Injustice and cruelty may escape retribution for a time, but they cannot for ever prevail against the order which God's justice, wisdom and goodness has established; and, likewise, patient endurance in self-sacrificing goodness, forgiveness, unrequited devotion to justice and charity, these, too, rise above time and space and find their culmination in union with the God of truth, justice and love. Man's freedom, given by God, makes him, under God, the arbiter of his eternal destiny, for wretchedness or for happiness.

Seen in this light, both the general law written in man's heart, to do good and not to do evil, and the more detailed rules of truth, of justice and of charity, appear not as abstract laws which are somehow almost hanging in the air, but as unshakably founded on the rock of the fatherly and just authority of the supreme personal Being, the Lord our God.

But God is not merely the supreme Authority for man, the guarantor and the vindicator of the order which governs the creation of free unity among men. Primarily, he is the builder of this unity, a loving Father of the human family all of whom are made in his image and owe their existence to him, and owe to him their life, their development, and their attainment of the final purpose of their existence. All men, as individuals, as communities and as one whole family, depend upon the goodness of God. And so, if man invokes God in times of crisis and of danger, there is surely reason why man should turn to God when he realizes the multiple, complex and powerful forces that threaten the well-being and even the very survival of the human race, and when he lifts his thoughts and hopes toward the overcoming of these forces in the great vision of a mankind united in freedom. During his space flight, while he was thrusting into the unknown with his life dependent upon such delicate calculations and instrumentalities, Major Gordon Cooper composed a prayer, in which he placed ultimate hope, for himself and for his enterprise, in God.[1] This prayer made a deep impression when read to the United States Congress. In this enterprise of achieving the effective unity of the whole human race, in which so much is dependent upon psychological influences and ideological fixations unknown or incalculable, men must place their ultimate hope in God, and with unshakable faith see in him alone the absolute guarantee that the great enterprise will ultimately succeed, in spite of all the attacks of evil in men and in the world, in spite of all inertia, resistance and machinations of the powers of darkness and unreason.

WHAT OF THIS IN PRACTICE?

In a sense, the rest of this work is an attempt to give some answer to this question. But the problems involved—psychological, social, economic, national and international, with reference not only to the whole world, literally, "from China to Peru" but even to outer space—ultimately depend upon the spiritual, or, as perhaps some would prefer to say, upon the ideological attitudes of men, and consequently it is not possible to lay down an exact blue-print applicable in detail to each situation everywhere. Yet the overall lines are sharply defined : truth, justice and charity. As regards truth, after some general considerations about the connection between truth and charity (ch. 2), certain reflections will follow about modern media of communication (ch. 3). Next, some consideration is given to the multiple and complex questions of justice as regards the rights of individuals and of various forms of society, including also a vision of the world authority which is yet to be established. These are drawn mainly from Pope John XXIII's statements about peace (ch. 4). Then follow chapters on the relevance, to general human problems, of the spirit, vision and efforts of Christians who seek unity among themselves as a preparation or even means to a wider human unity. At the end come some reflections upon the connection between the unity

[1] Cf. Appendix II, p. 239.

of men as men and the unity of Christians among themselves and upon the hopes of a convergence of the two.

In practice, there are numerous organizations and agencies working, each in its way, toward human unity: the United Nations and its subsidiary agencies; the activities of various governments in giving aid in money and men where it is needed; a variety of Institutes and Foundations directly or indirectly concerned with inter-group relations; Universities and Institutes of learning, many of which have special departments or courses about international affairs, and many of which interchange Professors; world Conferences of various professions, lawyers, doctors, scientists and even the police; commerce and industry, with rapid travel, plays its part in world relations. I merely refer to these in passing, and add that there is still room for greater support of all that is good and wise in them, and still room for further initiatives. Charity, as they say, is ingenious and inventive and can still find new ways of encounter, collaboration and mutual assistance, having regard to concrete situations, circumstances and possibilities.

Rarely, if ever, in history has the anxiety for peaceful co-existence been so strong, so deep and so universally felt by mankind as it is today. This is, perhaps, because mankind has never before felt so grievous a threat to its very existence. Faced with the terrible weapons of destruction which man has invented and produced, and locked in the fatal vice-like grip of the arms race, the mass of men feel helpless and almost driven to give up effort in despair, and the wisest of leaders are not immune from bewilderment and doubt, oppressed by the weight of their responsibility. And yet from very desperation comes hope. The armaments race and the threat of atomic bombs, deplorable as they are in themselves, at once increase the general yearning for peace, provoke a spiritual turmoil, and lead to deeper realization of the bonds which ultimately link all men, and of the urgent need to build the unity in freedom of the human family in truth, justice and charity. Moreover, if means of destruction are unparalleled in human history, so too are there unparalleled means of constructive influence, in spite of the mountainous obstacles. There is no reason for dismay or dis-couragement : look at the good in men, at the ever-growing forces for good, at the ever-greater number of men of good will, who love man and mankind. Above all, look to the Originator and Prime Builder of this unity, God on high, the loving and provident Father of all men, who made men in his image and likeness.

2

The Love of Truth and Charity

TAKING AS HIS TEXT THE FAMOUS DICTUM OF the Latin poet: *"trahit sua quemque voluptas"*—"Everyone has his own dear delight which draws him on", St Augustine remarks with his usual insight and clarity: "If our senses can afford us so much delight, the spirit, too, must have its delight". Surely he who had sought for the truth in all the haunts of men in Africa and Italy, knew—none better—what the desire for truth can mean. Yet so often even diligent quest for truth has only entangled men in doubts or falsehood, in spite of their sincere and deeply felt yearning for truth.

I was once told a tale about a craftsman or small shopkeeper who in the course of a conversation with a priest remarked: "You see, Father, to me philosophy seems like the pathology of thought". Of course this was far from just; but it must be confessed that sometimes the reading of philosophy leaves a similar tragic impression. Is it then so surprising that, in the course of history and even in our own day, zeal for the truth and the quest for truth have often led to disagreements, disputes, conflicts, and even to war between brother-Christians?

Too many men regard the truth as identical with their own ideas or with ideas similar to their own. They over-emphasize their differences with others, making no attempt, as they should do, to see things from other people's point of view. Thus ill-feeling arises. Yet truth is many-sided, having a thousand facets of which one given person, however talented and intelligent,

17

can see only a few. This, unhappily, is too often forgotten.

Nevertheless we ought not to follow the example of that judge in olden times of whom it is related that, when called upon to pronounce sentence in court, he first declared in favour of one party to the dispute and then went on to declare in favour of the other. Thereupon his small son, who was playing at his feet, very sensibly objected : "But, father, they can't both be right !" —to which the judge calmly rejoined : "How right *you* are, too !"

No, we cannot be as comprehensive as that. Yet it is compatible with a sincere and earnest love of truth to admit that our knowledge has limits and to recognize, even while firmly upholding an undoubted truth, that certain facets of it, unseen by us, may be visible to others.

Nor is there need to fall into the snare of giving so much consideration to the views of others as to reduce everything to a mere matter of opinion; or crudely to assert, as some people do, that all statements are equally true and equally false.

It is of vital importance to hold firmly that we can attain certain truths, even though not the full truth. The world today is a veritable welter of conflicting ideas, a world in which even a balanced firmness in the assertion of any truth, whether purely human or religious, is often taken as intransigent fanaticism and is abhorred as such. And still modern man in his heart longs for certainty, for assured and conclusive knowledge, however limited.

An authentic love of the truth compels us to recognize it wherever we find it, whatever its source may be. We must be ready to heed the voice of truth in whatever circumstances.

Misunderstandings and differences are often explicable by the difficulty in expressing the exact truth in human language. The gift of speech is undoubtedly a splendid gift from the Creator, enabling us to open our minds to others, to convey to them spiritual truths, all kinds of knowledge and the assurance of our affection. Yet speech is imperfect as a medium, vague and imprecise, limited in its scope. It gives rise to countless misunderstandings, even in the sacred domain of religious faith.

TRUTH AND ITS EXPRESSION

Everyone knows that the Catholic Church is conservative in regard to the traditional formulae in which her traditional doctrines are enshrined. Yet Pope John XXIII, on the occasion of the solemn opening of the Ecumenical Council, declared that the truths of which the Church is guardian must be proclaimed to the world of today in new language, that is, in the language of modern man which alone he regards as meaningful.

"An idea," Pope John went on to explain, "is one thing, its concrete expression in words is another. Pure doctrine can be faithfully preserved even though couched in phraseology adapted to modern modes of thought and ways of expression."[1]

One aberration, indicative of a false idea of what the love of truth requires, was exemplified by the tragic wars of religion. In the name of truth, an attempt was made to impose certain religious views by force on other men, in complete disregard of an equally fundamental aspect of the love of truth, namely, man's freedom. This freedom means that man has the right to decide freely how to direct his life in accordance with the dictates of his own conscience.

Each man has both the duty and the right to follow his conscience. It therefore follows that both individuals and society must respect this liberty of personal decision. Moral anarchy is, of course, to be excluded; for it must be assumed that every man has moral obligations implanted in his very nature as a rational being. Included in these moral obligations are the duties of man to his fellow-men; and, in the ultimate analysis, man fulfils these obligations by obeying his own conscience. What I say here about freedom of conscience is not merely my own personal conviction but also the age-long teaching of the Church. And this although it is true that in some places certain members of the Church have not respected the right to freedom

[1] Est enim aliud ipsum depositum Fidei, seu veritates quae veneranda doctrina nostra continentur, aliud modus, quo eaedem enuntiantur, eodem tamen sensu eademque sententia.

of conscience. This aberration, however, was not confined to ecclesiastics, as history bears witness.

ERROR HAS NO RIGHTS?

But what if a man's conscience is wrong and erroneous? Some would say, in such a case, that error has no rights. But the answer to them is cogent: error is an abstract concept and so it is meaningless to talk of it as having or not having "rights". It is a man who has rights, and he maintains just possession of them even when he is in error, the more especially when he errs in good faith. It is true, of course, that if a man led by an erroneous conscience should attack the rights of others or of society, those whom he attacks have the right to defend themselves. They have not, however, any right to attempt to correct the erroneous consciences of others by force or violence.

Latent in what I have just said are problems at once practical, complex and delicate. Pope John XXIII said plainly: "Every human being has the right to honour God according to the dictates of an upright conscience, and the right to profess his religion privately and publicly."[1] The right publicly to profess a religion has sometimes been the subject of dispute, as has the right of religious associations to legal incorporation in order to hold property. But greater difficulties have arisen about the right to persuade others of the truth of a faith and to draw them to accept it.

In certain countries concern for the religion, whether Christian or non-Christian, which has been traditional, has been intermingled with concern for national unity, for cultural heritage and for due order, especially where the mass of the population is less highly educated. This concern has led civil governments to take measures restricting the right to persuade others to change their faith, or the right of citizens to depart from the national religion. In some cases these measures have been an unjust invasion of liberty. On the other hand some

[1] *Pacem in Terris*, n. 14.

"missionaries" have tried to spread their faith by offensive means, without due regard and respect for the traditions and conditions of the countries to which they go. The World Council of Churches, after nearly ten years of investigation and study, published a document entitled *Christian Witness, Proselytism and Religious Liberty*, which competent Catholic scholars find, with one or two possible modifications, fully acceptable. This document, however, wisely said that "specific rules cannot be prescribed for all national and local situations".[1]

Is there any means of avoiding all the aberrations into which men fall through mistaken love of truth? Is there any general answer which can be applied to all the problems involved in reconciling zeal for the truth with respect for liberty, in reconciling unity with conflicting claims to the truth? The answer is immediate and final : "True charity towards our fellow-men".

FRIENDSHIP AND TRUTH

Take, for example, a mother's love or the love of a true friend. This love teaches them to put themselves in another's place, to be aware of another's point of view, to enter into his mind, to grasp what is reasonable in his way of thinking, to see others as he sees them, to make themselves understood by him. A true friend regards his friend and his friend's opinions with indulgence and respect. And why? Simply because of the love he bears him. Because in the words of St Paul, "Charity is long-suffering, is kind. . . . It rejoices in the truth, forgives all, believes all, hopes all things, endures all things. . .". (1 Cor. 13 : 4-7). Indeed these words by the great Apostle give a true picture of all authentic human love. Here again, however, a word of warning is required, so as to avoid pitfalls and aberrations similar to those already mentioned. How often, for example, does a mother's love become over-indulgent, blind to the danger of weakly granting the loved one's every request and compassing thereby his ruin ! And all because in her infatuation

---

[1] Cf. Appendix III, where the document is printed in full, p. 241.

she ignores the voice of reason and of common-sense; charity is here not combined with real love of truth. The example may sound unduly simple; but it can be applied to many cases and situations. It can apply to love of country, to love of unessential religious traditions, to love of accustomed ways and of the many non-doctrinal factors with which a cherished religion is associated.

Love of truth, love of people, that is, of our neighbour—both are essential and must be harmoniously combined each in its right proportions. How much this double love can do to draw men together and to bring about an increase of harmony in their relations with one another!

When men are united both by a love of truth and quest for it and by a true spirit of mutual goodwill the deepest needs of their inmost nature are satisfied. What more perfect union between two human beings is possible than when one spirit kindles or is kindled by the other, when one heart is drawn towards another by true affection and feels that affection returned?

The whole difficulty in such relationships is that of harmonizing the two tendencies, putting each in its proper place and according to each its right priority, without either gaining at the other's expense.

Indeed the love of truth divorced from charity can degenerate into intolerance and become repellent, while charity without truth lacks insight and cannot last. A distinguished Protestant writer, theorizing on the Christian doctrine of original sin, that is, of the disorder in man's nature resulting from his origin, sees one of the disastrous consequences of the Fall in man's capacity of disassociating truth from charity.

Man is not born with perfect balance between reason and desire; his psychological co-ordination is imperfect; various urges, some perhaps unconscious, press upon him, disturb his judgement and even impair his capacity to perceive the truth and to desire the real good. Against this tragic disorder inherent in his very nature, man must contend wisely and perseveringly. In order to do this effectively a man must ask himself this question: "Where am I to look for help, enlightenment and strength sufficient to enable me to fight life's battle with success?"

Every religion which recognizes the power of prayer advises man to turn to his divine Creator not only in his material needs but above all in the deeper and more essential needs of his soul. He should pray for the intelligence and wisdom that will enable him to lead his life wisely. In his prayers to his Creator man should seek that harmony which is so difficult to achieve, a harmony between truth and charity.

In his radio message of December 23rd, 1962, Pope John XXIII said that of all the blessings of this life, the most important and the most precious, alike for individuals, families and peoples, far and away the most important and the most precious is Peace. The echoes of this statement in the world press, of whatever creed and political colour, proved that the Pope expressed the most deeply seated desire of mankind today, a mankind haunted by the possibility of renewed strife and longing with all its soul for peace.

Today we have come to realize that peace does not depend only—one might almost say principally—on national leaders, but on the individual members of the population of the world.

Thus the most urgent task that lies before mankind is to ensure peace by means of love, by practising the love of truth in charity.

3

"Mass Media" of Communication

SAVING HUMAN PERSONALITY

IN MARCH THIS YEAR I WAS PRESENT AT A symposium held in Assisi for university professors. The subject was "The Great Discoveries of Modern Times at the Service of the Moral Progress of Humanity". About four hundred professors took part and the session at which I was present was addressed by Professor Ugo Papi, the President of the University of Rome, which numbers some fifty thousand students. Professor Papi, who is a well-known expert in economics, announced his intention of limiting himself in his address to certain salient matters affecting our modern civilization and culture. He first drew attention to a generally admitted fact, namely, that the modern world is assisting at the passing of one civilization, that of the élite, and at the birth and growth of another, that of the mass of the people. Professor Papi went on to outline what he considered to be the most important tasks devolving from this most significant change in human affairs. Amongst these he of course included the necessity of providing the minimum of subsistence for hundreds of millions of human beings in order to save them from starvation. But alongside this problem and on a level with it, he placed what he called the need for "saving the human personality". Mechanization, mass production, automation, efficiency methods, the "processing" even of food, the dealing with men in groups and not as individuals—all this makes for regimentation, organized uniformity and a generally standardized existence. Relations between groups and between individuals are affected by this and mankind is being depersonalized and dehumanized. "Organizational man" is a sign of the new age.

I confess that I was impressed by the fact that these strictures were not pronounced by a theologian or a philosopher, an artist or a classicist, but by an economic expert, which adds weight to his testimony. Amongst the numerous dangers noted by Professor Papi we shall here deal only with those which spring from such popular media of information and entertainment as the Press, the cinema, the radio and television. The reason why we choose to deal particularly with these is primarily because they possess such immense potentialities for helping or hindering the cause of unity in the human family. Moreover the very character of these mass media illustrates dramatically the paradoxical dilemma in which modern man finds himself. On the one hand these media provide him with undreamt-of opportunities for spreading civilization and culture on a worldwide scale and admitting millions to privileges which for centuries were reserved to an élite. On the other hand, as is only too well-known, these media may be used for ends which are debasing to mankind. This is true not only because entertainment is not seldom provided which appeals mainly to men's lower instincts. It is true also because, in their present form, these media appeal mainly to the senses—eyes, ears, imagination, emotion—and viewers and listeners tend to a certain passivity, and to an almost unconscious acceptance of the attitudes, outlooks and emotional reactions presented to them in such vivid ways. Mere repetition also has its effect. These media undoubtedly can lessen independence of mind and the making of conscious, personal and responsible decisions.

The influence exerted through these mass media is immense, and the responsibility of those who direct them is heavy. This influence certainly has great importance as regards the unity in freedom of the human family. It has huge potentialities for spreading real education, culture and, in the right sense, civilization among the broadest strata of mankind. In fact, however, these mass media are all too often handled and operated in an undesirable manner. Instead of spreading genuine culture, or of contributing to man's spiritual progress and to the production of truly cultured men, they too often succeed in creating in hearers and viewers a herd-mentality; and in producing a crowd of unformed nonentities who follow, if not their lower instincts, at least a sort of blind mass compulsion.

This subject is of great interest, by reason of its relationship to the theme of this book : that is, the sharing among men, in accordance with the needs of each, of those gifts, especially spiritual gifts, which individuals and communities possess (cf. Chapter 1). This involves mutuality and reciprocity, each giving to his neighbour and to society whatever he has to give, and receiving from them what they can give in return, especially in the realm of the mind and the spirit. Thus everybody contributes his share towards the quest for truth, towards the creation of unity, always, however, respecting the freedom and dignity of his neighbour.

THE POTENTIALITIES OF MODERN MASS MEDIA

In the limited space of one chapter it is of course impossible to deal adequately with the almost incredible development of mass media during the last few decades. I shall, therefore, give some statistics illustrating this development; and after that some reflections on the important role these media can play in the sharing of mental, artistic, and spiritual possessions, and so in bringing men closer together and helping towards real unity in the human family.

The following figures speak for themselves. The world is informed, influenced, importuned and almost besieged every day by 8,000 newspapers, three hundred million copies of which are printed daily; to this we must add 22,000 other periodicals, with 200 million copies printed monthly or weekly. To meet the needs of 170,000 cinemas, which attract 17,000 billion spectators annually (who spend a total of at least 35,000 billion hours watching them), 2,500 new films are produced each year. There are also 6,000 radio broadcasting stations in operation

which transmit to 400 million receivers. There are 1,000 tele-
vising stations, transmitting to a good 120 million subscribers
who spend 200,000 billion hours *per annum* before their sets.
To these may be added the hundreds of millions of gramophone
records manufactured yearly. Even as long as five years ago,
60 million had been sold of Bing Crosby's alone.

These media of information bring men into mental relation
with one another. They produce a continuous flow of news,
and they communicate ideas, opinions, suggestions, experiences
and emotions. A few decades ago, news was spread slowly and
with difficulty. Today news reaches every part of the world
simultaneously. Even the most remote parts of Asia and Africa
receive the news at the same time as the great world-capitals
which at one time had so great an advantage over other parts
of the world in this respect. Nowadays whoever has a cheap
radio set of his own or, even without that, has opportunity to
listen to the radio in the village inn or some public place, is
abreast with the news: in this respect Eskimos amid the snow
and ice, Africans in huts amid the jungle, Bedouin tent-dwellers,
all receive the latest news as soon as the well-to-do citizens of the
great American and European capitals.

These channels of information do not merely convey news
in an abstract way. They often reproduce actual experiences in
a manner which appeals directly to the senses, imagination and
feelings. They lead the audience to share the experience presented to them, almost as if they themselves were actual parti-
cipants, and even in giving news, the colour and tone can be
subtly "slanted" so as to try to arouse passionate support or
indignant repudiation of certain actions or policies.

This wholesale communication of ideas and experiences to a
larger and larger number of people, almost, one might say, to
the totality of mankind, tends to weld the human race into one
family within which a continuous exchange of news is contin-
uously in process. Thus experiences, sad and joyful, aspirations,
resolutions, are communicated to and shared in by all alike.

Another result of this continuous exchange of information
can be seen in the modification, adaptation and progressive

similarity in modes of speech, of fashion and taste in clothing and in amusements. This undoubtedly breaks down barriers whether cultural, political, or what you please, which have hitherto appeared to be insurmountable. This means that ideas, opinions, convictions, cultural, political, moral and religious, which have for ages been regarded as closed to discussion and immune, owing to habit and tradition, from all change, are now being called into question, subjected to criticism and re-examined more or less thoroughly in the press, on the radio or on television. This shake-up of ideas occurs all the more readily because the views which these media convey are often an interpretation of life and of outlooks towards life's problems and life's meaning, and are conveyed with a certain emotive emphasis which solicits and attracts sympathy and support.

THE BRIGHTER SIDE

All this has its good side and its bad. On the good side : through these media of communication—newspapers, cinema, radio, and television, and recordings—true information is widely conveyed; not seldom noble emotions are aroused; the miseries and calamities of others can be brought home to people; wise men have a wider forum; and the unifying influence of these mass media need not depersonalize and can tend towards a world community with common ideas and aspiration, yet not reduced to uniformity. Reasonable amusement and entertainment can alleviate the stresses and strains of modern life; and can do what Aristotle said of theatrical tragedies, rouse vicarious pity and fear and thus relieve tension and even purify the spirit. These media can be powerful agencies of real education. They can teach better methods of hygienic living and of agriculture. They can be used to teach languages, geography, sciences, philosophy and religion, and their efficacy in these respects has not yet been fully exploited. Certain films on religious themes have been noteworthy and inspiring; and television has brought religious ceremonies, such as the opening of the Second Vatican Council, into the homes and to the attention of vast multitudes.

Sermons, religious instruction and discussions on religion find
their place in many studios. Presentation of themes in all these
media gives scope for true artistic genius which has in fact produced much that is wholesome, unpretentiously uplifting and
in its own medium comparable to the work of the great artists
in sculpture, painting and music.

Thus these "mass media" of communication can have, and
to some extent have had results which it is a pleasure to applaud.

Finally, like a free press, the other media can be powerful pro-
tections of freedom against tyranny and corruption. In all these
ways they can diffuse love of truth, justice and charity, and thus
greatly contribute to a true cultural and human unity.

THE DARKER SIDE

First of all it must be realized that these media of communication have come to stay. They cannot be suppressed, even if
one wanted to; and if there is danger in them, danger is never
a reason for refusing the use of means which can be of real and
immense service in the cause of good. Next, there is considerable
difference in the media themselves. Newspapers and sound radio
are, in general, more used to give information and to instruct
than to interest and amuse, though this they also do. The
cinema, television and recordings, again speaking generally, are
more used for distraction and entertainment than for information and instruction, though these latter are by no means
excluded and are, in many regions, playing a more significant
role, especially in television. Thirdly, I am very well aware, and
should like my readers to bear this in mind, that conditions in
different countries differ very greatly. In some countries—it
must be said frankly—these media of communication are con-
trolled by the civil government and are used for indoctrination
to such an extent that wave-lengths from outside countries are
"jammed". Control of the means of information is a ready tool
in the hands of tyrants. In some regions of the world radio
is used as a means of propaganda which crosses national borders
and becomes a weapon in ideological or semi-political warfare,

used sometimes most unscrupulously. I forbear to give examples. In some countries there is a certain governmental control, direct or indirect, which may perhaps be justified in order to exclude excessive commercialization, and to try to maintain reasonable standards of objectivity and good taste. This does not necessarily involve denial of due liberty, though the danger in such control is subtle yet real, like the danger in any censorship. In still other countries, the whole matter is left to the initiative of individuals, or of groups, the guiding principle resting on the assumption that competition will in the long run weed out the inadequate, the inefficient and the wrong-headed. This, too, has its dangers, for it tends to gear the programmes to the lowest common denominator of recipients and to be too dependent on advertising.

On these matters I agree that nothing is perfect. I call attention, however, to dangers common to all these media, not with any puritanical or restrictive aim, but because of the importance of the matter and because the dangers may not be fully realized. I speak with no special country or region in mind, and ask readers to appreciate that what I say has its application not merely to countries and regions where the standard of education, culture and of living is in general high, but also to countries and regions which are comparatively underdeveloped, where illiteracy is common, living standards low and rapid social change is in process.

It is scarcely necessary to refer to presentations which are salacious, or horrifying, or which glorify violence or wrong-doing. The danger here is plain and obvious and consists in a threat to the self-control and the personal integrity of readers, hearers, or viewers. The exploitation of sex is nothing less than a crime against mankind, for it corrupts youth, attacks fidelity in marriage and reduces what should be sacrosanct and noble to something base and sordid.

Akin to this evil, though perhaps not so dangerous, is representation of a life in wealth and luxury as if such ought to be the possession of everybody, or, at least, as if it were the normal reward of "success". Thus a false standard of values is set up, and by omission there is an implicit depreciation of the worth of simple, hard-working and humble people. This danger, though often mitigated by the fairy-like quality of some presentations which are a kind of enacted Hans Andersen in pictures, is nevertheless real. Mass media, conjoined to advertising, can stimulate wants which it is not possible to supply, and can thus lead to unreasonable dissatisfaction with the actual conditions of life, to restlessness and a feeling of rebellion against the inevitable frustrations of life. This danger is greater when luxurious surroundings, habits and possessions of people in a wealthier civilization are vividly portrayed to people of a poorer.

The danger, too, is obvious of news being presented in a tendentious form, under an appearance of impartiality; so, too, is the danger of vulgarity and of that lack of reticence which pries into private life and exploits matters, like grief, which ought not to be subject to mere curiosity and profane interest. Similarly, though in general justice ought to be publicly administered and the proceedings of Courts of Law not held in secret, nevertheless there is no justification for exploiting and publicising all the sordid details of crime and of wrong-doing.

MORE SUBTLE DANGERS

These dangers are obvious. But there are others less obvious but more subtle, pervasive and slow to produce their effects. I shall try to indicate some because they affect the very nature of human thinking, the development of our civilization, and, perhaps saddest of all, they lead to an effective loss of true freedom.

The first of these is a general lessening of the rational critical power and of independent judgement and so of real intelligence. These media, especially the visual ones, bring people into continuous (though indirect) contact with concrete and actual events which are pictured to the eye. This has, of course, the advantage of correcting the excessive "abstractism" of former times. But it is generally admitted that in modern communication media there is a predominance of sense, sound, image, and to a certain extent, of emotion. This predominance springs partly from the nature of the media themselves and is partly contrived. Hence civilization today has been described as "a civilization of images". Advertising agencies and public relations officers are familiar with the techniques and processes involved. They try to present their product, organization or individual in an attractive picture-setting, which associates the object of this effort with things pleasing, attractive and emotionally satisfying. They do this by processes which appeal to the semi-conscious half-realized desires or attitudes of the recipients. The expression "hidden persuaders" is used of exclusively subliminal impacts of images or sounds too quickly transmitted to affect the consciousness; there may be, also, semi-subliminal impacts. People may be "conditioned" to react imaginatively and emotionally to certain stimuli. The process is, of course, not so crude as that of Pavlov's dog, which through an association set up between a bell and food, ultimately would secrete saliva at the sound of the bell even though no food appeared; in some of these media the process is far more subtle, complicated and complex. Nor could one say it is in itself illegitimate, but it is obviously dangerous.

The effect can be to substitute pseudo-convictions for conviction formed by personal and independent reasoning. These substitute convictions are built up, as it were, from the sediment or strata left on the mind by the half-assimilated ideas derived from the manipulation of the "image-creators", who control the media.

This arises partly through the predominance given by these media to sense, imagination and emotion. The intellect is too much neglected and the effort required in intellectual matters tends to be overlooked. Judgements are formed and decisions made on the basis of "impressions" which are in fact the effect of mass suggestion. Voluntary activity, which should be subsequent to hard thinking, tends to become merely a matter of likes and dislikes.

Akin to this danger is that of inducing in man a feeling that "events" and "historical processes" or even "history" enmesh him and carry him along irresistibly, do what he will. The actual sight of events taking place, in a series following inexorably one after the other, can lessen the sense of man's superiority to any "events" and his essential independence of "what happens".

Thus can come a certain atrophy of the will, manifest in the fear of making decisions and of accepting responsibility; and manifest in a certain desperation about man's own autonomy. The power of freedom comes to be felt as a burden instead of a lofty privilege and a magnificent joyful endowment.

If man's power to decide is weakened and his will and resolves subtly undermined he has lost all that is most noble and most human in him. He has lost that inner freedom which shows he is made in the likeness of God, since thereby he is master, not only of brute creation, but, more glorious, of his own acts and decisions, being inwardly bound to obey his own conscience and God, and outwardly being subject to human authority only in so far as it derives from God.

THE DANGER OF CONFORMISM

Yet another danger lies in what may be called the "levelling" influence of these media, that is, their tendency towards a uniformity in moral values and cultural standards; and in the assumption they often make that all hearers, listeners and viewers have the same discernment and capacity for judgement. As regards the first of these, moral values, the tendency is to level down and not up, since the directors of these media do not like complaints to be voiced and in order to avoid them rule out anything as regards morals which anyone, or at least any group, might object to. It may be doubted whether great moral or religious prophets or reformers would be granted access to these media, since prophets and reformers are apt to be controversial figures. Hence the tendency either to avoid moral and religious issues, or to treat them superficially and as if everyone should accept the colourless formless norms of all the uninstructed mass and what will rather please than admonish. Older people among Africans have lamented the effect upon their young people of films depicting violence, robbery and evil-doing. They lament, also, the decline in their customary hier-archical authority, by which the younger members of the family defer to the older and these in turn feel a responsibility according to their age and state. They lament the ideas about marriage which are spread by many films, and, even while recognizing that their own customs and laws may need revision, deplore the introduction of different customs without due preparation and due regard for tradition.

The levelling as regards cultural standards is perhaps of less consequence in regions where the generality of the population is already at more or less the same level. It is another matter, however, with underdeveloped regions. The impact upon their customs and their agricultural and patriarchal type of society can be disturbing and disintegrating. In many parts of the world there is regret that, mainly through the effect of the cinema, the traditional signs of respect, and of polite delay in dealing with one another, are going out of fashion. Much that is distinctively gracious and noble in traditions and culture can be, perhaps unintentionally, lost, to the detriment of the variety which ought to exist within the unity of the human family. Types of civilizations, with their language and traditions, are specific expressions of the human spirit and not only have a right to preserve their existence but by doing so they enrich the general human heritage, which ought not to be reduced to the dull uniformity of airports, even though airports are necessary.

There is another form of "levelling", this time social in char-acter. It is indeed necessary, as well as useful, in the interests of democracy, for citizens to be given the maximum of news that is possible by the press and other mass media. However, since there are human beings who, owing to their low cultural level, are scarcely capable of independent judgement and, owing to their low moral level, scarcely able to master their own instincts, ought not very careful consideration be given as to what should be provided by such media for these people? Otherwise there is a danger that such folk will imagine that they are capable of judging and deciding for themselves, whereas actually they will merely be the mouthpieces of those who have indoctrinated them and played upon their emotions whilst letting them imagine that they are acting freely and on their own initiative. Unfortunately there have been sad examples and proofs of the reality of this danger in recent unhappy events in more than one of those countries which in the past few years have acquired the precious gift of independence.

LIGHT OVERCOMING DARKNESS

From what has been said it must have emerged what an enormous influence these mass media of communication actually have on human thinking and so upon human conduct. This influence, which can be used for good or for ill, sets a serious problem before all men of good will who have at heart the unity of the human family and its fruitful development in truth, justice and charity. What can be done to help these precious inventions bring their due contribution to this cause?

I do not pretend to be able to give any ready answer to this question. The problem is world-wide, and assumes varied forms in different regions and countries. There is surely need for scientific research into varied aspects of the problem. Yet I venture to make certain reflections which may be of use.

First, there are already certain agencies at work to lessen the dangers. Many countries, if not all, have laws against defamation and libel, and against public displays which offend against decency and good morals. These laws, however, are often indeterminate in their incidence, and are difficult to enforce. There is, too, in many countries a certain governmental censorship of cinema films and children are excluded from certain exhibitions. In some countries groups have been organized in order to protest against indecent displays and even to boycott them.

There are, in some countries, professional associations of journalists which try to maintain proper standards in newspapers; and such associations may in some ways be compared to the associations of the medical and legal professions which have large power in dealing with unprofessional conduct. But journalists, cinema and television directors and producers deal so much with intangibles that it is difficult to establish any effective norms.

Newspapers and weekly periodicals often carry columns devoted to critical reviews of films and television items, making recommendations for readers. Awards, too, are given for artistic merit, a practice which must tend towards higher general standards.

Some television and radio authorities assign definite hours to religious broadcasts, and leave to churches, who act through their representatives, selection and arrangement of programmes. In certain countries religious groups have purchased transmitting equipment and broadcast their own programmes.

There are, too, some natural correctives inherent in the media themselves. A saturation point can be reached in sensationalism, in advertising and in propaganda. Repetition stales and a certain healthy scepticism results, especially in people more mature. Moreover, many countries are too poor to afford television, which may give time for greater maturity to develop before it is introduced.

By these means some of the dangers are avoided or mitigated. But these means are limited in their effects, do not exist in all countries and hence cannot dispel all the shadows, especially as regards children and people immature in age or in judgement. Further, in great areas of the world, mainly where educational and material conditions are low, television is not in use, but when it is introduced, as it surely will be, the dangers in such areas will be increased. Colour television in three dimensions will also sharpen the vividness of the impact upon the senses.

Printing came into use only gradually, and books at first were expensive and comparatively rare. But with the steam-engine, railways, postal services, the cheaper manufacture of paper and the telegraph, newspapers became cheaper and more common. The production, however, of printed matter required considerable skill and ability in those who communicated ideas, and required in those to whom they were communicated sufficient education to be able to read, which involved a certain intellectual training and capacity for mental concentration. But the cinema, radio and television came comparatively suddenly, require practically no education in the viewers or hearers, and less power of abstract thought in the performers. On the screen physical appearance counts greatly, and even the illiterate can talk on the radio or appear on cinema or television. Financial incentives and rewards are quicker and greater, if more precarious, than in the case of those who produce books, periodicals or even newspapers.

Looking at these wonderful inventions in the broad, a comparison occurs to me. The men of today, both those who operate these inventions and those who benefit from them, often seem to be like simple folk of modest estate who, through a sudden stroke of fortune, e.g. a lottery or a football pool, come into possession of a sum of money larger than they ever imagined really possible. Though they may try to conceal it, they are almost out of themselves with joy, and they think : "Now I can actually have what I dreamed about, eat and drink what I want, dress splendidly, drive about in an expensive car, enjoy myself . . . and be happy". Alas! Bitter experience will teach them how little happiness such things bring. They are besieged with requests for help, sometimes by plausible rogues, and learn, one hopes, the responsibility wealth brings; they find it hard to choose between attractions and pleasures, and learn, again one hopes, what self-discipline is needed to avoid complete loss; and they discover, one also hopes, that it is not so easy to be benevolent and do some service, however small, to their fellowmen. Great gifts are only given by God for the good of men and to further truth, justice, charity, and freedom.

PERSONAL RESPONSIBILITY

The comparison fails, of course, in many respects. Yet it holds in this that mankind has come, relatively suddenly, into possession of the great gift of these media of communication. Both those who control and operate them, and those who receive from them, ought to have a deep sense of responsibility, realizing that they are dealing with most powerful forces which affect the most precious endowment of man, his reason, will and spirit. Power for good and power for evil is immeasurably increased.

Is it possible that readers, listeners and viewers might arrange to meet in groups to exchange opinions, to criticize, form equitable judgements, and to help one another in selection of programmes? If so, it would help to obviate the dangers of passivity, mental sloth and subtle indoctrination, to strengthen reasonable independence of mind and a resolution of will to overcome the dominance of mere amusement-seeking. Is it possible that directors and operators of these media might meet to discuss the standards which should guide them and to help one another in resisting pressures upon them from exclusive commercialism, or even from political agencies? I put these questions because I know how greatly conditions differ in different parts of the world. But the rule of truth, justice and charity should hold sway everywhere, and to reconcile that rule with right freedom requires co-operative efforts.

Finally, human freedom is at stake. The liberation of man from colonial status, from imperialist rule and from material and political bondage is certainly a great thing, a thing of fundamental importance. But such liberation would be of small avail if men's inner freedom were destroyed, if they were to fall into the embrace, deadly though insidious and enticing, of those who, by working on their emotions and passions, would lull their nobler faculties, intellect and will, into inertia and apathy.

I believe this danger to be real, and believe that to meet it calls for most intelligent and dedicated efforts on the part of all who have at heart the true unity of the human race. There is need of initiative, resource and sacrifice not only on the part of individuals, but on the part of groups who see the danger and can take means not only to ward it off but to enable these media to exert their full force in overcoming suspicions and hostilities, in fostering understanding, in sharing intellectual and artistic gifts, in defending and spreading truth, freedom and justice and in uniting all men in the charity which comes from God.

4

The Impact of Pope John XXIII

POPE JOHN'S HUMANISM

JOHN XXIII, IN THE SHORT PERIOD OF HIS leadership of the Catholic Church, won the esteem and regard of many men and women of diverse religious faiths and even of no religious faith. People liked his welcome to other Christian leaders like Archbishop Fisher, to Rabbis and to non-Christians like Buddhist priests. They liked his visit to a famous Roman gaol, to meet, as he put it, "his good (yes, good) children who could not come to see him". They appreciated the almost startling directness of his speech, the simplicity of his manner, his touches of humour, his frankness about his peasant origin, his humility in summoning a Council, and, perhaps above all, his deep concern for humanity and its welfare. I propose, then, in this chapter to select some extracts from Pope John's *Encyclical* on Peace, and to give a few personal recollections of him as I knew him by personal contact.

The *Encyclical* on Peace received a general welcome, even though it had to be read in translation, and no translation can convey the full flavour of an original. This welcome, I think, sprang from an instinctive realization that Pope John voiced the feelings and the aspirations of all humanity. People felt, too, that he voiced the authentic Christian message applicable to the conditions of our time; they approved his unequivocal assertion that Christianity must be concerned for the welfare of men as men. They rejoiced at his active concern for the whole human family even on the purely human level. Many, of course, did

40

not hold the faith that he held, or admit the claims inherent in his position; but there were few who failed to appreciate his broad humanity, to welcome it and to respect the faith that inspired it. A Jewish Rabbi, Louis Finkelstein, Chancellor of the Jewish Theological Seminary of America, wrote: *"Pacem in Terris* is a great step toward the implementation of the world community which he felt must be the basis of enduring peace. For this courageous statement—which must be of far-reaching effect—men of all faiths will long arise and bless him."[1]

The basic ideas in the preceding chapters of this book are no mere opinions of my own. They are key-ideas, basic to Christianity, regarding the unity of mankind in freedom. They reflect both the spirit of John XXIII in his own life, and the doctrine of his Church as it was expressed by him in what may be called his last will and testament—the *Encyclical* on Peace.

This chapter is not merely an expression of my own personal veneration for John XXIII. It is designed to help a reader to grasp more easily the main standpoint of the document and its principal affirmations about human unity and freedom. The citations are in no sense meant to be an abridgement or summary of the whole document, which deals with very many more questions than are here mentioned. They are intended merely to be samples of the spirit and of the doctrinal principles which pervade the whole *Encyclical* and to be an encouragement to read the whole. The citations I arrange under six main headings to which the citations have general relevance.

1. THE RIGHTS OF MAN

Rights derive from personality: "Any human society, if it is to be well-ordered and beneficial, must lay down as a foundation this principle, namely, that every human being is a person, that is, his nature is endowed with intelligence and free will. By virtue of this, he has rights and duties of his own, flowing, directly and concomitantly, from his very nature. These rights

[1] *America,* June 15, 1963, p. 859.

are therefore universal, inviolable and inalienable." (N. 9)

Rights to moral values: "By the natural law[1] every human being has the right to respect for his person, to his good reputation, to freedom in searching for truth and—within the limits laid down by the moral order and the common good—in expressing and communicating his opinions, and in pursuit of art. He has the right, finally, to be informed truthfully about public events." (N. 12)

Public authority and human rights: "The chief concern of civil authorities must be to insure that these rights are acknowledged, respected, co-ordinated with other rights, defended and promoted, so that in this way each individual may more easily carry out his duties. For to safeguard the inviolable rights of the human person, and to facilitate the fulfilment of his duties, should be the essential duty of every public authority." (N. 60)

Universal Declaration of Human Rights by UN: "An act of the highest importance performed by the United Nations was the Universal Declaration of Human Rights, approved in the General Assembly on December 10, 1948. In the preamble of that declaration, the recognition and respect of those rights and respective liberties is proclaimed as an ideal to be pursued by all peoples and all countries.

"Some objections and reservations, we observed, were raised regarding certain points in the declaration, and rightly so.[2] There is no doubt, however, that the document represents an important step on the path toward the juridico-political organization of the world community. For in it, in most solemn form, the dignity of a human person is acknowledged in all men. And as a consequence there is proclaimed, as a fundamental right, the right of free movement in the search for truth and in the attainment of moral good and of justice, and also the right

---

[1] "The natural law" here does not refer to the ways in which beings act under given conditions in so far as their actions are not free; it means the "moral" law, concerning right and wrong, as an imperative derived from right reason as affecting free choices. It does not directly depend upon any special revelation from God.

[2] The reference here may be to the dissolution of marriage, or to the rights of an unborn child.

to a dignified life, while other rights connected with those mentioned are likewise proclaimed." (N. 143 and 144)

2. THE FREEDOM OF MAN

Human dignity and freedom: "The dignity of the human person
also requires that every man enjoy the right to act freely and
responsibly. For this reason, in social relations especially man
should exercise his rights, fulfil his obligations and, in the countless forms of collaboration with others, act chiefly through his
own personal decision. This means that each should act from
sincere conviction, on his own initiative, accepting his own
responsibility, without being moved by force or pressure
brought to bear on him from without." (N. 34)

Human society and freedom: "The unifying force in human
association must be found in freedom, that is to say, in ways and
means in keeping with the dignity of its citizens, who accept the
responsibility of their actions precisely because they are by
nature rational beings." (N. 35)

No threats or fears: "Where the civil authority uses as its only,
or its chief, means either threats and fear of punishment
or promises of rewards, it cannot effectively move men to promote the common good of all. Even if it did so move them, this
would be altogether opposed to their dignity as men endowed
with reason and free will." (N. 48)

Economic order and freedom: "For this principle must always
be retained : that the activity of the State in the economic field,
no matter what its breadth or depth may be, ought not to be
exercised in such as to curtail an individual's freedom of personal initiative. Rather it should work to expand that freedom
as much as possible by the effective protection of the essential
personal rights of each and every individual." (N. 65)

The freedom of nations: "Relations between states should be
based on freedom. This means that no country may unjustly
oppress others or unduly meddle in their affairs. On the
contrary, all should help to develop in others a sense of responsi-

bility, a spirit of enterprise and an earnest desire to be the first to promote their own advancement in every field." (N. 120)

3. CORRELATIVE DUTIES

Rights imply duties: "The natural rights with which we have been dealing are, however, inseparably connected, in the very person who is their subject, with equally many respective duties. And rights as well as duties find their source, their sustenance and their inviolability in the natural law which grants or enjoins them.

"For example, the right of every man to life is correlative with the duty to preserve it; his right to a decent standard of living, with the duty of living it becomingly; and his right to investigate the truth freely, with the duty of pursuing it and gaining more complete and exact knowledge." (N. 28 and 29)

Practical respect for others' rights: "Since men are social by nature, they are meant to live with others and to contribute to one another's welfare. Hence, a well-ordered human society requires that men recognize and observe their mutual rights and duties. It also demands that each take his full share in the establishment of a civic order in which rights and duties are progressively more conscientiously and effectively acknowledged and fulfilled.

"It is not enough, for example, to acknowledge and respect every man's right to the means of subsistence. One must also strive to ensure that he actually has enough food and nourishment.

"Associations of men ought to be not only well-ordered, but ought also to be the source of real advantages. This certainly requires that they recognize and fulfil their mutual rights and obligations. It likewise requires that there be co-operative effort towards the multiple forms of progress which modern civilization allows or encourages or even demands." (N. 31, 32 and 33)

Racialism: "The conviction that all men are equal by reason of their natural dignity has been generally accepted. Hence,

racial discrimination can in no way be justified, at least, not by
any sound doctrine or theory. And this is of fundamental importance and significance for the formation of human society
according to those principles which we have outlined above.
For, if a man becomes conscious of his rights, he must become
equally aware of his duties. Thus, he who possesses certain rights
has likewise the duty to claim those rights as marks of his dignity,
while all others have the obligation to acknowledge those rights
and respect them." (N. 44)

What is the moral order: "The order which prevails in society is
by nature moral. Grounded as it is in truth, it must function
according to the norms of justice, it should be inspired and perfected by mutual love, and finally it should be brought to an
ever more refined and human balance in full freedom." (N. 37)

4. CHARITY AND SHARING

Fellowship in the Spirit: "An association of human beings is
well-ordered, beneficial and in keeping with human dignity if
it is grounded on truth. This demands that reciprocal rights
and duties be honestly recognized. Furthermore, human society
will be such as we have described it, if its members, guided by
justice, have a real interest in the rights of others and in dis-
charging loyally their own duties; if they are animated by such
charity as to feel as their own the needs and the wants of others
and share with others their own goods; if, finally, they work for
a progressively closer fellowship in the world of spiritual values.
Moreover, the unifying force in human association must
be found in freedom, that is to say, in ways and means in keeping with the dignity of its members, who accept responsibility
for their actions precisely because they are by nature rational
beings.

"Human society ought to be regarded above all as a reality
of the spirit, in which men communicate knowledge to one
another in the light of truth; in which they can enjoy their
rights and fulfil their duties, and are inspired to strive for moral
good. Society should enable men to share and enjoy beauty in

all its noble expressions. It should encourage them constantly to pass on to others all that is best in themselves and strive to make their own the spiritual riches of others. These are the values of the spirit which constantly give life and basic direction to civilization, economic and social institutions, political movements and forms, legal enactments and all the other external structures in which society manifests and expresses itself in its ceaseless development." (N. 35, 36)

Recognize and encourage good wherever it is found: "It must be borne in mind, furthermore, that neither can false philosophical teachings regarding the nature, origin and destiny of the universe and of man be identified with historical movements that have economic, social, cultural or political purposes, not even when these movements have originated from those teachings and have drawn and still draw inspiration therefrom.

"This is so because the teachings, once they are drawn up and defined, remain always the same, while the movements, working in constantly evolving historical situations, cannot but be influenced by these latter and cannot avoid, therefore, being subject to changes, even of a profound nature. Besides, who can deny that those movements, in so far as they conform to the dictates of right reason and are interpreters of the lawful aspirations of the human person, contain elements that are positive and deserving of approval?" (N. 159)

"It can happen, then, that meetings for the attainment of some practical end, which formerly were deemed inopportune or unproductive, might now or in the future be considered opportune and useful." (N. 160)[1]

Negotiations in mutual trust: "There is reason to hope, however, that by meeting and negotiating men may come to discover better the ties—deriving from the human nature which they have in common—that unite them, and that they may learn also that one of the most profound requirements of their

---

[1] This passage has been the subject of much comment and speculation. The meaning is clear: it is possible to distinguish between mistaken doctrines with which a movement is allied, and the movement itself, just as it is possible to distinguish between an error and the man who errs.

common nature is this: that between them and their respective peoples it is not fear which should reign but love, a love which tends to express itself in a collaboration that is loyal, manifold in form and productive of many benefits." (N. 129)

Interest in the welfare of the entire human family: "Once again we deem it opportune to remind our children of their duty to take an active part in public life and to contribute toward the attainment of the common good of the entire human family as well as to that of their own political community. They should endeavour, therefore, in the light of their Christian faith, and led by love, to insure that the various institutions—whether economic, social, cultural or political in purpose—should be such as not to obstruct, but rather to facilitate or render less arduous man's self-betterment both in the natural order and the supernatural." (N. 146)

Loyal and Careful Co-operation with other Christians and with non-Christians: "The doctrinal principles outlined in this document derive from or are suggested by the requirements of human nature itself, and are, for the most part, dictates of the natural law. They provide Catholics, therefore, with a vast field in which they can meet and come to an understanding both with Christians separated from this Apostolic See, and also with human beings who are not enlightened by faith in Jesus Christ, but who are reasonable men with a natural and operative integrity.

"In such relations let the faithful be careful to be always consistent in their actions, so that they may never come to any compromise in matters of religion and morals. At the same time, however, let them be, and show themselves to be, animated by a spirit of understanding and unselfishness, and disposed to work loyally in the pursuit of objectives which are of their nature good, or conducive to good." (N. 157)[1]

Disarmament—peace based on mutual trust: "Justice, right reason and humanity urgently demand that the arms race

---

[1] Cf. Encycl. *Mater et Magistra. Acta Apostolicae Sedis* 53 (1961), 456.

should cease; that the stockpiles which exist in various countries should be reduced equally and simultaneously by the parties concerned; that nuclear weapons should be banned; and that a general agreement should eventually be reached about progressive disarmament and an effective method of control.

"In the words of Pius XII, our predecessor of happy memory : The calamity of a world war, with the economic and social ruin and the moral excesses and dissolution that accompany it, must not be permitted to engulf the human race for a third time.[1]

"All must realize that there is no hope of putting an end to the building up of armaments, or of reducing the present stocks, still less of abolishing them altogether, unless the process is complete and thorough and unless it proceeds from inner conviction; unless, that is, everyone sincerely co-operates to banish the fear and anxious foreboding about war, with which men are oppressed. If this is to come about, the radical principle on which our present peace depends must be replaced by another, which declares that the true and solid peace of nations can consist, not in equality of arms, but in mutual trust alone.

"We believe that this can be brought to pass, and we consider that it will prove to be the source of many benefits." (N. 112 and 113)

5. A WORLD COMMUNITY

A general convergence towards unity: "Recent progress in science and technology has profoundly affected human beings, and its influence has been towards recognition of general interdependence and of the need of co-ordination on a world scale. There has been a great increase in the movement of ideas, of people and of goods from one country to another, so that relations have become closer between individuals, families and

[1] Cf. Radio Message, Christmas Eve, 1941, *Acta Apostolicae Sedis* 34 (1942), 17; and Exhortation of Benedict XV to the rulers of peoples at war, Aug. 1, 1917. *Acta Apostolicae Sedis* 9 (1917), 418.

intermediate associations belonging to different political communities, and between the public authorities of those communities.

"At the same time the interdependence of national economies has grown deeper, one becoming progressively more closely related to the other, so that they become almost integral parts of the one world economy. Likewise the social progress, order, security and peace of any one country are vitally linked with the social progress, order, security and peace of all other countries.

"At the present time no political community is able to pursue its own interests and develop itself in isolation, because its prosperity and development are both a consequence and a component part of the prosperity and development of all the other political communities." (N. 130, 131)

Ethnic characteristics and the common good: "Furthermore, the universal common good requires that in every nation friendly relations be fostered in all fields between the citizens and their intermediate societies.

"There are, in many lands, groupings of people of more or less different racial backgrounds. However, the elements which characterize an ethnic group must not be transformed into a water-tight compartment in which human beings are prevented from communicating with their fellow men of other ethnic groups. That would ill befit our contemporary situation, in which the distances separating peoples have been almost wiped out. Nor can one overlook the fact that, even though human beings differ from one another in their ethnic characteristics, they all possess certain essential common characteristics and are inclined by nature to meet each other in the world of spiritual values, in which progressive unifying development opens to them the possibility of improvement without limits. They have the right and duty, therefore, to live in communion with one another." (N. 100)

A world community of peoples: "It is a mistake too commonly made, to imagine that the relationships between men and states can be governed by the same laws which regulate the unreasoning forces and elements of the universe. The laws governing these relationships are of quite a different kind and are to be sought elsewhere, namely, where the Father of all things wrote them, that is, in the nature of man.

"By these laws, men are most admirably taught, first of all, how they should conduct their mutual dealings among themselves; next, how the relationships between the citizens and the public authorities of each state should be regulated; then, how states should deal with one another; finally, how, on the one hand individual men and states, and on the other hand the community of all peoples, should act toward each other. The establishment of such a world community of peoples is urgently demanded today by the requirements of universal common good." (N. 6 and 7)

The United Nations: "As is known, the United Nations (UN) was established on June 26, 1945, and to it there were subsequently added inter-governmental agencies with extensive international tasks in the economic, social, cultural, educational and health fields. The United Nations had as its essential purpose the maintenance and consolidation of peace between peoples, fostering between them friendly relations based on the principles of equality, mutual respect and varied forms of co-operation in every sector of human endeavour.

"It is our earnest prayer that the United Nations—in its structure and in its means—may become ever more equal to the magnitude and nobility of its tasks. May the day come as quickly as possible when every human being will find therein an effective safeguard for the rights which derive directly from his dignity as a person, and which are therefore universal, inviolable and inalienable rights. This is all the more to be hoped for, since all human beings, as they take an ever more active part in the public life of their own political communities, are showing an increasing interest in the affairs of all peoples, and are becoming more consciously aware that they are living members of a world community." (N. 142 and 145)

6. GOD, THE FIRST TRUTH AND THE HIGHEST GOOD

The infinite greatness of God: "Peace on earth, which men of every era have most ardently yearned for, can be firmly established only if the order laid down by God is dutifully observed.

"The progress of science and the inventions of technology bear witness first and foremost to the infinite greatness of God himself, who created the universe and man. He created all things out of nothing, pouring into them the abundance of his wisdom and goodness.

"The Creator of the world has imprinted in man's heart an order which his conscience reveals to him and enjoins him to obey : 'They show the work of the Law written in their hearts'. Their conscience bears witness to them.

"And how could it be otherwise ? For whatever God has made shows forth his infinite wisdom, and it is manifested more clearly in the things which have greater perfection." (N. 1, 3, 5)

God the source of order among men: "Now an order of this kind, whose principles are universal, absolute and unchangeable, has its ultimate source in the one true God, who is personal and transcends human nature. Inasmuch as God is the first truth and the highest good, he alone is that ultimate source from which human society can draw its vitality, if that society is to be well ordered, beneficial and in keeping with human dignity." (N. 38)

God perceived in spiritual values: "When the relationships in human society are organized in terms of rights and duties, men become conscious of spiritual values and understand the meaning and significance of truth, justice, charity and freedom. They become deeply aware that they belong to this world of values. Moreover, when moved by such concerns, they are brought to a better knowledge of the true God, who is personal and transcendent. Thus they make the ties that bind them to God the solid foundation of their lives, both of that life which they live interiorly in the depths of their own souls and of that in which they are united to their fellows in society." (N. 45)

All authority ultimately from God: "Since authority is chiefly
concerned with moral force, it follows that civil authority must
appeal primarily to the conscience of individual citizens, that is,
to each one's duty to collaborate readily for the common good
of all. Since by nature all men are equal in human dignity, it
follows that no man can demand internal compliance from
another.[1] That is in the power of God alone, who sees and judges
what is hidden in men's hearts. Those, therefore, who have
authority in the state may oblige men in conscience only if their
authority is intrinsically related to the authority of God and
shares in it.

"By this principle the dignity of the citizens is protected.
When, in fact, men obey their rulers, it is not merely as men that
they obey them. It is God, the provident Creator of all things,
whom they reverence through their obedience, since he has
decreed that men's dealings with one another should be
regulated by an order which he himself has established. Moreover, in showing this due reverence to God, we not only do not
demean ourselves, but rather perfect and ennoble ourselves. For
to serve God is to rule." (N. 48, 49, 50)

Requirement for an order truly human: spiritual values: "We
call attention to the fact that scientific competence, technical
capacity and professional experience, although necessary, are
not of themselves sufficient to elevate the relationships of society
to an order that is genuinely human, that is, to an order whose
foundation is truth, whose measure and objective is justice,
whose driving force is love, and whose method of attainment
is freedom.

"For this end it is certainly necessary that human beings
carry on their own temporal activities in accordance with the
laws governing them and following the methods corresponding
to their nature. But it is also necessary that they should carry
on those activities as acts within the moral order and, therefore,

[1] The Latin here reads: nemo valet alium ad aliquid intimis animi
sensibus efficiendum cogere. The Italian: nessuno puo obbligare gli altri
interioramente. The version released by the Vatican Press office: "no
one may be coerced to perform interior acts".

as the exercise or vindication of a right, as the fulfilment of a duty or the performance of a service, and as a positive response to the providential design of God directed to our salvation.

"In other words, it is necessary that human beings, in the intimacy of their own consciences, should so live and act in their temporal lives as to create a synthesis between scientific, technical and professional elements on the one hand, and spiritual values on the other." (N. 149, 150)

An immense task: "There is an immense task incumbent on all men of good will, namely, the task of restoring the relations of the human family in truth, in justice, in love and in freedom—relations between individual human beings, between citizens and their respective political communities, between political communities themselves, and finally, between individuals, families, intermediate associations and political communities on the one hand, and the world community on the other. This is a most exalted task, all will agree, for it is the task of bringing about true peace in the order established by God.

"It is an imperative of duty; it is a requirement of love.

"Every believer in this world of ours must be a spark of light, a nucleus of love, a vivifying leaven amidst his fellow-men. And he will be this all the more perfectly, the more closely he lives in communion with God in the intimacy of his own soul.

"In fact, there can be no peace between men unless there is peace within each one of them, unless, that is, each one builds up within himself the order willed by God." (N. 163 and 164, N. 165)

Help from on high: "There is so noble and so elevated a task that human resources, even though inspired by the most praise-worthy good will, cannot bring it to realization alone. In order that human society may reflect as faithfully as possible the King-dom of God, help from on high is necessary." (N. 168)

Pope John's own prayer: "This is the peace which we implore of Christ with the ardent yearning of our prayer. May he banish from the hearts of men whatever might endanger peace. May he transform them into witnesses of truth, justice and brotherly love. May he enlighten the rulers of peoples so that in addition to their solicitude for the due welfare of their citizens, they may guarantee and defend the fairest gift of peace. May he enkindle the wills of all so that they may break through the barriers that divide them, cherish the bonds of mutual charity, understand others, and pardon those who have done them wrong. By virtue of his action, may all peoples of the earth become as brothers, and may the most longed-for peace spring forth and reign always among them." (N. 171)

POPE JOHN'S PERSONAL RESPECT FOR FREEDOM

To a very great extent the ideas in the *Encyclical* on Peace reflect the spirit and the character of Pope John XXIII himself. The man shines through the formality of phraseology necessary in a document of this kind—the man, with his warmth, his humanity and, one can say, his true greatness.

Pope John XXIII had a deep and personal respect for man's freedom. In an audience given to a group of bishops during the first session of the council, he remarked that some people were anxious about the forceful language used in the Council by several bishops. "But what do you expect them to do?" he remarked, "they are not a bevy of nuns who always have to agree with the Mother Superior." Indeed, only the history of these last years, when it comes to be written, will reveal how solicitous was John XXIII about the freedom of the bishops and how many troubles he had in securing it for them. His famous intervention, towards the end of November, about the *Schema* (or draft proposals) on the Sources of Revelation, showed his respect for the independence of the Council. The question was whether the *Schema*, which was thought to favour the view of Scripture and Tradition as two independent sources, should be accepted with minor modifications, or whether an entirely new *Schema* should be drafted. A majority in the Council wanted a new *Schema*, but this majority fell short of the two-thirds required by the rules of procedure. The Pope intervened and appointed a new "mixed" Commission (or Committee) to prepare another *Schema* on the subject; but he took the greatest pains to see that his new special Commission should include representatives of all the main currents of opinion represented on the Council. He overrode the letter of procedure rules; but he did so only after the Council Fathers had discussed freely and fully, and he intervened in a way which enabled free expression of opinion to be more effective.

Another instance of his respect for freedom may be mentioned in general terms. At the very beginning of his Pontificate, he said he intended to work hard and make others work hard. Those who were in a position to be aware of the way in which he observed the work of the Congregations (that is, the ecclesiastical Civil Service) know how careful he was to respect the just freedom of initiative and of action in those in positions of responsibility—even in cases where he would personally have preferred different methods, and where certain action caused him, with his inclination toward kindness, very deep suffering. His forbearance sprang from his sincere respect for human persons and their freedom and shows that he deeply believed what he said in his *Encyclical* about the due freedom of thought and of initiative, of action and of decision which should be allowed all men as endowed with intelligence and freedom by their Creator.

This respect for others' freedom came more easily to him, because of his almost innate inclination to see and to stress the good in men and in situations. He often used to repeat : "Look at the good which there is and try to encourage it as much as possible; that itself will lessen the bad". The following citation from the *Encyclical* on Peace is typical of Pope John's outlook : "One must never confuse error and the person who errs, not even when it is in the moral or religious field that there is error, or inadequate knowledge of truth. (N. 158)

"The person who errs is always and above all a human being, and in every single case he retains his dignity as a human person. He must always be regarded and treated in accordance with that lofty dignity. Besides, in every human being there is a need that is congenital to his nature and never becomes extinguished, and that is an incentive to break through the web of error and open his mind to the knowledge of truth. And God will never fail to act on his interior being, so that a person, who at a given moment of his life lacks the clarity of faith or adheres to erroneous doctrines, can at a future date be enlightened and believe the truth." (N. 158)

THE PROPHETS OF GLOOM

Even more revealing, especially as it was made in his address at the solemn opening of the Council, is a fragment of autobiography, perhaps his only public reference to some who could not bring themselves to share his outlooks: "In the daily exercise of our pastoral office, we sometimes have to listen, much to our regret, to the voices of persons who, though burning with zeal, are not endowed with too much sense of discretion or balance. In these modern times they can see nothing but prevarication and ruin; they say that our era, in comparison with past eras, is getting worse; and they behave as though they had learned nothing from history, which is nonetheless the teacher of life, and as though at the time of former Councils everything was a full triumph for the Christian idea and life, and for proper religious liberty.

"We feel we must disagree with those prophets of gloom who are always forecasting disaster, as though the end of the world were at hand.

"In the present order of things, Providence is leading us to a new order of human relations, which by men's own efforts and even beyond their very expectations, are directed toward the fulfilment of God's higher and unexpected designs; and everything, even human differences, leads to the greater good of the Church."[1]

It was not that he did not see, with sober realism, the imperfections and the evil. In the *Encyclical* on Peace, "admittedly," he stated, "there are not many who are trying to

[1] *Acta Apostolicae Sedis* 54 (1962), pp. 788-789.

reconstruct the relationships of social life according to the criteria we have just explained." But he at once takes any sting out of this statement by giving warm recognition to these few zealous workers and hoping their numbers may increase : "To them we extend our fatherly appreciation and invite them to persevere with even greater zeal. We are comforted by the hope that their numbers will increase, especially among those who believe. It is an imperative duty and a demand of love." (N. 164)

His combined optimism and sober realism was likewise shown by the passage in the *Encyclical*[1] about disarmament and the relations between nations and between the alignments of nations which at present divide the world. He saw and said that disarmament must begin with disarmament of the spirit, with a change of threats and fear into mutual trust.

From his belief in the goodness in men sprang his understanding, patience, kindness and affection. The first Christmas of his Pontificate, he paid visits to the hospital for sick children in Rome and to the prisoners in the *Regina Coeli* gaol. After his death, there were wreaths of red roses on his catafalque, paid for out of the meagre savings of the convicts of Rome and of Parma, in mute witness that his radiant faith in human goodness could find a response even in those who might be expected, from the harsh conditions of their life, to bear resentment against the whole of society.

PERSONAL TRIALS

But there is something more : trials more testing for the unselfishness of real goodness, the trials of meeting opposition and obstruction to holy and generous aims, plans and exertions. Here I can speak from personal intercourse with Pope John, since more than once he spoke to me of his difficulties with various people, difficulties which caused him real suffering. Yet he never complained or made any harsh judgement, bearing it not only

[1] Cf. above, p. 48.

with patience and forbearance, but with sincere efforts to understand and excuse.

The sufferings of refugees touched him : "Since, by God's
grace, we feel towards all men a fatherly regard and affection,
we look with deepest distress upon the lot of political refugees;
their number is immense and their sufferings countless and
grievous." (*Encyclical* on Peace, n. 103)

And, after pointing out that political refugees do not lose
their rights as persons by losing their nationality, nor their right
to enter another political community, he thanks all those who
are labouring to mitigate the sufferings of these refugees,
almost as if they were doing a service to himself :

"Wherefore, on this occasion, we publicly approve and commend every undertaking founded on the principles of human
solidarity or Christian charity which aims at making the
migration of persons from one country to another less painful.

"And we will be permitted to single out for the attention and
gratitude of all right-minded persons the manifold work which
specialized international agencies are carrying out in this very
delicate field." (*Ibid*. nn. 107, 108)

THE MEDICINE OF COMPASSION

From his concern for mankind sprang, likewise, the hope he
expressed at its opening that the Council would use the kind of
language which modern man understands and so make really
intelligible the message entrusted to the Church for the good
of all humanity. There was, too, another statement at the opening of the Council which was evidently the result of his mature
reflections and made in full awareness of its applicability and
importance on this occasion. The Church, he said, intends to
change her method of dealing with men. In other days what
may be called severity was used, but now the Church means
to use kindness. "The Church," he went on, "has always opposed
the various false teachings which have arisen. Not seldom she
condemned them with great severity. Today, however, the
spouse of Christ prefers the medicine of compassion to the

severity of condemnation. She judges that the needs of the present time are to be met by actual and living evidence of the validity of her teaching, rather than by repeating condemnations.

"The Catholic Church, through the Council, wishes to show herself to be the loving Mother of all, kind, patient, full of compassion and goodness."[1]

There was another conspicuous trait in John XXIII, partly the fruit of his goodness, partly its root, that is, his deep humbleness, mildness and meekness. He frequently spoke of himself as "the humble Pope", "the humble and unworthy Vicar of Christ", "the humble successor of St Peter", and did so quite naturally, not, as it were, parading his humility, but like a simple man aware how modest were the claims of his person, his attainments and his activities. He wrote in his will : "I ask forgiveness of those whom I have unwittingly offended, and those whom I have not edified. For my part, I feel I have nothing to forgive anyone. Those who knew me and had contacts with me, even if they offended me, or thought little of me, or, perhaps justly, disapproved of me, or caused me pain—these I look upon only as brothers who did good to me, to whom I am grateful and for whom I pray and will always pray."

OPPOSITION AND RESISTANCE

Here also is the explanation of his attitude towards opposition and resistance to his plans and wishes. More than once, I had certain knowledge that he fully realized that such opposition was unjustified and had bad effects; but he never doubted the good faith and good will of the individuals concerned. He excused them, tried to explain their actions and their motives in the best sense and to treat them with fatherly patience and charity. I never came out of an audience with him without being deeply impressed by his character; he was so large-minded, so tolerant and so forbearing, and yet so strong, so inflexible in his

---

[1] *Acta Apostolicae Sedis* 54 (1962), p. 792.

principles and in his purposes. Such he was as I knew him, and I admired him as a man great in his humility and humble in his greatness.

In his coronation address he asked his children throughout the world to pray that God might give him a special gift during his Pontificate; and the nature of the gift he wanted caused surprise to some. He said this:

"Of the divine teachings, certain words of the Gospel are the central point and precept, which sums up and includes in itself all the others: 'Learn of me, for I am meek and humble of heart.' (Matt. 11:29.) This is the great principle of gentleness and lowliness. All of you throughout the world, devout and 'fervent in spirit' (Rom. 12:11), should pray assiduously to God for your Pontiff, with this intention: that he may advance more and more in the gentleness and humility of the Gospel."

In retrospect one can see that that prayer was granted. When he was nearing death in his slow agony, the Italian radio (and it was not alone in this) returned again and again to this thought of meekness, and almost spelled out the words, "the meek, the humble Pope". It is written in the Gospel that the meek shall inherit the earth: it was true of him, for he made an unparalleled impact upon the Church and the world of our day, and men of every faith and no faith felt for him an affection as for a personal friend.

It is not easy to speak of his religious life. Yet in all my contacts with him I felt his faith in God and his trust in God somehow shining through, or glowing like a fire within him. He judged everything by the principles taught by the faith: failures, obstruction, difficulties, opposition. Success consoled him, but he attributed it to God, and, in sincere modesty, to the exertions of those who worked with him. He was not disheartened by obstacles, for his courage sprang from reliance upon nothing human, but upon the all-powerful help of God. He was well aware that it was an enormous and risky task to call an Ecumenical Council. In the audiences he gave, the constant theme was prayers for the success of the Council. It was astonishing how insistent he was about it, as well as how felicitous he was in finding ways of bringing home his request not only to mixed assemblies of people in general audiences, but to each group in the smaller audiences—children, the sick and suffering, professional people, theological students, nuns and priests. He always found a special reason why each group should pray for the Council and for trust in God's help.

HIS COURAGE

It has been very truly said, by a writer well acquainted with the circumstances and the situation, that the Council was first of all, and above all, an act, and the fruit, of Pope John's faith and confidence in God. No other explanation meets the facts. He succeeded in inspiring others with this faith and his courage. How often have I heard him utter the word "Courage"—for he was not spared opposition and resistance, which he felt acutely, above all when they impeded and planned to obstruct his pastoral efforts. To a bishop who complained about the difficulties he encountered in his diocese, Pope John answered, very simply and gently: "Excellency, I, too, have a diocese, and sometimes I, too, have difficulties. At such times I go to my chapel. And once it seemed to me that Jesus said to me 'Now, Johnny, don't take these things too hard. There's me, too, still in my Church'."

Because of this humility, and humble trust in God, he was lion-hearted in facing the gigantic problems of the modern world, in seeking a solution to them; he had a dynamic yet sober optimism and a surprisingly youthful zest. In his exhortation for work for the unity of mankind, he spoke thus: "All human beings ought rather to reckon that what has been accomplished is but little in comparison with what remains to be done. This is so because organs of production, trade unions, professional organizations, insurance systems, legal systems, political regimes, and institutions for cultural, health, recreational or sporting and other similar purposes must all be adjusted to the era of the atom and of the conquest of space, an era in which the human family has already entered on its new advance toward limitless horizons." (*Encyclical* on Peace, n. 156).

The Pope was over eighty years old when he wrote so. Dr Douglas Horton, retired Dean of Harvard Divinity School, wrote that "his updating of the thought of the Church makes Pope John a primary point in its history". The following statement, about the Russian space flight in August, 1961, shows how Pope John welcomed all progress, wherever found :

"We look on with sympathy," he said, "and we follow with prayer and blessing these enterprises for the conquest of space. And we wish true success to them, so that they may contribute to human brotherhood and to true civilization. This last is a task which transcends all heights, all velocities and all triumphs of technology, the task which should engage resolute and trustful efforts, that is, to bring mankind nearer to God and to permeate all social life with the ferment of the Gospel."

5

World Problems in a
World Assembly

JOHN XXIII BECAME POPE AFTER A VERY VARIED
experience of life and of men. He had been Secretary to
Bishop Radini-Tedeschi, and had tried to apply in
Bergamo the social teachings of Leo XIII; then a soldier and
an Army chaplain; he had written a life of St Charles Borromeo,
and a history in five volumes about the Apostolic Visitations by
St Charles Borromeo to the diocese of Bergamo; he had dealt
with the financial side of the Society for the Propagation of the
Faith, which brought international contacts; he had represented the Holy See in Bulgaria (1925-1935), in Turkey and
Greece, during the Second World War (1935-1944), and in
France during a period (1944-1953) which included the trouble-
some adjustments involved in the change from Vichy to the
new régime; and during the last five years of Pius XII (1953-
1958) he had been Patriarch of Venice, where the traditional
links of the Venetians with the East no doubt reinforced the
interest in Eastern Christendom roused by his lengthy stay in
Bulgaria and Turkey.

In his coronation address, three matters stood out: first,
his equal regard for the Eastern church as for the Western;
second, his distress at the denial of freedom to the Church in
several parts of the world and at the sufferings of the faithful
in those lands; and third, his concern at the quarrels and dissension among the leaders of nations. On this last point, he spoke
feelingly:

Why are the resources of human genius and the riches of the peoples devoted more often to turning out pernicious instruments of death and destruction than to increasing the welfare of all classes of citizens, and particularly of the poorer classes?

We know that there are grave and intricate problems which must be solved to carry out a programme so praiseworthy and to untangle the knots of discord. But these difficulties must be victoriously overcome, even at the cost of great effort. Set to work, therefore, with courage and faith.... Turn your eyes to the people who are entrusted to you and hear this voice. What are they asking of you, what are they supplicating? They are asking, not for those monstrous instruments of war, invented in our times, which cause fratricidal destruction and universal massacre, but for peace—a peace under which the entire human family can live freely.[1]

Quarrels and dissensions: a look at the map of the world will bring recollection of sad events even after the end of the last world war: Korea, Malaya, Kenya, Colombia, Suez, Hungary, Indonesia, Thailand, Iraq, Burma, Vietnam, the Lebanon, Germany and Berlin, India and China, Quemoy and Formosa, the Congo and Katanga, Algeria, Cuba—all recall wars great or small, conflicts between nations or groups of nations, or between fellow-citizens, resorts to arms, sometimes savagely repressed, guerrilla fighting, assassinations, forced migrations of multitudes of innocent people, the rapid increase in population with consequent hunger, the unrest incidental to rapid social and political change, and all this against a background of multiplying nuclear tests, and repeated crises with the threats of a war incalculable in its effects.

No doubt all of this, or much of this, was in the mind of Pope John when he spoke of "quarrels and dissensions" and of the human misery they entail. Moreover, he was doubtless aware of the general mood of depression or even despair about the human predicament, the mood of "escapism" and the decline in firm convictions about ultimate values which cuts the nerve of resolution and destroys the basic motives for persevering and

[1] *Acta Apostolicae Sedis* 50 (1958), p. 840.

patient efforts. When he said, "all these difficulties must be victoriously overcome. . . . Set to work with courage and faith," he was making a large demand, and as his subsequent conduct shows, he applied his admonition to himself, and asked himself "How can *I* set to work with courage and faith to help mankind?"

THE BIRTH OF AN IDEA

In 1962, speaking to Venetian pilgrims led by the new Patriarch, Cardinal Urbani, he explained his state of mind during the last months of 1958 :

> In a private conversation with the Secretary of State, Cardinal Tardini, we agreed that throughout the wide world there was distress and turmoil. We noticed, among other things, that protests of desire for peace and agreement unhappily often ended in sharper disputes and intensified threats.[1] What ought the Church to do? Should the mystic barque of Christ remain at the mercy of the waves or drift with the currents? Surely not. On the contrary, is it not from the Church that the world had a right to expect not merely some new warning but also the illumination of a great example? What form should that illumination take?
>
> The Cardinal listened expectantly, and reverently, to hear our solution, if any. Suddenly a great idea lit up our mind, and was instantly accepted with inexpressible trust in the divine Master. A single word sprang to our lips, solemn and challenging, a word which we spoke for the first time : a Council.[2]

The idea of the Council, then, sprang from Pope John XXIII's concern and anxiety for the world and for humanity, and from his conviction that the Church has a responsibility for the welfare of all mankind. This was a recurrent theme in

[1] The year 1958 saw the Soviet resumption of nuclear tests, the Quemoy crisis, military *coups* in Siam and Iraq, civil war in Burma and in the autumn, the breakdown of negotiations between the Russians and the Western countries over the question of a German peace treaty and Berlin.

[2] *Osservatore Romano*, 11 May 1962, p. 1

almost all of his subsequent utterances, spoken and written, and the theme became clearer in outline and content as time went on.

At the opening of the Commissions preparatory to the Council, in November, 1960, he gave a diagnosis of the fundamental problem of the modern world. "The Church," he said, "is faced by a strange new world, a world torn between the fascinations and the perils of our almost exclusive pursuit of material prosperity, with enfeebled grasp of the spiritual and supernatural dimension of existence. . . ." He went on, "To deplore the deviations of the human spirit, tempted and drawn towards mere enjoyment of the earthly good things which modern scientific inventions put within easy reach of the children of this age . . . to deplore this is a duty." But here, with characteristic trust in goodness, he immediately added: "Yet God preserve us from losing a sense of proportion and exaggerating, as if we believed the heavens of God had closed above our head, that darkness had truly covered the earth or that nothing were left but to sprinkle our weak way with our tears. . . . No! Christ, the Son of God, Saviour of the world, has not disappeared from the world he redeemed."[1]

In the Bull, *Humanae Salutis*, of Christmas Day, 1961, formally convoking the Council, he declared that the service of humanity must be the first aim of the Council:

The Church is today witnessing a crisis in the history of human society. Mankind is at the verge of a new era and the tasks confronting the Church are as vital and as formidable as any which have ever faced her, even during the most tragic epochs in her history. The primary need of our day is to transfuse into the life-stream of this modern world of ours the renewing, deathless and divine energy of the Gospel; this modern world, proud of its technological and scientific conquests, suffers the inevitable consequences of efforts to bring stability and peace which too often leave God entirely out of account. Material progress has not been accompanied by moral progress. Appreciation of the things of the spirit grows feeble,

[1] *Acta Apotolicae Sedis* 52 (1960), pp. 1006 ff.

and men set their hearts almost exclusively on those earthly enjoyments which modern techniques place within easy reach. Finally, a new and frightening fact, the rise of a militant type of atheism, operating on a world scale.[1]

Yet here again, Pope John refused to look only on the dark side, and went on to explain that the very fear of wars stimulates the desire for peace, and even brings a new openness of mind, possibly even a readiness to listen to the Church, and that this obliges the Church to gather all its resources and show itself more and more able to answer the questions being asked by men of today. This is the first reason he gave for summoning the Council.

EVERYMAN'S CHURCH

The Radio Message of September 11th, 1962, was no doubt based on the work of the Commissions preparing for the Council. It stated in energetic terms that "the world needs Christ, and the Church must give Christ to the world". It listed some of the main problems confronting humanity today, the problem of the family, the food situation, the preservation of peace, internal and external. It affirmed the fundamental equal rights of all nations, and their duties towards the whole family of nations. It declared that to underdeveloped countries the Church must present the true image of what she is, and what she means to be, that is, the Church of everyman, and especially the Church of the poor. Then comes the social responsibility which must not be shirked, because of which "men must measure what is superfluous by the light of other peoples' needs and must be awake to the urgent need of a fair distribution of the goods of this world to all the human race". Mention is then made of religious freedom, "which is not merely freedom of worship ... the Church cannot surrender this freedom, for it is an inherent necessity for the service she must render mankind".[2]

[1] *Acta Apostolicae Sedis* 54 (1962), p. 6.
[2] *Acta Apostolicae Sedis* 54 (1962), pp. 678-683.

WORLD PEACE

Finally, the Pope turned to the greatest ideal and the great problem, world peace. The previous Christmas he had said: "The world is bewildered, confused, and deeply apprehensive under the constant threat of new and frightful conflicts. The coming Council will, we hope, prove an occasion for suggesting thoughts and even plans for peace to all men of good will: that true peace, which can and must come through forces of a higher and spiritual order, from the mind and the conscience of men, enlightened and guided by God, the creator and redeemer of mankind."[1] In the September radio "message", Pope John spoke of peace in penetrating and moving words:

> Mothers and fathers of families detest war. The Church, mother of all men, whoever they be, lifts up once again the voice that comes through the centuries from Bethlehem and Calvary, beseeching and commanding peace, peace which must have its source and its guarantee in the heart of each man.

> By peace, John went on, he did not mean "something negative, the mere detestation of armed conflict; but, far more than this, peace means something positive, and demands of every man an awareness and a fulfilment of his individual duties; it demands acceptance of a true scale of values, with sincerity, justice and charity placed first by everybody, so that possession and use of natural and technological forces be directed to raising both the spiritual and the economic standard of life of all peoples."

> Brotherhood and love, among all peoples and all races: this is a natural need and a natural demand. It is the command laid upon each Christian to govern relations between man and man, between peoples and peoples. The Council will proclaim this and exemplify this, solemnly and sacredly.[2]

---

[1] *Acta Apostolicae Sedis* 54 (1962), p. 9.
[2] Cf. *Acta Apostolicae Sedis* 54 (1962), pp. 678-683.

UNITY IN FREEDOM

The main import, then, of the Council, as conceived by Pope John XXIII, may be summed up as *Unity in Freedom*. The true worth of freedom springs from the dignity of each human person, endowed with intelligence and free will. This is the basic safeguard of human liberty; and that safeguard can be weakened and lost through exclusive interest in material goods and earthly enjoyments, through a materialistic technical progress which leads to selfish forgetfulness of the high dignity and worth of each individual person. Real freedom can be lost by reducing human persons to the status of mere parts in the machine of "progress", and assessing their worth by the exclusive standard of technological, scientific, or even financial "advance". Freedom is a value in the spiritual order, not to be measured in terms of wave-lengths, or the composition of atoms, or by means of statistics and graphs, and far less by financial balance-sheets. If esteem for moral worth declines, freedom inevitably suffers, and it is this that Pope John perceived and proclaimed.

But equally with freedom, the human race needs *unity*. It is clear that this need for human unity is insufficiently realized : the threats of war—indeed, the continuing existence of armed conflict in various parts of the world; the condition of under-developed countries by comparison with the more developed and wealthier; the troubles and ferment in race relations, which take differing forms in different regions; ideological oppositions, in the philosophical, economic and religious fields—all these tend to insufficient appreciation of the unity which ought to exist among all men. There is a fundamental equality of all peoples, without distinction of country, race, culture or religious faith, and this unity transcends all the differences. Right estimation and affirmation of this fundamental equality is an essential step towards the universal peace which all men desire. Consciousness of particularism in race, in nationality, in ideology, in religion, has tended to blunt the sense of common human unity, and to overlay the awareness of the duty, on the part of individuals and of peoples, to foster the common interests of all mankind and to work for the construction of a true community of all peoples, and thus to attain, not merely avoidance of war, but a truly international community fused together by a harmony of rights and duties, in brotherhood and love.

THE PURPOSE OF THE SECOND VATICAN COUNCIL

The announcement of a general Council by Pope John in January 1959 came as a surprise to many both inside and outside the Catholic Church. Generally the announcement was welcomed. But inside the Church there were some who were a little puzzled to know exactly what was the purpose of the Council, since practically all previous Councils had met in order to deal with some specific issue, and generally to declare the authentic Christian message as against some particular distortion or aberration. It has been said that one prominent prelate asked Pope John with some insistence what was the precise object of the Council and that the Pope went to the windows of the room and threw them open, saying : "This". The story may be invented : and it may be interpreted in two ways, first that the opening of the windows signified letting in new light and air; and, secondly, that the opening of the windows signified an opening to the great world outside. The two interpretations are perhaps only two sides to the same thing. If the Church was to increase and widen its impact on the problems of mankind, it would necessarily have to deepen and widen its own conception of itself; and its impact upon the world would, to some extent at least, depend upon a more general and co-ordinated effort which should affect the totality of the Church and not merely its comparatively few leaders. New ways of thinking in the Church might help to stimulate new ways of thinking in the world. A renovation of the Catholic Church might help on a reawakening to spiritual values in all human relationships. Moreover, as will appear later, Pope John regarded the Council as a more definite and more universal gesture towards the unity of all Christians, so that universal human brotherhood might be better fostered through a closer brotherhood of all those who profess to follow Christ.[1]

Pope John, also, felt and said that the Church of which he was head should give a concrete example of unity in freedom, of co-ordination and co-operation among free men who are brothers.

The secular press, and world opinion, speaking generally, welcomed the announcement of the Council and followed its preparation and its first Session not only with respect and even friendliness but with a surprising penetration and maturity of judgement. Though the Council represented a religion accepted by less than twenty per cent of mankind, and though in the minds of not a few it was a religion unduly authoritarian, narrow and suspected of intolerance, still it was recognized as a definite spiritual force throughout most of the world and the gathering of its representatives in a general Council was regarded as a significant event and development. There was a certain curiosity to see what would eventuate, an interest in the procedure of an assembly so large and so international, and even a certain readiness to listen to what this gathering might say about Christianity and world problems.

PREPARATION ON AN INTERNATIONAL SCALE

The first step was a consultation on a very broad basis, both as regards the people consulted and the form of the consultation. Some 2,800 letters were sent to Cardinals, Patriarchs, Archbishops and Bishops, to leaders of the Roman Congregations,

---

[1] I am aware that among our separated brethren there has been great interest in questions relating to human brotherhood, to problems of international justice and world order and their practical applications. For instance the Commission of the Churches on International Affairs, a subsidiary of the World Council of Churches, has made many most valuable studies and done most praiseworthy work in many fields. As the impulse toward full Christian unity grows, we may hope that all Christians may be able to make together more co-ordinated and effective efforts in the great cause of universal peace and human brotherhood.

and to all Faculties of Theology and to Catholic Universities. These letters did not contain anything in the nature of a questionnaire specifying what matters the Council might discuss, but contained an invitation of a most general kind to propose what subjects were judged suitable or urgent for the deliberations of the Council. Within eight months some 2,150 answers were received, the unanswered letters being accounted for partly by the fact that some bishops were denied freedom of communication with Rome, partly because some bishops agreed on a common answer, and partly because some were old and infirm. Cardinal Tardini, asked to indicate what things were suggested, answered : "Everything in heaven and earth—and more besides." The mass of these answers were classified and catalogued by the general preparatory Secretariat, and published in 14 folio volumes, running to about 10,000 pages.

This consultation was as universal as it was possible to make it.

The next step was the setting up of the Preparatory Commissions. The members of these numbered 877, and were drawn from 79 nations and from every continent, 27 from Europe, 17 from Asia, 13 from Africa, 20 from the Americas, North and South, and 2 from Oceania. They were men of varied positions, background and experience. Among them were 73 cardinals, 5 patriarchs, 363 archbishops and bishops, 212 members of the secular clergy and 284 regulars (drawn from 80 religious orders and congregations) and 8 laymen. Among the members were to be found not only bishops and priests engaged in ordinary diocesan and parochial work, but also teachers, administrators of various kinds, directors of charitable, social and cultural institutes, university rectors and professors, theologians, biblical scholars, specialists in canon law, liturgy and social sciences, journalists and radio and television experts.

It is noteworthy, also, that while the Commissions were concerned with subjects usual in ecclesiastical bodies, such as doctrine, morals, the customs and discipline of the Church and missiology, others worked in fields comparatively new, the lay apostolate, modern media of communication, and relations with our separated brethren (the Secretariat for the Promotion of Christian Unity). The basis of this work was the replies, over 2,000 in number, from the episcopate and the universities; but the commissions had access, also, to various sources of information, partly statistical, in the records of the Roman Congregations. They spent two years on the continuous and wearisome task of analysing the state of the Church, as shown in these documents, and in bringing to a focus the problems and the solutions suggested.

The preliminary consultation of the episcopate and the universities, with the analysis made by the Preparatory Commissions, broke new ground in the well-nigh two thousand years of the Church's history. It involved exchange of ideas, proposals and suggestions which was itself almost the equivalent of a Council. All this work, of the twelve Commissions and the two Secretariats, was summed up in *Schemata* and in this form was reviewed by the Central Commission. This last was composed of 60 cardinals, 5 patriarchs, 33 archbishops and bishops and the generals of the chief religious orders—a total of 103 members with voting rights. This Central Commission held some eighty strenuous sessions, each lasting from three to four hours.

It is interesting to compare this preparatory work with that done for the first Vatican Council of 1870, a Council which is not unimpressive compared with the previous series of Councils. Preliminary consultations for that Council took the form of a fixed questionnaire, to which there were some 224 replies, afterwards printed in a volume of 423 pages. The preparatory work was then carried out by a Central Commission composed of 9 cardinals, and by 6 special Commissions with a total of no more than 102 members. The First Vatican Council itself numbered only 764 Council Fathers, some hundred or so fewer than the number of members in the Preparatory Commissions for Vatican II.

It is not exaggeration to say that for none of the twenty Councils in the history of the Church was there greater industry and diligence in preparation, just as none had had so broad a scope or, one may say, so universal an aim.

INTERNATIONAL AND REPRESENTATIVE

After nearly three years of preparation the Council met on October 11th, 1962. What was immediately striking, as the long procession of 2,800 Fathers moved into the great nave of St Peter's, were the different races and the different dress. There were Asian and African cardinals, one Chinese, one Japanese, one Filippino, one Indian and one from Tanganyika. By residence, 40 per cent were from Europe; 16 per cent from South America; 14.2 per cent from North America; 13.2 per cent from Asia; 10 per cent from Africa; 3 per cent from Central America and 2.6 from Oceania (which includes Australia and New Zealand).

Again, a comparison with the first Vatican Council is interesting. In 1870, according to the most reliable statistics, there were 764 Fathers present, of whom 541, or 70.8 per cent, were from Europe; 113, or 14.7 per cent, from the Americas; 83, or 10 per cent, from Asia; 14, or 1.8 per cent, from Africa, and 13 or 1.7 per cent, from Oceania.

In the present Council, that is, after some ninety-two years, the European representation has declined from 70.8 per cent to 40 per cent; that from the two Americas and from Oceania has doubled, that from Africa has increased by a third and that from Asia fivefold. The increase of the general population may have been greater in the Americas, Africa, Asia and Oceania than in Europe; but even so, the decline of the European representation from 70 per cent to 40 per cent is striking and suggests that the Catholic Church is steadily becoming more international. A writer not of the Catholic faith has noted that "the Roman Catholic Church can demonstrate the universality of the Church, that is, its world-wide character, in most striking fashion". Please God, that may enable it to work more effectively for the unity and brotherhood of the whole human family.

Within the Church itself the Council is representative. Question has been raised whether representation might not be better if the ordinary clergy and the laity each had their own representation and spokesmen on the Council. The question, so put, is based on too close a comparison between political representation in secular assemblies and the "representation" in the Church of Christ. The Bishops are not "delegates" to speak for the interests and wishes of their particular diocese or area, but primarily are *witnesses*, able to affirm to the whole Church what is the faith of all the believers in their own diocese or area, and able to affirm to their own diocese or area what is the faith of the universal Church. Of the 2,800 "Fathers" who sit on the Council, there are 80 cardinals, 7 patriarchs, 1,620 archbishops and bishops in charge of dioceses, about 1,000 titular archbishops and bishops (some, e.g., rectors of universities, some in charge of particular apostolic organizations, some auxiliaries or coadjutors to diocesans), nuncios, apostolic delegates, vicars and prefects apostolic (who belong to missionary areas); 12 prelates *nullius*, 12 abbots *nullius* (i.e. independent of the local diocese); 73 generals superior of religious orders or congregations. Of those sitting with voting rights, 1,859, or 66 per cent, belong to the secular, or "diocesan", clergy, and 939, or 34 per cent to the regular clergy. The Council, therefore, is representative of everything which is most influential, and, one may add, best, in the Church, both among seculars and regulars. The members of the Council have had very varied experience, in different conditions, in different fields of work and in different forms of administration.

THE ATMOSPHERE OF THE COUNCIL

A fact, about the first session of the Council, which impressed many people, both within the Catholic Church and without it, was the presence, at each plenary session, of delegated observers from Christian communities not in communion with Rome. These "observers", some forty in number, came from no less than sixteen different countries[1] and represented all the major denominations which stemmed from the Reformation of

[1] Argentina, Ceylon, Denmark, Egypt, England, Ethiopia, France, Germany, Holland, Italy, Lebanon, Russia, Scotland, Switzerland, Syria, and the United States of America. A full list of the delegated observers, at the first and the second Sessions will be found in Appendix IV, pp. 252-258.

the sixteenth century, though the Baptists had no delegated observers, but one "guest observer" of the Secretariat. Observers also came from a good number of the ancient autonomous churches of the East, which are not in communion with many of the Orthodox churches. The Moscow Patriarchate sent "Delegated Observers" as did the Russian Church outside the Soviet Union. The "observers", then, came from nine of the great world "Alliances", "Communions" or "Conferences", "Federations" of the major Protestant denominations, from six Oriental Churches and from the Utrecht Union of Old Catholics. The World Council of Churches also sent an "observer" and the Secretariat for the Unity of Christians invited nine special guests, none of them being in communion with Rome, all, however, being eminent in the theological or religious world.

The invitation to send observers, its acceptance by the religious bodies concerned, the selection of capable and representative personalities, as well as the place of honour given them on the Council—all this is significant of the new atmosphere of frankness and mutual trust among Christians and impressed the world at large. As is well known, the Balzan International Foundation conferred its Peace prize for 1962 upon Pope John XXIII; and the reason assigned for the award—apart from mention of diplomatic efforts for peace—was his invitation of delegated observers to the Council. By this, the citation said, the Pope helped on and fostered "brotherhood among men and peoples" by bringing about "a greater degree of mutual understanding between members of the denominations invited to send observers and members of the Catholic Church, a fact which should have further important repercussions".[1]

[1] The Balzan International Foundation is patterned on the Nobel Foundation. Its first Chairmen were the President of the Swiss Federation and the President of Italy. It awards three prizes each year, one for services to the arts, literature and philosophy, a second, to peace and the humanities, and the third to natural sciences. The three prizes may, however, be merged into a single prize. The first award, in 1962 worth 1,000,000 Swiss francs—about $232,500, £80,000—was given to the Nobel Foundation; the second, in 1963, to Pope John XXIII, who directed that the money should be used to further the cause of peace.

Of the atmosphere prevailing at the Council the Rev. Dr George Williams, of Harvard, said this: "It is a new climate, a climate of trust, of mutual respect, which verges on the miraculous. I am a student of Church history and I have not been able to find any record of an atmosphere comparable to that prevailing at this moment of history, at this Council of the twentieth century."

FREE SPEECH

Professor Edmund Schlink was present as the official observer for the Evangelical Church in Germany. Later he wrote as follows: "Positively speaking, one must say of the Council that a genuine synodical event has taken place in an atmosphere which permitted free speech and free decision. Although the order of business and the appointment of the Council Presidency were in the Pope's hands and not in the Council's, it is clear that the Pope in no way imposed his own will on conciliar discussions as in the First Vatican Council."

Anyone who had dealings with the observers during the Council will know that these statements really do reflect the views of practically all of them and that it was the freedom of speech here referred to which made the deepest impression on them and on others from outside who followed the work of the Council. From the very beginning, the bishops were made to feel that in the course of the earnest discussions in progress they were perfectly free to express their own opinions and that the Pope would be the first to ensure that such freedom would always be fully safeguarded. The course of events during the first part of the Council made it abundantly clear that the function of the bishops was not simply to ratify the decisions of a central authority. They were on the contrary true members of the Apostolic College which, in union with the Pope, bore the heavy burden of responsibility for the welfare of the Church and of its mission to the world.

Clearly such freedom could not, in the eyes of Catholics, include the right to call in question any dogma already clearly defined by the Church. But, apart from such dogmas, there are many points of doctrine which are still insufficiently clarified, and there are countless questions of Catholic law and practice that need to be discussed. The bishops were able to deal with all these matters in complete liberty. Indeed so great was the liberty that discussions were sometimes perhaps unduly protracted, this being a lesser evil however than any restriction on the bishops' full freedom to express their views. It should here be noted that the existence of this freedom did not prevent the bishops from arriving quite often at practically unanimous conclusions. Indeed, in a number of secret ballots taken, two thousand votes being involved, only a few score were usually against the majority decision. Such unanimity, however, may not, and need not, always be found.

In this same spirit of complete sincerity, I said to the observers in my address of welcome :

> I beg you to put complete trust in us and to tell us in all frankness, especially during the course of the special meetings arranged for you by the Secretariat, whatever may displease you. Let us have your criticisms, your suggestions, your *desiderata*. I cannot of course promise to find a solution of every problem but I can assure you that we shall be thankful to be taken into your confidence. I can assure you that anything and everything you propose or say will be most seriously considered and weighed so that everything possible may be done, to the extent of our ability, both now and in the future.

This offer of mine was greatly appreciated and, what is more, it was widely accepted and acted upon. I can even add that certain suggestions made by observers were passed on through the Secretariat and put before the Council. One of the observers, during the audience given by the Cardinal Secretary of State, described the impression which our attitude had made upon him and his colleagues. He said : "We have had an extraordinary opportunity of getting to know members of your Church. We have had free access to all that has been going on, and have been able to see what genuine efforts have been made to understand our beliefs, our point of view, our hopes and difficulties. I am convinced that as a result not only have contacts been established—as the ecumenical phrase has it—but that genuine friendships have been formed, particularly between the observers and members of the Secretariat for Christian Unity, who have worked tirelessly for us and to whom we owe special thanks."

To conclude: the task of building up the unity, in freedom, of the human family is vast and challenging. It makes a demand upon each and every source of energy and of good will—a demand that these be brought together and that each of them be used to its fullest extent. But, to be used, they must first be known. It is for this reason—and not for any desire to make much of our own affairs or efforts—that I have used the Council as an illustration of one source of energy and good will, and of one group of men who are aware of the tumult of problems which press on mankind today, and are trying to co-operate in solving them. What I have said is meant primarily to give information; but I should rejoice if it were also an encouragement to anyone of good will to work to the best of his ability and as hard as he can for a better future for humanity.

6

The Dynamic Unity of the Church

GROWTH IN UNITY

MOST PEOPLE ARE AWARE, I IMAGINE, THAT THE Catholic Church is one single body. They know that all Catholics have the same fundamental outlook on human life, that all use the same religious rites, called sacraments, and that all owe religious allegiance to the Pope, the Bishop of Rome. This clearly gives the Catholic Church a manifest unity. This unity, however, is not static, nor is it merely external, nor is it merely legal; it is dynamic, it is internal to the mind and the hearts of men, and it is caused and maintained not merely by regulations but by the action of the Spirit of God on the spirits of living people. It is a unity which persists amid the various changes in the outlooks and activities of the people who make up the Church; and so it is a living, even a moving unity. In short, it is a unity among living human people.

Like other institutions, the Church can grow and develop; and in its growth and development its unity also grows and develops. It is, moreover, a unity in freedom, not a unity imposed by force and by fear, and hence, too, it is a unity, above all, of charity, which is meant by Christ to show mankind that unity among them does not demand an enforced conformity, does not lessen their freedom, but increases it, does not lower their dignity as human beings, but enhances it.

Let me, then, begin this chapter by speaking of the dynamism within this Christian body—a dynamism which has in the last year or two caused some surprise.

80

CAPACITY FOR RENEWAL

The New York *Times* wrote in December 1962 : "Millions of Catholics have discovered that their Church is as vigorous an institution as ever, keenly desiring renovation and reform. Non-Catholics are learning that this image of the Church as a huge, monolithic structure, is not an exact one."[1] The same opinion is expressed by Dr William A. Visser 't Hooft, General Secretary of the World Council of Churches, in an official report to the Central Committee :

> The Council has shown that the Catholic Church has greater capacity for renewal than most non-Roman Christians and in fact many Roman Catholics considered possible.[2]

The Catholic Church is a large body, containing perhaps 500,000,000 men, women and children; and it is part of Catholic doctrine that the members of the Church are not all saints, but sinners as well. It is well known that many who call themselves Catholics, and retain much of a Catholic outlook, yet are deficient in the practise of their faith. The "leakage", that is, the practical defection from the faith, is certainly great, how great perhaps no one knows. Many Catholics have been influenced by the materialism of their surroundings and fail to give the example they should. Moreover, it may be asked if the social teaching of Leo XIII and Pius XI has been every-where whole-heartedly accepted and real efforts made to apply it. Again, some countries have experienced a falling off in the numbers of vocations to the priesthood and to religious life; and in some areas, working people have felt that the Church was cut off from them and had no real message for them. Searching questions were raised : Was the Church's teaching being pre-sented in formulas, accurate no doubt, but often not meaningful to the modern mind? Was there a mental attitude which was too inward-looking, too defensive, too frightened of criticism?

[1] Quoted in *Ecumenical Youth News*, No. 9, Dec. 1962, p. 3.
[2] *Ecumenical Press Service*, 12 Feb., 1963, p. 1.

Was there such a concentration of authority that initiative was lessened, and a tendency induced in subordinate authorities to evade their responsibilities by throwing it upon the central authority? Were the resources of the Church being used to best advantage? Was enough use being made of modern media of communication? Was there danger, even among good and holy people, of confusing error which must be resisted with the people who err but must be loved? In short, was the Church presenting clearly enough her true image to the world?

MOVEMENTS IN THE CHURCH

Such questionings, based upon realization of the need of renewal, and of wide and deep consultation about the ways and needs of renewal, do not, of course, fail to recognize the renewal which had in fact been taking place in the Church. Many "movements" in the Church were encouraging and stimulating. I briefly list some of them, because their co-ordination and their further development has a bearing upon the renewal of the Church so that it may serve humanity the better. Each of these movements brought and is bringing its own contribution to the Church and so to the service of humanity: each, likewise, brings new problems of different kinds.

First, *the "missionary" movement*. The word "missionary" is almost out of date; but its real meaning is the effort to bring all men to Christ by founding the one Church, yet a thoroughly indigenous Church, in every land and nation. The term in Roman Catholic language usually designates territories or countries under the Congregation for the Propagation of the Faith. The dedicated self-sacrificing labours of many priests, brothers, nuns and lay people who have gone from their own countries to these territories (I can speak in praise of them since I have not had the honour of being of their company), has produced noteworthy results. Judging merely by numbers, in 1918 there were some 10,645,000 Catholics in "missionary" countries; in 1957 there were 37,564,000, a threefold increase in forty years. In 1926, there were 11 territories with Asian or

African bishops; in 1957 there were 128. The Encyclicals of Benedict XV in 1917, of Pius XI in 1926, and of Pius XII in 1939 and 1951 laid down wise and forward-looking policies for the "missions", based on evangelical principles; and their efforts certainly stimulated both vocations and far greater interest and help from countries where the Church has been longer established. The United States of America entered this field with its traditional immense generosity, and American missionaries showed an unexpected willingness and ability to adapt themselves to conditions and standards of living very different from their own. The principles governing this effort were : adaptation to local conditions, respect for older civilizations and in general the aim of making the Church as quickly as possible the Church of the inhabitants of the country, and in no sense a foreign importation. In 1936 the ancestor cult in Japan was admitted to be purely civil, and in 1939 a cult of Confucius in China was accepted as permissible to Catholics. In 1938 certain funeral rites in the Congo were admitted to be not contrary to Christian teaching and in Malabar a larger view was taken of their ancient rites. The number of institutes for the scientific study of missionary problems has multiplied, as has the number of periodicals. Christian art began to find new forms in Asia and Africa.

Changes in political, economic and social conditions, the grip of an atheistic Communism in China, in North Korea and Vietnam, the decline in the relative prestige of "European civilization" face the Church with new problems, but also with new opportunities.

BIBLE, LITURGY AND KERYGMA

Secondly, there were and, of course, are the biblical, the liturgical movements and the new "kerygmatic" methods in catechism. These are closely connected, for the liturgy, especially the missal and the breviary, is very largely composed of Scripture, and the new "kerygmatic" methods of teaching catechism apply to a considerable extent the brief, proclaiming sentences and phrases of Scripture, and teach, as so much of Scripture does, not so much by argumentation, as by announcement. Increased appreciation of the Bible brought deepened understanding of the action of God on the whole of human history. New translations in very many languages (in English, the Knox, the Westminster, the Confraternity and plans for a version acceptable to Catholics, Jews and "Protestants") were making the Word of God more accessible to the people.

The comparatively recent great increase in the number of people able to read ought not to bring forgetfulness of the fact that throughout the greater part of Christian history vast masses of people were illiterate : and their instruction in religion depended upon preaching, hearing the Bible read, the celebration of the various feasts of the liturgical year, the decoration of Churches, and the presentation of "mystery plays". Even today vast numbers cannot read, and many cannot command the concentration needed; a fact which should be a stimulus to artists, and to those engaged in visual artistry, to find inspiration in the great and moving themes of the Old and the New Testament.

These last years have witnessed a great impetus in biblical scholarship, which manifest in numerous lexicons, dictionaries, commentaries and in almost innumerable meetings, conferences and associations, and this impetus is having its effect upon theological insights and upon the general life of the Church. At the Council, the book of the Gospels was laid open in the centre of St Peter's, and, as Professor Karl Barth observed, was far more "than just a necessary piece of liturgical and ornamental scenery";[1] it was the symbol of God's Word in the living Church.

Changes in liturgy—that is, in the common worship of priests and people—had been gradual but significant : a new Latin version of the Psalms, in 1945; priests made extraordinary ministers of confirmation, in 1946; approbation of Mass in Chinese, 1949; the Easter Vigil, 1951; change in Eucharistic

[1] "Thoughts on the Second Vatican Council", *Ecumenical Review* XV, 4 (July 1963), p. 360.

fast and permission for evening Masses, 1953 and 1957; extended use of the vernacular in sacraments other than the Eucharist; "dialogue" Masses, and changes envisaged which should meet the needs of different countries, since there are parts of the world where there is no one single "vernacular" language; the Constitution on the liturgy approved in the Second Session of the Council (Dec. 4, 1963), synthesized the fruits of some decades of the liturgical movement, extending them, by official approval, to the whole Church. Wider horizons were opening in the manner of man's worship of God and service to God and to all God's children.

THE LAITY

Thirdly, the position and function of the laity in the Church had for the last fifty years and more been stirring deeper thought about "the apostolate of the laity" and the meaning of the priesthood of all the faithful. One of the most significant developments has been the work of the laity in literary fields : many influential Catholic weekly newspapers and a variety of monthly and quarterly periodicals, are edited and produced entirely by lay men and women. It would be invidious to mention even some of the authors of books in various fields, many of high value not only by literary or historical standards, but also in philosophy and theology; and in the publishing world Catholic laymen not only print and sell many excellent religious books, but have an influence in suggesting to authors the type of book they desire. Associations of lay people have multiplied almost beyond count : doctors, lawyers, journalists, employers, trade unionists, University dons and professors, University graduates, students, police, factory and other workers, including young workers—all have their own special association; and it would be almost impossible to count the number of guilds, "legions", and similar associations either for public, charitable, apostolic or purely spiritual purposes. In 1951 and 1957 there were World Congresses held in Rome to discuss and formulate doctrine and aims regarding the apostolate of the laity; in 1957,

2,000 persons represented some eighty nations and approximately fifty international organizations. A permanent committee was formed after the 1951 world meeting, to co-ordinate, to exchange information, and foster international contacts.

A development towards a more evangelical following of Christ which is new in the Church is that of "secular institutes", that is, groups of people who live in the world and not in community, wear secular dress, and dedicate themselves by promises in common to follow a special rule of life and to serve Christ in some particular way. There are over a hundred of these "secular institutes" which have been formed and approved, and about two hundred in process of formation.

Akin to this development has been, for the last fifty years or so, increased interest in the ascetical and mystical elements in religion, manifest by a large number of books, dictionaries and periodicals; there have been excellent studies on the history of monasticism, on Eastern spirituality, as well as on the various "schools" or trends of asceticism in the Western Church. The lives of saints have been written in a more critical and independent spirit and their real holiness and their heroic service to humanity are presented the more convincingly.

Fourthly, there was the "ecumenical movement", that is, the endeavour to attain the unity of all Christians. About this I shall have more to say in chapter 9 (p. 144).

Fifthly, there has been developing a movement towards greater consultation and co-operation among the bishops. By 1963 some fifty Episcopal Conferences were organized and have regular meetings to discuss common problems and to combine in solutions, for instance, in such matters as new catechisms; and published reports of the Second Vatican Council show that groups of bishops meet together, and that proposals have been made both for greater importance to be given to national or regional Conferences of Bishops and for something in the nature of a senate of bishops to assist at the centre.

All these movements for renewal—which were taking place in various ways and various degrees in different regions of the Church—were undoubtedly doing much to enable the

Church to carry on its task in a changed world. The question was, however, whether they were doing enough, whether new directives were needed about modifications in Church organization, in its emphasis upon different facets of its message, and, indeed, in its general orientation towards this rapidly changing world. Such directives would best be given by the combined experience and wisdom of the whole Church, as far as it could be gathered together.

"CONSERVATIVES" AND "PROGRESSIVES"

When the Council began its proceedings, surprise was expressed by very many at the freedom of discussion used by its members. Astonishment was expressed that one Cardinal could strongly disagree with another Cardinal. This surprise is explained by the current image of the Church : it is well enough known that the Catholic Church stresses the principle of authority, a stress which led many people, even well-informed people, to imagine that all Catholics, including the bishops, are almost subjugated by the authority and lack independence of mind and fearless expression of honest opinion. The freedom with which members of the Council spoke was not something that could have been improvised for the occasion; it indicated an attitude of mind, even a tradition, which in fact had existed, but was unrealized by many—and it was this which caused the surprise.

Even during the sittings of the Central Preparatory Commission there had been talk of a "conservative" and an "opposition" party; and later, as the Council proceeded, there was a tendency to dramatize the opposition between "traditionalists" and "progressives". The fact was, of course, that thoughtful leaders in the Church were concerned and even worried not so much about freedom—they knew the bishops well enough to know they were not men readily to be overawed or even curtailed in speech—but about unity. How was it possible to achieve fruitful unity in an assembly so large, and so heterogeneous? In 1962 there were 2,908 persons with a right to vote, although only 2,540 were present at the opening and the average attendance at the sitting was 2,300 or less. They came from 133 countries in all the continents, representing many races, and speaking many languages. Pope John XXIII, in his introduction to the rules of procedure, had said that the number and variety of those present on the Council were a source of anxiety as well as of comfort. "It will be no easy matter," he said, "to take in the import of the advice proffered in so numerous an assembly, to listen to the different voices, to take serious account of the wishes and proposals of everyone, and then to put all the final decisions into effect."[1]

Difficulties of procedure there certainly were, some overcome fairly quickly, some persisting, at least in the background. These difficulties were inherent in an assembly so large in which all members have absolutely equal rights to be heard, and whose decisions would have to win something approaching unanimity among the bishops if the decisions were to be implemented gladly and effectively. It is true that the Council has supreme authority in the universal Church (Can. 228, par. 1). It is also true that the Council works within the framework of the "deposit of faith", which means that it has no authority to change the faith handed down from the Apostles. The whole Council, the Pope included, joined on the first day in a solemn profession of faithfulness to the traditional belief of the Church, as contained in the Nicene creed and in the teachings of previous Councils. The Council cannot change the faith "once delivered to the saints" and this is the fundamental presupposition in its meeting; yet, holding always the unalterable faith, there is a large field of action and decision open to the Council. It can, for instance, both give explanations of doctrines that have been misunderstood and it can set into the whole context of the Christian faith certain doctrines which may have been considered too much in isolation (especially by separate brethren). One instance of this is the infallibility of the Pope. The very wording of the first Vatican pronouncement connected the infallibility of the Pope with the infallibility of the whole Church of Christ.

[1] *Acta Apostolicae Sedis* 54 (1962), p. 610.

The one cannot stand without the other. Indeed some have maintained that the real import of the doctrine of papal infallibility was the rejection of the theory which would make the Church a mere federation of independent national churches, each able to enforce its own particularism against all the others.[1]

This, however, is merely an instance to show how the Second Vatican Council has a certain freedom even within the unalterable framework of doctrine held to be revealed by God. The Council, also, within that framework can show the interconnection of doctrines one to another, can lay stress on certain aspects of doctrine as more relevant to the conditions of our time, can show the application of the faith to existing conditions, can issue prudential guidance and directives, and can modify ecclesiastical rules and customs. On all these matters those deliberating in the Council give their frank opinion; and it is natural that these opinions should differ. In the press—which sometimes dramatizes things a bit to rouse interest—a good deal has been made of "conservatives" and "progressives" in the Council; and there are in the Council, as in every group of human beings, those who feel drawn to traditional ways and those who stress the need for adaptation to modern conditions. It is good that it should be so, for thus a balance may be struck. And it is noteworthy that, though in matters of procedure

[1] It is insufficiently known that the famous words, *definitiones ex sese, non autem ex consensu ecclesiae, irreformabiles esse*—(the Pope's) "definitions are irreformable of themselves, and not from the consent of the Church" —were against the fourth "Gallican article" of 1682, which read: "... yet his (the Pope's) judgement is not irreformable unless the consent of the Church is given to it." cf. Cuthbert Butler's *The Vatican Council 1869-1870*, London, revised ed. by Christopher Butler, London, 1962, pp. 31, 379. Mgr. Vincent Gasser, Bishop of Brixen, Austrian Tyrol, gave an exposition of the definition which is generally accepted. For instance, he said that the infallibility "is not personal to the Pope as a private person, or private doctor. So we do not speak of personal infallibility although we attribute it to the person of the Roman Pontiff, not as an individual person, but as a public person, the Head of the Church in his relation to the Universal Church. Nor is the Pope infallible simply as Pope, but as subject to the divine assistance guiding him". Cited in Butler, p. 387, from Mansi, IV (52), 1204 ff.

votes were sometimes fairly evenly balanced, on matters of substance there has been something approaching unanimity, and a unanimity attained not by the intervention of the Pope, but by free discussion, good sense and the reasonableness of the conclusions arrived at. Many of the matters discussed, it is true, do not seem to have an immediate and direct bearing upon the question of the unity of mankind as a whole; but they have a definite bearing upon the renewed vitality of the Church, and hence ultimately will lead to a wider and more vivid realization and better fulfilment of the Church's mission to all mankind.

THE UNITY OF MANKIND AND OF THE CHURCH

As we said in Chapter 1, the unity of all men flows from possession of the same nature as free and intelligent beings. As such they are reflections of God, in the image of God, who is the infinite Intelligence and the utter Freedom. Moreover, men are also linked together by their relationship to God their creator, to whom—whether they understand it or not—they owe their being and existence, their intelligence and their freedom. God loves all men, the work of his desire to share his goodness and has a fatherly providence over them. On men's side, they are aware of their community in nature, from which springs a real brotherhood, guided by the principles of truth, of mutual respect for the freedom of others, and of justice and of love.

The Christian teaching, however, while accepting this natural unity of mankind, holds that God, without in the least lessening or harming this natural unity, has lifted it to a higher plane. God has freely given to mankind a new vital principle of unity, a transfusion into human nature of the very life-blood of God himself—in so far as one can use such language of God.

FOUNDATIONS OF CHRISTIAN UNITY

The Christian concept of unity must and does completely depend upon the truth that God himself became man, a truth difficult indeed for anyone to accept, but yet a fundamental truth of Christianity. Christians are well aware that the idea of God becoming man is not only mysterious, but practically incredible to the sophisticated or worldly mind. "This is indeed," said the Theologian of the Orthodox Church, St Gregory Nazianzen, "an unheard-of commingling and a paradoxical fusion. He who is, becomes: the Infinite is created and contained in space ... the Word becomes reachable by the senses, the Invisible is seen, the Inaccessible touched, the Timeless steps into time, the Son of God becomes the Son of Man."[1]

Yet all Christians not only accept the mystery, but find it consoling beyond power of expression. And, indeed, leaving aside the question of its truth, it is a conception at once sublime and inspiring: the Ultimate in all existence, being all love and all freedom, did not merely create men and leave them to the sorrows and afflictions inherent in the limitations of a created human nature, but willed himself to share those sorrows and afflictions and to become "in all things like unto us, sin excepted" (Heb. 4:11). It is part of Christian belief that it was God himself who suffered and died; God, indeed, not in his divine nature, but in the human nature which God, the Son, made to be absolutely his own, so that it was he who was really as much a man as any and all of us are men. God, then, knows what men are like and what they have to endure, not merely by spiritual knowledge but by actual experience.

And the purpose of this? It was to convince men of God's real love for them, since love is a sharing and God in becoming man shared all that is man's, sin alone excepted. It was to bring into the world a counterpoise and an offset to the pride, selfishness, hatred, cruelty and sin among men, and to show one Man who is utterly humble, self-giving, loving, kind, pure and sinless. One man, true man, but a man who also transcends the limitations of human personality and thus changes the very concept of what a man can be.

[1] Orat. 38, ch. II and XIII; *P.G.* 36, 313b and 325c.

THE NEW BROTHERHOOD

Yet this does not say everything. By becoming man the Son of God wished to share with men not only his own understanding of God, as far as men could grasp it, not only to tell men and show them how the ultimate reality of truth is united with the ultimate reality of love, but even to share with men his very nature, and make men, remaining men, to become divine. (2 Peter 1 :4.)

This, then, is the Christian solution of the "human predicament" : the Infinite entered into the finite, so that the bonds of the finite might be broken. God became man, as the earliest Christian writers so often say, that man might become divine. Christ is true God and yet true man : God, limitless, timeless, omnipotent, all-knowing, all pure : man, limited, bound to history, weak, ignorant, sinful : in Christ the two are united, save only that Christ was sinless, and in him a bridge is built that spans the fathomless chasm between God and man.

This is the foundation of all Christian belief, and the new and higher basis for the brotherhood of men. It is a noble conception, even looked at merely as an expression of the aspirations of the human spirit, and the telling of it in the sacred books of Christians is impressive even as literature :

> Sing for joy, O heavens, and exult, O earth :
> Break forth, O mountains, into singing.
> For the Lord has comforted his people,
> and will have compassion on his afflicted.
> But Zion said, "The Lord has forsaken me,
> my Lord has forgotten me".
> Can a woman forget her suckling child
> pity no longer the son she bore in her womb?
> And if she should forget,
> yet I will not forget you.
> Behold, I have graven you on the
> palms of my hands;
> Your walls are continually before me. (Isaiah 49 :13-16.)

And, with reference, though obscure, to Christ :

> Behold my servant, whom I uphold,
>> my chosen, in whom my soul delights;
> I have put my spirit upon him,
>> he will bring justice to the nations.
> He will not cry or lift up his voice,
>> or make it heard in the street;
> A bruised reed he will not break,
>> and a dimly burning wick he will not quench;
> He will establish justice in truth.
> He will not fail or be discouraged
>> till he has established justice on the earth,
>> and in the far-off islands men wait for it.
> Thus says God, the Lord,
>> who created the heavens and stretched them out,
>> who spread forth the earth and what comes
>>> from it,
>> who gives breath to the people upon it and
>>> spirit to those who walk in it :
> I am the Lord, I have called you,
>> true to my purpose, I have called you,
> I have taken you by the hand and kept you;
> I have given you as a covenant to the people,
>> a light to the nations
>> to open eyes that are blind,
> to bring out the prisoners from the dungeon,
>> from the prison those who sit in darkness. (Isaiah 42.)

And in the New Testament :

In the beginning was the Word, and the Word was with God, and the Word was God. . . .

And the Word was made flesh and dwelt amongst us . . . (and we beheld his glory, the glory as of the only-begotten of the Father) full of grace and truth. (John 1 :1, 14, 16.)

God so loved the world that he gave his only Son, that who-ever believes in him should not perish but have eternal life. For God did not send his Son into the world in order to judge the world, but that the world might be saved through him. (John 3 :16, 17.)

As many as received him, he gave them power to be made the sons of God; their birth comes, not from human stock, nor from nature's will or man's, but from God. (John 1 :13.)

Behold what manner of love the Father has bestowed upon us, that we should be called the sons of God; and so we are. (1 John 3 :1.)

Jesus Christ, "by whom he has given us most great and precious promises, that by these we should be made partakers of the divine nature." (2 Peter 1 :4.)

For Christians, Christ is the way, the truth and the life : and Christ is brought to them by the Spirit of God, the Spirit of Christ, enlightening minds, inspiring wills, sustaining love,—and this not only in men as individuals, but in the whole collectivity which we call the Church.

The Spirit is the spirit of sonship :

because you are sons, God has sent the spirit of his Son into our hearts, crying, "Abba! Father!" Gal. 4 :6.) "And all who are led by the spirit, they are the sons of God." (Rom. 8 :14.)

St Paul speaks of a "new creation" of those who are thus "made conformable to the image of God's own Son". (2 Cor. 5 : 17; Rom. 8 :29.) And here is a new equality of men, a new unity and, as I hope to show in the following chapter, a new freedom :

As many of you as have been baptized in Christ, have put on Christ.

There is neither Jew nor Greek, there is neither slave nor freeman; there is neither male nor female. For you are all one in Christ Jesus. (Gal. 3 :27, 28.)

The unity in Christ transcends race, nationality, standing in society, even transcends difference in sex; and here, too, is the reason why Christians should respect one another, even reverence one another, because they know that the very Spirit of God dwells in them.

Not that this denies difference of function. The comparison of the Church to a body was used by St Paul :

For as the body is one and has many members : and all the members of the body, whereas they are many, yet are one body, so also is Christ.

For in one Spirit were we all baptized into one body, whether Jews or Gentiles, whether bond or free; and in one Spirit we have all been made to drink. . . .

And if one member suffer anything, all the members suffer with it; or if one member is honoured, all the others rejoice with it.

Now you are the body of Christ and individually members in it.

And God has set some in the Church, first apostles, secondly, prophets, thirdly, teachers; after these miracles, then the grace of healings, helps, power of administration, and the speaking of tongues. (1 Cor. 12 :12-13, 26-28.)

The analogy is a most fruitful one : the Church has diversity in its unity and the very diversity contributes to the good of the whole. In a physical body, each organ is correlative to the other organs; and so in the Church laity, priests, bishops, and Pope are only conceivable as correlative to each other and to the whole. Each organ in a body helps the others—the heart, the circulatory system, the brain, the nerves—and depends upon the others; and so too, in the unity of the Church each group, each different function, at once helps the others and is dependent upon the others.

The analogy holds, too, in this, that as a natural body needs food for sustenance and health, so, too, does this body of the Church; and St Paul tells us of this food :

The chalice of benediction, which we bless, is it not the communion of the blood of Christ? And the bread which we break, is it not a partaking of the body of the Lord?

For we, being many, are one bread, one body, all that partake of one bread. (1 Cor. 10 :16, 17.)

The nourishment of the body of the Church, and its sustenance, like its unity, come from what Christians call "the Eucharist", which is at once a sign of the unity and its cause. Here, of course, arises the mystery of "sacraments" and the mystery of the union with Christ brought by the ever-present sacrificial food of the Eucharist. The mystery of the Incarnation, of the sacrificial death of Christ, the mystery of the union of Christians in the body of Christ, all stand together, all imply one another and depend on one another. The unity of the Church is not a natural union, like the union of a nation, based on geographical location, memories in common, political ideals or ideas, social intercourse and perhaps language and material interests, all intertwined : it is a union caused and preserved not only through common belief about the ultimate meaning of human existence and about the right way of life as revealed by God in Christ, but also through the action of the Spirit of God both in individual members and in the body as a whole.

THE ACTION OF THE SPIRIT OF GOD

The influence of the Spirit of God upon individuals is a constant theme in the New Testament : the Spirit of Truth (John 14 :17, 26; 15 :26; 16 :13), of charity (Rom. 5 :5), of holiness (Rom. 1 :4, etc.) of freedom (2 Cor. 3 :17), of sonship (Rom. 8 :15), of life (Rom. 8 :1; 1 Cor. 15 :45). The Spirit of God gives truth, charity, holiness, freedom, sonship, life to men, in and through Christ, for the Spirit of God is the Spirit of Christ. (Rom. 8 :9) This is almost a commonplace among Christians. But the Catholic Church believes, also, that the Spirit of God acts upon the whole body to ensure that it will throughout all time and in all places faithfully bring to men both the true message and the healing and inspiring power of Christ. In spite of external attacks and persecutions, in spite of sinners in the Church, and even in the sanctuary, in spite of internal corruption and periods when faith grew cold and worldliness too prevalent, nevertheless the Catholic faith holds firm that Christ's promises did not fail and will not fail, and that Christ through his Spirit has kept and will always keep the unity of the body of Christ : "one body, and one Spirit ... one Lord, one faith, one baptism." (Eph. 4 :4, 5.)

To his apostles Christ promised that the powers of hell would not prevail against the church (Matt. 16 : 18; 18 : 18); that as the Father had sent him, so also he sent his apostles (John 20 : 21) and, after commanding them to carry his teaching to all nations, he promised to be with them even to the end of the world (Matt. 28 : 20). The Catholic Church has understood that implicit in the universality of Christ himself and consequently of his Church, and implicit in his commission to the Apostles, is the obligation, upon those who succeed the apostles in that commission, to proclaim Christ's whole message, to give not only advice and admonition, but also directives to all the followers of Christ, who are thereby summoned both to closer unity of faith and of spiritual action. The followers of Christ must "obey truth" (Gal. 3 : 1; 5 : 7), must "obey the gospel" (Rom. 10 : 16; 2 Thess. 1 : 8); Christ's followers are "children of obedience" (1 Peter 1 : 14), and St Paul even speaks of "taking every thought captive to obey Christ" (2 Cor. 10 : 5) and in the letter to the Hebrews the command is explicit : "obey your superiors and submit to them, for they keep watch as having to render an account of your souls." (Heb. 13 : 17.)

The Catholic community in general does not find this authority burdensome, and, again in general, feels instinctively that a clear and firm authority, deriving from God, is at once a protection to them and a stimulus to a nobler life, and that it helps to maintain the supernatural dimension of human life. Especially since St Pius X gave a new impetus to frequent Holy Communion, there has been an increased sense of man's need for help from God against his weakness, and an increased aware-ness of the meaning of Christ's sacrificial life. Obedience to the Church is obedience within a family, and, though it may make exacting demands sometimes, usually in connection with mar-riage, it is not generally felt as burdensome. There is, in greater or less degrees, of course, a certain tenderness of piety, a certain delicacy and reverence towards the Christ-child born for us and for us "obedient unto death, even the death on the cross" (Phil. 2 : 8), and with devotion to Christ, a certain awareness, varying in vividness, of union with the martyrs and all the saints, especially the Mother of the Saviour, the Mother of God, and an awareness of the universality of the faith, and of the unity of the faith, symbolized and centred in its chief shepherd, successor of St Peter, the "Holy Father", or "the common Father". No doubt there may be some mixture of human elements in Catholic loyalty to the Pope, bishops and clergy; and no doubt there are grumblings at various failings. Yet a clear distinction is drawn between the man and his office : it would be, for instance, unthinkable for a Catholic today to distinguish between the Mass said by a holy priest and a priest less holy, or to imagine even for a second that Holy Communion could differ, by whatever priest the sacrament was consecrated. Moreover, though the Catholic Church is very definitely hierarchical, it is possibly more democratic in opening its hierarchy to merit, independent of wealth or social position, than any organization in the world. The people feel, generally, that the priests and bishops are theirs, and the more theirs since celibacy, which admittedly has its difficulties, is a sacrifice made for the benefit of the people.

To sum up, then, Catholic unity has elements both visible and invisible. The visible elements include outward profession of the same faith, participation in the same worship of God with reception of the same means of holiness called sacraments, and acceptance of the same visible religious authority, the shepherds with the chief shepherd of the flock. The invisible elements include the action of God's Spirit upon the souls of men, and upon the whole body to ensure that the essential message and the essential means of salvation, for this world and for the world to come, will never be corrupted or lost. It is a unity which transcends race, nationality, social position and individual gifts and talents. It is a unity, which is one of the signs making the Church not only visible but recognizable as Christ's Church, "that they also may be one in us, so that the world may believe that thou hast sent me" (John 19 : 21). Because the Church is made up of sinners as well as of saints, this unity may shine forth more conspicuously at some periods than at others, but Catholics believe that it never has failed nor ever will fail.

It is a unity flowing from the Son of God becoming man, and therefore exists for the good of all mankind; and the present second Vatican Council is meeting to try to make the Church in its unity better fitted to fulfil its task of helping all mankind to truth, unity and freedom, love and peace.

7

The Defence of Freedom

THE MODERN WORLD HAS UNHAPPILY SEEN A vast number of restrictions placed by men on the liberty of their fellow-men : tyranny, government by foreign nations, domination by groups, or by countries, by means of military, economic or financial pressures. There have been "totalitarian" states, claiming the right to subject the persons and even the thoughts of men to the control of a dictator or of a dominant minority. There have been arbitrary arrests, secret trials, denial of a free press, ruthless suppression of differing opinions, confiscation of property, concentration camps, exile, even the attempted extermination of racial groups by deliberate infliction of death.

Such dangers to human freedom are obvious. So, too, is the danger from materialism and atheism which deny in theory the basis of religious liberty. But in addition to these obvious dangers there are other dangers to liberty, more subtle and more difficult to meet. One of these is control of the means of information, which I discussed in chapter 3 on Mass Media of Communication. I now list some of the others.

THREATS TO FREEDOM

(a) The increasing "socialization" of modern life, the growth of what is called "the welfare state". As Pope John XXIII pointed out in his *Encyclical* "New Light on Social Problems"

(*Mater et Magistra*), "socialization" is becoming very generally embedded into social, economic and legal frameworks. "This development," says the Encyclical, "in the social life of man is at once an effect and a cause of the growing intervention of the State even in matters of such intimate concern to the individual as health and education, the choice of a career, and the care and rehabilitation of the physically or mentally handicapped. It is also the result and the expression of a natural, well-nigh irresistible urge in man to combine with his fellows for the attainment of objectives which are beyond the means or the capacities of single individuals."

The Encyclical then points out some of the advantages of this development :

> Clearly, this sort of growth in social relationships brings many advantages in its train. It makes it possible for the individual to exercise many of his personal rights, especially those which we call economic and social, such as the right to the indispensable means of obtaining a livelihood, preserving good health, receiving further education and a more thorough professional training; the right to housing, work, suitable leisure and recreation. Furthermore, the progressive perfection of modern methods of thought-diffusion—the press, cinema, radio, television—makes it possible for everyone to participate in human events the world over. (N. 61 of *New Light on Social Problems*)

Together, however, with these advantages go dangers to liberty :

> At the same time, however, this multiplication and daily extension of forms of association necessarily entails a multiplicity of restrictive laws and regulations in every department of human life. As a consequence, it narrows the sphere of a person's freedom of action. The means it uses, the methods it follows, the atmosphere it creates, all conspire to make it difficult for a person to think independently of outside influence, to act on his own initiative, exercise his responsibility and express and fulfil his own personality. (N. 62)

Pope John XXIII, however, by no means rested content with the negative aspect : "What then ?", he goes on, "Must we conclude that increased social action necessarily reduces men to the condition of being mere automatons? By no means." He suggests, to meet the danger, a general increased respect for human personality and for freedom, the formation and development in the State of subsidiary associations having a real autonomy yet working for the common good, and timely encouragement by the State of various forms of private enterprise.

(b) There is also, in many regions of the world, a tendency, if not a determination, to identify national or economic or cultural interests with the religion of the majority of the population. From this *tendency* and the danger it carries to religious liberty few countries and few religions in the world are absolutely immune, though the danger is more conspicuous in some than in others. In some regions it has proved impossible for peoples of different religions to live together in one State, and in many countries the position of minorities is made difficult, and charges of practical denial of civil rights are voiced. In not a few countries a change of religious allegiance would be regarded as an affront to the religion of the majority and would be followed by various social and even economic penalties, or at least definite disadvantages. I deliberately refrain from giving instances since they will probably leap to the mind of any reader.

(c) In many parts of the world religious "pluralism" exists, that is, people of different religions live in the same country or state, and this has been increased by various migrations of population. The danger here to real religious freedom is possibly so subtle as to be almost unnoticed; but the danger is real that religious convictions be weakened through the idea, subtly spread, that religion is a mere matter of opinion, that religious truth is impossible to attain and that all religions are more or less equally good. Social pressures against firm religious convictions and definite religious practice can be insidious and the way to a real indifferentism in religions is open and easy. Thus real religious freedom is lessened or even destroyed by a subtle process of erosion.

Recognition of this danger can lead to an excessive reaction towards intolerance and intemperance in vindicating the right of truth and the obligation to follow it.

DEFENCE OF RELIGIOUS FREEDOM

The importance of the question in its practical applications in various conditions, and in various parts of the world, demands most serious thought in order to fix principles on which true religious liberty can be established and defended. In the Secretariat for the Promotion of Christian Unity, for over two years the question was discussed by experts from various countries and in the *Schema* on Ecumenism our conclusions were set out for the consideration of the Council. Time did not permit full discussion in the Council; but I state here some general principles which seem to me fundamental:

1. Pope John XXIII, in the Encyclical on Peace, affirmed :

Every human being has the right to honour God according to the dictates of an upright conscience and therefore the right to worship God privately and publicly.[1]

2. This right Pope John XXIII lists among those which derive from human personality :

Any human society, if it is to be well-ordered and beneficial, must lay down as a foundation this principle, namely, that every human being is a person, that is, his nature is endowed with intelligence and free will. By virtue of this, he has rights and duties of his own, flowing, directly and concomitantly, from his very nature. These rights are therefore universal, inviolable and inalienable. (*Ibid.* n. 9.)

The right, then, to religious liberty is inalienable, and no human law can take it away. The truth and the law of God are too great to be fit only for slaves or to be imposed by compulsion :

---

[1] The Latin text reads: *ad rectam conscientiae suae normam*. The exact translation would be "according to the right norm of his own conscience" clearly meaning that it is right to follow one's own conscience.

they are meant to be accepted consciously and freely, by men who grasp something of their grandeur and magnificence. God wills the free service of his creatures, and this, too, excludes external coercion.

It is most pertinent to observe that Pope John XXIII defended the liberty of the Church on the ground of the liberty due to all men. In his Encyclical of June 29, 1959, on *Truth, Unity and Peace,* after speaking of the afflictions and sufferings of his children in some parts of the world, he went on :

> We have no desire to offend anyone. On the contrary, we freely pardon all and pray God for their pardon. But the consciousness of our sacred duty requires that we do all in our power to uphold the rights of these our brethren and children. We must insist therefore that the legitimate freedom to which everyone—and therefore God's Church—has a right should accordingly be granted to all men. Men who are concerned for truth and justice and the welfare of the individual and of State, they are not the men to deny freedom, to fetter freedom, to crush freedom. They have no need to act in such a way. Therefore the well-being of the citizens, if it is to be just, can never be attained by the use of force, nor by the fettering of minds and souls.[1]

Pope John did not ask liberty for the Church upon any ground special to the Church, but he appealed to a right which belongs to all men, and is founded on truth, justice and the general well-being of individuals and of commonwealths, or States.

3. This liberty includes two elements equally essential. It

[1] *Acta Apostolicae Sedis* 51 (1959), p. 528. The Latin reads: Sed sacri officii Nostri conscientia postulat ut horum fratrum filiorumque iura pro facultate tueamur; utque legitima libertas, quae omnibus debetur ideoque etiam Ecclesiae Dei, omnibus, ut oportet concedatur etiam atque etiam rogemus. Qui ea sequuntur quae vera, quae iusta, quae utilia singulis hominibus et civitatibus sunt, libertatem non renuunt, libertatem non restringunt, libertatem non opprimunt; non enim hac agendi ratione indigent. Quamobrem ad civium prosperitatem quae iusta sit, non vi, non mentium animorumque oppressione unquam deveniri potest.

excludes any compulsion by other men or society, and it enables a man to follow, conscientiously and freely, the laws of God, according to the norm of his own honest conscience. This liberty involves not merely the right to worship God, but also the right to profess his faith privately and publicly, to bear witness to it and to propagate it, always, however, with due regard for the general good, and for the rights of others. Thus, for instance, "suttee" or the burning of a wife on the bier of her dead husband, was forbidden in India; polygamy was forbidden in the United States, although some religious groups advocated it; "ritual murder" must rightly be forbidden, and in some regions, where feeling between people of different religions runs high, certain religious processions may be forbidden for the safety of life and property. The appeal to the "general good", however, cannot be made a pretext or an excuse for a denial of real religious freedom. It only enters in to protect either the rights of individuals such as the right of the widow in "suttee", or good order in the State.[1]

4. The right to religious freedom remains intact, even in the case where, in good faith, there is invincible error about religion, granted, as has been said in n. 3, due regard for the common good and the rights of others.[2]

5. The right of religious liberty which each man has carries with it the obligation that others, and particularly civil society, should respect it, safeguard it, defend it, and, if need be, regulate its exercise so as to protect the rights of others and of society at large as said in n. 3. It is a right that pertains to man as man,

[1] Article 29 of the Universal Declaration of Human Rights reads:
"(1) Everyone has duties to the community in which alone the free and full development of his personality is possible.
(2) In the exercise of his rights and freedoms, everyone shall be subject only to such limitations as are determined by law solely for the purpose of securing due recognition and respect for the rights and freedoms of others and of meeting the just requirements of morality, public order and the general welfare in a democratic society."
[2] Cf. Chapter 2, pp. 20 and 21. No man loses his right to freedom because he is in error.

and hence to each individual man, and to every religious group, granted a sincere following of conscience.

6. From this right to religious freedom follows the obligation of responsible religious decision. Religious liberty does not imply caprice, lawlessness or indifference to truth. On the contrary, since it is based, ultimately, upon the gifts of intelligence and freedom, it presupposes reasonable use of intelligence about religion and responsible use of freedom.

These principles apply to the whole human family and to men of all religions, Christian and non-Christian. As Pope John XXIII declared : "If we look upon the dignity of the human person in the light of divinely revealed truth, we cannot help but esteem it far more highly : for men are redeemed by the blood of Jesus Christ, they are by grace the children and friends of God and heirs of eternal glory."[1]

Thus Christians have an added motive for respecting the honest convictions of all men, whatever their race or religion. Christians, indeed, feel constrained by the "great commandment" of Christ, "Go, make disciples of all nations, teaching them to observe whatsoever I have commanded you" (Matt. 29 : 19). But, obviously, men can become disciples only by their own decision, and to teach presupposes willingness to be taught. Christ, during his life-time, did indeed lament the hard-heartedness and pride which led some to reject his message; but he never forced men to believe him. He relied upon the power of truth and of goodness and the evidence he gave that God was with him.

INADEQUATE REASONS

The importance of religious liberty demands that its justification be sound and unassailable. Merely pragmatic grounds, for instance, are not adequate. It is easy to say : "In fact, men of

[1] *Encyclical* on Peace, n. 10.

different religions have to live together, and this they can only do with mutual tolerance. Pluralism in religion is a fact of our times and serves as a means of securing liberty, since none can claim what they are not willing to concede to others." This reason is surely inadequate as a final and ultimate reason. In certain countries religious pluralism is a fact; but in others the vast majority may belong to one religion, and the rights of minorities are not protected by such a justification for religious freedom. Furthermore, Christians do not, and cannot, envisage a permanent state of religious pluralism as being the will of God.

Another justification sometimes alleged is that truth is a matter of opinion and that all opinions are equally good and hence all should be equally tolerated. That defence of liberty is self-destructive; for if it is accepted as a true statement, it denies what it affirms—at least it is true that truth is a matter of opinion and all opinions are equally good. The opinion, then, of those who deny the general assertion would, on the hypothesis, not be as good as those who affirm it. This, of course, pushes the matter to logical extremes, but does, I think, show that liberty must be based upon some commonly accepted truth or truths.

The dilemma facing some concepts of the basis of liberty is this: can toleration extend to the propagation of ideas that deny the basis on which toleration is justified? This is not a merely theoretical question. Recent years have shown that many governments are greatly concerned about "security"; those who have access to secret information are "screened", and the role of "security services" has widened very greatly, including investigation into character and into family and social connections which would make a man a "bad security risk". The case, of course, of those in particular positions of trust is exceptional; nevertheless their case does serve to show that a universal defence of liberty cannot be based on an amorphous general feeling that everyone has a right to his own opinion, no matter what it may be. Liberty cannot be defended on the assertion that all truth is relative, for the very defence of liberty depends upon the absolute truth that liberty is a good thing and worth defending. Despair of truth leads to the apotheosis of power, and not seldom to the worship of brute force.

It is, of course, quite another matter to say that in religious affairs the State should give equal rights to all conscientious convictions, provided they do not attack the basis of social order and do not cause public upset. It is, too, another matter to say that one must have not only charitable tolerance for those who hold religious views other than one's own, but must also have real respect for their personal dignity, as Pope John XXIII so truly said.[1] But this only proves that religious freedom cannot be defended if truth is regarded as relative. Such a defence leads inevitably to indifferentism in religion, and indifferentism is rejected by the majority of the great religions of the world, and notably by Chrisians and Muslims. Moreover, if it is a matter of indifference what religion a man holds, then there is no great reason why he should not be compelled to accept one religion rather than another, and the door is open to religious tyranny. The right to follow an honest conscience, with due regard for the common good, can be based, as Pope John XXIII said, only upon the inherent dignity of man and upon the intelligence and free will which God has given him and intends him to use responsibly and conscientiously. The law of conscience is written in men's hearts, as St Paul affirms. (Rom. 2:15.)

CHURCH AND STATE

In her long history the Church has experienced many different attitudes towards her on the part of different civil powers: some were hostile and persecuted the Church. Some were friendly and meant to help the Church, though in doing so not seldom they tried to gain complete control of the Church and use it for their own purposes; and sometimes churchmen became practically officials of the State and forgetful of their religious calling. Sometimes States were, and are, neutral to-

[1] Cf. above Ch. 4, p. 43.

wards religion and left the Church free to develop her own life, neither helping nor hindering. I confess that I now speak of matters outside my field of work; and yet I venture to record my impression that, making all allowance for the sins, defects, worldly ambition, exaggerated claims of churchmen, and for widespread corruption in the Church at certain periods, for instance, the tenth and eleventh centuries, nevertheless, striking a balance over the centuries, the Church has been a bulwark against despotism and tyranny and the protector of the poor and the weak against the savage lawlessness of the strong. The words of Christ echoed down the ages "Give unto Caesar the things that are Caesar's and to God the things that are God's" (Matt. 22:22), and echoed as a denial of state absolutism, and a defence of the soul of man against secular domination.

After a visit to the United States, which, though brief, warmed my heart, Archbishop Paul J. Hallinan sent me a question about the relation of Church and State, and I am happy to reproduce the question and my answer.

Question: The Catholic Church in the United States has flourished under our particular relationship with the State, as is evident from her pastoral experience and from the public statements of her bishops beginning with Archbishop John Carroll and continuing down to the present time. Can the American experience not be considered as enriching the historic teaching of the Church on this subject of Church-State?

Reply: Permit me to be brief and not to attempt any full discussion of all the aspects of the general question, since this is not my particular field. Of course, I realize that this question is intimately connected with the question of religious liberty. I believe, then, that I can briefly say that the truly flourishing state of the Church in the United States, even if due to a whole series of factors, undoubtedly constitutes an irrefutable proof that your particular experience in this area has been truly fruitful and that it can make a weighty contribution to the solution of this perennial and thorny problem. I can add that this experience is particularly useful today and will become more so since it involves an experience which developed in a particular form of society, that is, a pluralistic society. Now since religious differentiation is becoming more and more widespread today, the importance of your experience is clear. Consequently, without wishing to make suggestions (which does not fall within my competence), it is my desire and hope that, out of love for the Church, the leaders of the Church in your country—together with other Fathers of the Council—will, at the appropriate time and place, give to this question their forceful and fruitful witness, based on a rich practical experience.

By this answer, of course, I did not mean in any way to reflect on other systems or arrangements of relations between Church and State. Pope John XXIII summarized Catholic teaching when he said "It is not possible to give a general ruling on the most suitable form of government, or the ways in which civil authorities can most effectively fulfil their legislative, administrative and judicial function. In determining what form a particular government should take, and the way in which it should function, a major consideration must be the prevailing circumstances and the condition of the people; and these are things which differ in different places and at different times".[1] He likewise affirmed the need of adaptation to changing conditions :

Social life is so complex, varied and dynamic in this modern age that even a juridical system which has been established with great prudence and foresight often becomes inadequate to the needs of society.

It is also true that the relations of citizens with each other, of citizens and intermediate groups with public authorities, and the relations between different public authorities of the same State, are often so complex and so sensitive that they cannot be regulated by inflexible provisions.[2]

"Inflexible legal provisions" are not easily applicable to relations between Church and State, as experience has demonstrated. The general principle was laid down, of course, by Christ : Caesar has his rights, but so too has God. The Church has always opposed the idea that the State is a self-contained

[1] *Pacem in Terris*, nn. 67, 68.
[2] *Ibid.* nn. 71, 72.

and self-sufficient reality, which in itself is competent to be the guardian and promoter of all human good; but, similarly, the Church has never supported the idea that the Church should in any way usurp the functions of the State. Pope Gelasius in 495 declared that "the spiritual power should keep its distance from the entanglements of this world and, fighting for God, it should not become involved in secular matters; while in its turn the secular power should take care not to take over the direction of divine matters. Thus with both powers remaining dutifully in their places, both would handle competently the things which fall within its sphere."[1]

Nevertheless there are areas in which Church and State impinge upon one another : such matters, for example, as the holding of property by the representatives of the Church, education, marriage legislation, access to modern media of communication, public manifestations of beliefs which are offensive to the majority of citizens and may cause disorder or riots. In such matters solutions can generally be found by good sense, restraint, kindliness and patience, though admittedly it is difficult to secure even-handed justice in all respects, and to avoid a sense of grievance on the part of minority groups. Where civil liberty is denied, the Church is usually the first to suffer, as indeed the Church in some regions is suffering today, and the absence of certain bishops from the Council is an eloquent example, although only an example.

INNER FREEDOM

All this, however, concerns merely civil liberty, which consists mainly in freedom from external constraint. But within a man himself are impulses, urges, desires which can be constraints

---

[1] *De Anathematis Vinculo*, P.L.59, 108-9. The same doctrine appears in Leo XIII's *Immortale Dei*, Nov. 1, 1885. I may repeat here what I said in Chapter 7 of *The Unity of Christians* about need to interpret all theological formulations in the light of the historical situation and of the intellectual climate of the times, pp. 97-99. Certain declarations of the Popes, if read without awareness of the historical conditions in which they were made, may be completely misunderstood.

upon true freedom. The case of the "compulsive drinker" and of the drug addict are clear examples; they arrive at a stage at which, as one says, "they cannot help themselves", and their freedom is effectively destroyed. They do, in a sense, what they want to do; but even they, at certain moments, can understand that they are ruining themselves precisely by doing this thing that they want. At what stage they could "have pulled themselves up" probably no one can say, and certainly they get to a stage when they are beyond self-help, and beyond censure in each individual act of drinking or drug taking. But the example shows that real freedom does not consist merely in "doing what one wants or desires". Freedom is not merely satisfaction of desire. Animals satisfy their desires but they are not free.

Conscience places certain restraints and controls upon human beings; but it is a self-restraint, a self-control, and by it human beings are not made less but more human. Desires can be toward the good or the bad, and only reasonable judgement can distinguish between them, and only self-control can ensure that the good is both chosen and followed, the evil rejected. And the good is that which befits a human being in the wholeness of his being and in all his relations. There are, of course, differing judgements about what in particular is befitting and becoming to a human being; generally speaking, however, the rule is accepted "do to others as you would be done by", and hence truthfulness, honesty, faithfulness to the pledged word, fortitude, moderation, consideration for others, diligence, are generally accepted as befitting to men and are called "virtues", whereas lying, theft, betrayal of friends, cowardice, cruelty, arrogance, sloth, are accepted as worthy of dislike and are reprobated as "vices". Man can freely decide between his desires, and as he chooses to desire and follow the good, his freedom is perfected, not taken away.

This shows that freedom is not an end in itself. Sometimes civil freedom, that is, the throwing off of tyranny, and the attainment of a national self-government, may be a temporary and a most important end. But when the tyranny is overthrown and liberty attained the question is what the nation does with its freedom, what kind of a state is set up and what objects are pursued in freedom. Much more is this true of an individual man. He may, in a certain sense, be free in sin, and he surely is free in virtue; but his own conscience, and other men, do not approve him merely because he acts freely, but because he uses his freedom well.

In recent times, there has been a mood which tends to feel freedom as a burden. Part of the reason for this is confusion about what really is a good decision, what a bad, and this confusion tends towards avoidance of responsibility and to what may be called "a loss of nerve". Part of the reason springs from the difficulty of self-control, the difficulty in making right reason prevail over the various and varying impulses and desires which arise from lack of perfect balance between judgement and desires. Part of it springs from a sense of the unattainability of absolute perfection; whatever good a man chooses will be, in the concrete, a limited good, and, instinctively seeking a limitless good, man can become too acutely conscious of the imperfection involved in all his decisions. Together with this mood goes a feeling that the individual is caught up in a world so complex, so full of dangerous possibilities, that whatever an individual does can make little difference and therefore he had best get what satisfaction and pleasure he can manage during his short span on earth.

Against this mood fearing freedom, Pope John XXIII made an energetic protest in his *Pacem in Terris*, though the protest was put in a positive, not a negative form. Men are free and can use their freedom to control the forces that make for human misery; and his message gave hope and consequent energy to multitudes.

ST PAUL, PSYCHOLOGIST OF FREEDOM

Apart from Paul's strictly religious message, or perhaps embedded in it, is a view of human psychology which is of universal application, even though he was speaking to Christians :

> You have been called to freedom, brethren, only do not use freedom as an opportunity for the flesh, but through love serve one another.
> For the whole law is fulfilled in one word, "Thou shalt love thy neighbour as thyself".
> But if you bite and devour one another, take heed that you are not consumed by one another. (Gal. 5 :13-16)

Here two aspects of freedom are stressed : the negative aspect, that freedom does not mean excess or mere self-indulgence; the positive, that freedom fundamentally involves charity to others and mutual service. By the term "an opportunity for the flesh", St Paul means to include, as he goes on to say, "enmity, strife, jealousy, anger, selfishness, dissension, party spirit and envy", things which strike at the root of all human society, and through them people do "devour" and "consume" one another, and so destroy real freedom in human living together.

Paul makes plain that the law of God is only meant to ensure freedom, not destroy it. Indeed he says that the law does not apply to a good man :

> The law (given by God in the Old Testament) is not made for a just man, but for the lawless and disobedient, for the ungodly and sinners, for the wicked and defiled, for murders of fathers and murders of mothers, for manslayers, for whoremongers, for them that defile themselves with mankind, for kidnappers, liars, perjurers—and for whatever else is contrary to sound instruction. (1 Tim. 1 :9-10)

God's law, then, does no more than prevent man's destruction, the destruction of all that is most noble, holy and estimable in him; it is the highest sanction and guarantee of the innate worth and nobility of man's being, safeguarding the image of God in man and looking to his free and harmonious development.

Paul speaks often of the slavery of sin (Rom. 6 :6, 20), and of sin being a tyrant who dominates over man (Rom. 6 :6, 17,

20). Nor does he mean by this "slavery" merely the slavery of habit, though doubtless that is included; he means, also, subjection to the death-principle, which involves corruption, disintegration, dissolution, taken in the widest sense. (Cf. Rom. 5 : 12-15; 6 : 16-21; 7 : 13)

This principle, however, is not merely external to man but somehow has entered into his psychological make-up. There is a certain split in every human personality, which leads to interior conflict or complexes. The passage from his letter to the Romans on this is well known, but never trite :

> I am made of flesh and blood, sold into the slavery of sin. My own actions bewilder me; what I do is not what I wish to do, but something which I hate. Why then, if what I do is something I have no wish to do, I thereby admit that the law is worthy of all honour; meanwhile, my action does not come from me, but from the sinful principle that dwells in me. Of this I am certain, that no principle of good dwells in me, that is, in my natural self; praiseworthy intentions are always ready to hand, but I cannot find my way to the performance of them; it is not the good my will prefers, but the evil my will disapproves, that I find myself doing. And if what I do is something I have not the will to do, it cannot be I that bring it about, it must be the sinful principle that dwells in me. This, then, is what I find about the law, that evil is close at my side, when my will is to do what is praiseworthy. Inwardly, I applaud God's disposition, but I observe another disposition in my lower self, which raises war against the disposition of my conscience, and so I am handed over as a captive to that disposition towards sin which my lower self contains. Pitiable creature that I am, who is to set me free from a nature thus doomed to death? (Translation by Knox; Rom. 7 : 14-25)

St Paul does not specify to what extent all this is true of each individual man in the whole of his life. He generalizes about the human predicament, and certainly if one looks at the course of human history, evil seems to have a strange dominance : conflicts and wars, into which peoples are drawn against their deeper will, knowing that everyone will lose by them; the rise of tyrants who deceive people under appearance of good; social institutions and customs which make justice and kindness a mockery; "the law's delay," as Shakespeare puts it, "the insolence of office, and the spurns that patient merit of the unworthy takes"; the cynicism and cold-hearted selfishness; the eyes and minds shut to the sufferings of others . . . . if Paul was speaking of mankind in general, few could deny the truth of the sad picture he draws of mankind made captive to "the sinful principle which dwells within me".

Yet of individuals, too, what Paul says will be seen to be correct if one has a true standard and ideal of the nobility of man, and if selfishness, indulgence, and soft conditions of living have not dimmed the higher vision. Who does not feel, in his better moments, that he has failed to follow his nobler aspirations? Who can feel that he has done absolutely all that he could? Whose heart is absolutely pure?

And the remedy? The ancient Gnostics thought to find it in knowledge, in man's intelligence; but experience shows that the fruits of knowledge and intelligence can be used for evil as well as for good. The atomic bomb is a token of this. The ancient Stoics and Pelagians thought to find it in the strength of man's will, reinforced by good example; but, here again, experience shows that the conflict between desire and decision is too acute, that human decision for good is too wayward and that the basic presupposition of man's self-sufficiency is arrogant and in the long run unreal and ineffective. Still others—various "enthusiasts" and puritans—have tried to find a remedy in a rigidly austere and regimented form of society; but too often they made the false supposition that matter was evil and only spirit good, and the vast majority of men felt instinctively that their disdain or fear of human joy was unbalanced and unappealing to the generality.

The Christian solution, from the beginning, has been "the grace of God", which alone can give man interior freedom, for it gives a share in the very freedom of God. Throughout the centuries, the Christian Church withstood philosophies or theologies that denied free will: the Manichees, the Gnostics, the

Predestinarians, the Jansenists. However great the theoretical difficulties in reconciling God's omniscience and omnipotence with the contingency and indetermination of man's free choices, the Church stood firm to the truth of man's responsibility for his decisions. However great the theoretical difficulty of explaining how God's grace exerts an internal influence upon man's choices and yet leaves him free, the Church held firm to the need of God's grace in order that men may be truly free : "For the law of the Spirit of life in Jesus Christ has made us free from the principle of sin and death". (Rom. 8 : 2)

That "spirit of life" is the Spirit of God, brought and given by God incarnate; and the Spirit of God is charity. It is this Spirit which can heal the split in the human psychological make-up, can overcome the rebellion of the lower self, bring unity to the whole man, and light and warm his life with the fire of charity. "You shall love the Lord your God with all your heart, and with all your soul, and with all your mind. . . . You shall love your neighbour as yourself. On these two commandments depend all the law and the prophets." (Matt. 22 : 37-40) Love widens the heart, raises the spirit, knits the mind's conviction with the feelings and emotions, and increases and multiplies strength and power; as Paul says, he who has charity "is long-suffering and kind", for "charity does not envy; is not puffed up; is not ambitious, is not self-seeking, is not provoked to anger, thinks no evil, does not rejoice over wrong, but rejoices with the truth. Charity bears all things, believes all things, hopes all things, endures all things". (1 Cor. 13 : 4-7)

"Where the Spirit of the Lord is, there is freedom." (2 Cor. 3 : 17) This Spirit is the Spirit of love; and so St Paul can say :

> He that loveth his neighbour, has fulfilled the law. "For thou shalt not commit adultery, thou shalt not kill : thou shalt not steal : thou shalt not bear false witness : thou shalt not covet"; and if there is any other commandment, it is included and summed up in this word : "thou shalt love thy neighbour as thyself".
>
> The love of the neighbour works no evil. Love therefore is the fulfilling of the law. (Rom. 13 : 8-11)

Here is the summit of Paul's teaching on freedom. It is charity that brings independence of passion, victorious resistance to the strange compulsions of sin, and triumph over the confinement of selfishness which would destroy the true nobility of man's nature. Charity is the life-force of the Spirit, which finds its health, its growth and its happiness in love of God and of other men. Thus the possession and the practice of charity represents supreme freedom, and the true nobility of man.

Broken homes, juvenile delinquency, crowded prisons, corruption in business and political life—all these spring from a misuse of the God-given gift of freedom. They cannot be corrected merely by force. They cannot be corrected merely by making new laws. They can only be remedied by a more general attainment of true "inner freedom", by a wider and deeper appreciation of the real values of life. Some readers may disagree with the Christian conviction about the need of God's grace. Let them, then, address themselves to the problems involved in educating mankind at large, and young people in particular, about the need for the self-control which inner freedom connotes and which is essential to the well-being of society.

The expression "self-control" may sound negative and restrictive, and it may be better to speak of "responsible self-determination". The word "responsible" means that a man must be ready to answer for his conduct, sometimes to his fellow men, and always to his own conscience and to God. "Self-determination" means that in the last analysis each man must decide for himself about right and wrong and no compulsion from without can reach the inner recess of his conscience. The shape and character of a man's real life must be chosen and decided, under God, by himself alone. Others, of course, can help by wise counsel and heartening example. Society can help by maintaining worthy standards. But still each man remains free. Not even God will force him, though God can and does draw him, even through his freedom. And this is man's greatest glory, that he can give himself with complete freedom to the cause of truth, justice, charity and to the cause of the freedom of all mankind.

8

The Church and Freedom

NO MAN HAS ABSOLUTE FREEDOM OF THOUGHT, for all thought is bound by truth. Two and two make four: a man may, if he will, question or doubt this, but he cannot conduct his life in that doubt, for his dealings with others must rest on the hypothesis—accepted by most as true—that two and two do not make three or five but four. Scientists are not free to reject the results of experiments. The import, indeed, and the wider implications of the experiments may cause judgement to be suspended, but the results, within their due limits, bind the freedom of scientific thinking and all sciences rest on this supposition.

Moreover, every man in a very great deal of his life must trust in the witness of other men. He must trust, at least in the broad, the instruction given him by parents, teachers, professors and text books, for it is impossible for him to verify everything for himself. He must trust—again in the broad—to the competence of those who plan and manage transport by ship, train, automobiles and aeroplane. He must trust—again in the broad —the judgement of doctors, lawyers and experts in various fields. And lastly, he must, and does, trust the love of friends, of husband or wife, of children and parents, of parents and children.

In all these cases there is awareness that the trust cannot be absolute; nevertheless, using reasonable judgement to ascertain that the person or persons in question have sufficient knowledge and reasonable integrity, a man puts in them his practical trust, because if he did not, life would be impossible. He has, as we say, faith in them—a faith that he knows may perhaps be mistaken, but is still sufficient—and indeed necessary—in order that life may go on. Such faith and trust in other men is no abdication either of reason or of freedom; it is, speaking generally, a necessary prerequisite for the very exercise of reason and of freedom. Nor does it involve a mere conformity to conventional views and standards, for the scientific, medical, legal and other outlooks and standards change, even radically, and it is good that they should. It does mean, however, that it would be unreasonable to say one would not believe in the existence of Patagonia unless one had actually been there; or in the existence of whales or wombats unless one had actually seen them; or that one would not ride in an automobile unless one had first tested the steering for oneself. There are some things, at least, that one must take on trust. The mutual love of husband and wife for the founding of a family is perhaps the most conspicuous example.

To apply this to religion, first of all faith rests upon the testimony of God. As St John says: "If we receive the testimony of men, the testimony of God is greater". (1 John 5 : 9) Belief therefore springs not from immediate vision, nor from a series of logical arguments, but from the reliability of God himself; and in awareness of that reliability is contained some apperception of the goodness and love of God, who gives directions for human life because of his love for men. Faith therefore and trust are absolute, since God is absolutely true and absolutely good. By believing God, and accepting his guidance about life amidst the mysteries of life and death, man pays a tribute of love and of esteem to God; and in this way faith is a free and responsible tribute. It is not compelled by the evidence of our senses, nor by the force of logic; the very mystery of God himself is involved in the self-committal of faith. It is, indeed, reasonable to believe; but no reasons, like the evidence of the known truth, force the mind to assent. Faith must be a personal act, springing from the whole man and involving the self-giving of the whole man to God in utter trust. "We see now as in a glass darkly, but then face to face" (1 Cor. 13 : 12); we do not see God, there is still a curtain hung over our futurity, the life after death may seem unreal or even impossible; but the witness of God outweighs all the mystery and the apparent impossibility, and so faith commits itself to God, because the word of God is trustworthy and penetrates through all the mysteries and gives assurance in spite of what seem natural impossibilities.

Because, then, faith is necessarily a personal act, involving a personal relation to God, it is likewise necessarily a free act; and being both personal and free, it excludes all compulsion or coercion. This, as has been said, is the essential basis for religious liberty; not that all beliefs are equally true, or have in them equal proportions of truth and fasehood, but that faith is a personal free act, and demands respect from all creatures for the personality and the freedom which God has given. This, too, is why religious persecution is hateful, for it is an attempt to come between God and the creature he has made, from whom God asks only free service and love.

Faith, too, in the concrete, involves obedience to God, even the obedience of the mind. And this is at once reasonable, and, far from restricting man's freedom, makes man more free. Of old the psalmist said : "I walked at large (or at liberty) because I sought after thy commandments" (Ps. 118 :45). God's commandments are for our good, and for our freedom, just as traffic regulations are for the good and the freedom of those who use the roads. Nothing would be more fallacious than to imagine the believer is less free than the unbeliever, or that the unbeliever is less "committed" than the believer. An unbeliever is a believer in fact, for he commits himself to his unbelief, and this unbelief cannot be a mere "neutrality", a serene superiority to all religious decisions. That "neutrality" is itself a self-committal and a decision, and a decision which may have momentous practical consequences. If a doctor refuses to give any opinion about the illness of a patient, the very refusal is a decision which may mean life or death to the patient. Similarly, the unbeliever's very refusal of decision inevitably affects his judgement about practical issues and binds him just as much as the self-committal of the believer binds him. Secularism can erect itself into a religion, with its prophets, its dogmas, its commandments and its prohibitions, especially its prohibitions against any manifestation of religious belief in public life. One of its main dogmas is the dogma of human self-sufficiency, and denial of this is a heresy which must be banished into the hidden recesses of "private life".

The difference between a believer and an unbeliever is that the believer has a map of life which shows him where there are impassable swamps and trackless deserts and unclimbable mountains; and he knows where he can advance in safety towards better things in this life and the next. The unbeliever is too often inhibited by doubts and fears and loneliness in the recesses of his heart; the sufferings and the injustices of life are to him unrelieved by any "greater hope" and it is easy for him to sink into the narrowness of cynicism, or the apathy of practical despair, or the defeat of mere pleasure-seeking. The believer, indeed, is not relieved of problems, nor does his belief free him from responsible decisions, but belief enables him to face his problems and make his decisions with freedom of mind and heart.

FREEDOM IN THE CHURCH

The Catholic Church claims to be the bearer of God's revelation, a claim which raises deep and complex problems both in the theoretical and the practical orders. How is it possible to know that God in Christ spoke to certain men and commissioned them to carry his message through the centuries to all men? How establish the fact that God has revealed truth to these particular men? To answer these questions is not easy and involves the whole of what is called "Christian apologetics". Moreover, my purpose in this chapter, as, indeed, in the whole book, is not to try to establish the truth of either Christianity or of Catholicism, but to show that that Catholic belief accords with human freedom. I may say, however, that there are a multitude of converging reasons which have in fact convinced millions and millions of men, many of them highly intelligent, that God did reveal himself in Christ and that Christ entrusted this revelation to his immediate followers who left behind them both written records and a community in which the message is contained. Men who came later can satisfy themselves by many reasons that this is so : the character of Christ himself, the content of the message itself which befits at once the character of God and the natural aspirations of good men, the astonishing spread of the Christian belief in spite of the harshest of persecutions, the beneficent effect on those who accepted the revelation as from God, and its power in lifting the ideals of men towards freedom, justice and charity and in so wide an effective realization of those ideals. But I merely mention some of the reasons which have led so many to accept as true the revelation of God in Christ and its faithful and authoritative transmission through the centuries. All this concerns the theoretical level.

THE OBJECTION

On the practical level, it may be objected that even granted God's revelation, one organized body which claims faithfully to hand on God's message, that is, the Catholic Church, in fact became a centralized, monolithic, monarchical body enforcing a kind of iron military-type discipline which stifles freedom of thought, of initiative and of personal decision. Is it adequate to answer—referring to the Council which is now in process—"No one could say that there is any suppression of freedom of expression or of consultation in the Council"? But to this it may be retorted that this is a new development in the Catholic Church, that it has not always been so, and that the principle of papal supremacy and infallibility contain within themselves a theory of absolutism which has inherent possibilities of misuse of authority and of practical tyranny. Moreover, even the present Council only mitigates the essential authoritarianism by diluting it a little. The radical objection still stands, that the Catholic Church claims to bind the consciences of men in a way which is contrary to modern thought and to the democratic principles which more and more are being accepted as normative and alone in keeping with human dignity and freedom. In consequence, the Catholic Church must be mistrusted, for even its affirmations of human freedom may be only specious pretexts by which to aggrandize its power and entrap the unwary into surrender of their true freedom. The actual conduct of the Catholic Church where it is in a majority, makes clear that the Catholic Church in practice denies, for instance, the freedom of anyone baptized as an infant to change his religious allegiance and hence to marry except as the Catholic Church prescribes (Canon 1099, n.1, par. 1); the Head of the State in some countries must profess the Catholic religion; and all conscript soldiers are obliged to attend, on occasion, Catholic services and to pay a homage to "the host" which may be contrary to their conscientious convictions.

Before giving any "answer" to these "objections", let me say at once that I consider the most important question to be the direction of human thought towards the principles which can unite mankind in peace and love. It is true to say that neither Pope John XXIII nor Pope Paul VI had or have any great interest in controversy. The need to defend the dignity and the freedom of men is too urgent to allow time and energies to be wasted in controversies which rouse emotions and generally do small good.

Viewed, however, in the perspective of the unity of the human family, the charge that a body numbering over 500,000,000 denies real liberty to its members assumes importance, since that body would be an obstacle to attaining the unity in freedom of mankind. Consequently, I state briefly some Catholic principles as regards the freedom of its members and the use of its authority.

AUTHORITY EXCLUSIVELY RELIGIOUS

First, the authority extends only to religious matters and secular activities, as such, are outside its scope. It has, indeed, been objected that since the Church can settle what in the concrete is "secular" and what is "religious", the Church effectively claims that every activity of members of the Church falls under its authority. At least in modern times, this objection is concretely answered by the fact that Catholics, in many countries, belong to different political parties and have very differing views on matters of methods of government, economics and of culture generally. There are, as I said above (p. 111) areas where the distinction between the secular and the religious is difficult to define, and this applies, perhaps, with special force to the question of education. Good sense, however, forbearance and charity can find solutions on the practical level; and the danger to liberty, in an equitable judgement, must seem to come rather from the claim of secular governments to control, through education, the total thinking of their citizens, and thus "condition" them to a materialistic or secularist outlook.

In times past it is true that churchmen may have made exaggerated or unjustified claims; but here there is need for equitable historical judgement, taking into account all the circumstances and the prevailing mentalities. Catholic historians have no hesitation in admitting, and indeed revealing, the darker side of church history.

In some countries religion and the national ethos and culture are closely connected. This, however, is true not only of Catholicism, but also of Protestantism and of several non-Christian religions. In several countries a "Protestant" religion is "established". This "establishment" takes different forms, but it is defended as not denying freedom of religion to everybody nor as giving churchmen any control over the secular activities of citizens, but as being merely a practical recognition of the fact that the vast majority of citizens do belong to one religion and desire some recognition of that fact in national life. Doubtless, there may be some discomforts and difficulties in the position of a small Catholic minority in a predominantly Protestant country, and of a small Protestant minority in a predominantly Catholic country, and this is particularly true where there are memories of persecutions on one side or the other. The same is true of the position of Christians in countries predominantly non-Christian.

In times past, abjuration of the predominant faith in some countries was regarded as practical treason to the State, and this both in Catholic and in Protestant countries; and this gave rise to hateful persecutions. But those days are past, thank God. It need not, however, be denied that an individual who passes from one religion to another, whether from Protestantism to Catholicism or *vice versa*, or from a non-Christian religion to a Christian, may incur social disapprobation more or less severe. This is especially true in non-Christian lands, where "conversion" to Christianity is too often regarded as an affront to the prevailing religious convictions. For this reason it is important that Christians should defend religious freedom on the unassailable grounds of respect for human personality and dignity, and of the essential freedom involved in faith.

This is becoming more universally recognized by Catholics and in some Catholic countries a process of adjustment is in action, which will, it is hoped, remove all grounds for complaint.

The principle, however, stands firm and clear : the Catholic Church claims authority exclusively in the religious sphere; and in this sphere its authority presupposes the freedom of the act of faith in its adherents.

AUTHORITY IS CONSTITUTIONAL

Secondly, this authority is exercised, one may truly say, "constitutionally", that is by laws designed to prevent arbitrary exercise of authority. In practice, the Pope's authority, though supreme, is limited by the divine constitution of the Church, and by accepted Church law. The Pope, for instance, could not suppress the bishops, could not declare that there are ten or five sacraments instead of seven, and could not define anything which was not the universal faith of the Church. The definitions of the Immaculate Conception and of the Assumption were preceded by consultations of the whole Catholic world, and merely, in fact, made unmistakably clear what was and is the existing belief of the whole Church.

The meaning of these doctrines has, I think, been much misunderstood; they do not glorify an individual because of personal merits, but glorify, rather, the supreme freedom and the supreme kindness of God in his dealings with mankind; they protect the outposts of the doctrine that it was the Son of God who really became man; and they lift human hope to more vivid faith in God's supernatural activity in the world. But, whatever be opinion about the doctrines in themselves, the Pope could not have defined them unless they had been already part of the universal faith.

Similarly, bishops, priests and laymen have their rights and obligations fairly clearly defined and bounded.

In a body so large and so variegated as the Catholic Church, laws are at once necessary to maintain essential unity and to protect the liberty of everyone.

There have been, indeed, revisions of the Canon Law, and the present Council is in process of supervising further revisions. Pope Paul VI has indicated that changes are to take place in the *Curia*, that is in the permanent central civil service of the Church, and the changes will probably be in the direction of bringing the Curia into closer touch with the bishops, and of making it more international and more responsive to modern needs in a changing world.

The principle, however, stands firm and clear: religious authority in the Catholic Church is exercised in a constitutional manner and not arbitrarily. Abuses, naturally, there have been and may still be; but they are recognized as such and are generally corrected in due course.

Thirdly, a clear distinction must be drawn between (a) what is a matter of faith, (b) what falls under prudential guidance and (c) what is freely open to theological discussion.

(a) *Truths which are a matter of faith* are those which constitute the essential message of Christianity. It is part of Catholic belief that God protects his Church from propagating a distortion or falsification of the message of Christ to mankind; and that he assists the Church in that commission of transmitting faithfully and reliably the truth revealed by God in Christ. In practice, the Church believes that the decisions of general Councils, that is, gatherings of all the bishops as witnesses to the faith (of which there have been some twenty before Vatican II), have been a providential means of rejecting falsifications of the message by individuals or groups, and of safeguarding the faith in its transmission. Instances were the rejection of distortions which denied that Christ was a true man, or denied that he had a true human mind, or held that Christ was merely a man and not the Son of God.

There are, of course, truths contained in the Christian message which have not been defined by any general Council; such for instance, are all the truths contained in the Scriptures, granted right understanding and interpretation according to the mind of the inspired writer. Such, also, was the truth of the bodily Assumption of the Mother of God, which was believed in the Church before Pope Pius XII defined it.

The ordinary teaching of the Church is found in Catechisms, in the normal preaching, in episcopal pastoral letters and in papal *Encyclicals,* such as those of Leo XIII, Pius XI and John XXIII on various applications of Christian doctrine to social problems.

GUIDANCE BY THE CHURCH

(b) *Prudential guidance* is concerned in its positive aspect with affirmations of truths judged of practical importance, and with the application of those truths to existing conditions. In its negative aspect, which is more relevant to the question of liberty, the guidance is concerned with outlooks or views which do not clearly and manifestly contradict or overthrow the purity of the Christian message, but which, in concrete circumstances, form a danger to the faith of ordinary people. This prudential guidance is usually given to those in positions of some authority, such as teachers in theological colleges, writers and leaders of various "movements" in the Church. They may, however, sometimes be directed to the whole body of the faithful. The guidance may concern not so much the truth or falsity of certain views, but the stress laid upon certain aspects of the truth which could effectively overshadow other truths and lead to unbalance in presenting the Christian message. It may concern the advocacy and propagation of truths for which the generality of the faithful are not mentally or spiritually prepared. It may concern the issuing of a firm directive in a question disputed among Catholics; it may concern the application of Christian principles to concrete situations. In short, the area in which the authorities of the Catholic Church may give "prudential guidance" is extremely wide, and, to some extent, impossible to delimit by general principles, beyond the general principle that the Christian message must not be distorted or falsified.

In this area, infallibility is not claimed for the authorities of the Catholic Church. But this admission—or, indeed, this proclaimed truth—does not say all that ought to be said. Though in particular cases—that of Pope Honorius, who is generally admitted to have failed in due prudence, is an example—directives may be defective, and directives may not be forthcoming when many may think they should be forthcoming; nevertheless a Catholic is convinced that in the main the prudential guidance given by the authority of the Church does not fail in essentials over the centuries. A Catholic does not feel this guidance as a restriction upon his freedom; rather, he welcomes it as enabling him to unite his own thinking with a wisdom larger, wider and deeper than his own individual insights and judgements. Even though—as may happen—a Catholic scholar may find himself unable to grasp the reasons for certain directives given, he is glad, or at least willing, to obey in practice because he is convinced that God can and will direct even the mistakes of authority to ultimate good.

This prudential guidance may be given in papal encyclicals, or formal letters, which are to be interpreted according to their mind, intent, language and hearing in the whole existential context. Sometimes these encyclicals state the ordinary teaching of the Church, and then their authority is greater and more binding. Guidance is given, also, in various pronouncements of organs of the Church, such as the Holy Office, and the Congregation for Universities and Ecclesiastical Studies; and the norms of interpretation are, in general, the same as those for papal encyclicals. Usually these latter directives refer to teaching given to future priests.

PRUDENTIAL GUIDANCE AND CENSORSHIP

Books and articles written by Catholics upon religious topics must have *nihil obstat* and an *imprimatur* from the diocese where they are published or where they are printed, or from the author's own bishop. The grant of such approval for publication means only that a book or pamphlet is considered to be free from doctrinal and moral error, and does not mean agreement with the contents, opinions or statements expressed. Such censorship may in some cases be a restriction upon an author; but it is also a protection to an author, since it gives a guarantee against possible charges of unorthodoxy or laxity. Writers and authors, on any subject, very often are glad when friends read their manuscripts and make friendly suggestions; and usually those who read manuscripts before the grant of a *nihil obstat* do so in a friendly spirit. There are, of course, variations from diocese to diocese and from country to country in the standards applied in the grant of the *nihil obstat*; and there are, too, occasional instances of obscurantism, which is not encouraging to scholarly initiative and forward-looking thinking. But to imagine that the censorship keeps the minds of Catholics in chains would be unreal, as the not inconsiderable literary output of Catholics shows. The Church, after all, is not a research institute engaged in investigation and experiment to make new discoveries or to advance knowledge of science. The primary purpose of the Church is to communicate the saving message of Christ, and, though on that task new insights and advancement in knowledge can help better communication of that message, nevertheless on the whole intelligent Catholics, while regretting some conservative attitudes which regard the Church as a

beleaguered fortress, recognize the need for doctrinal correctness and the danger of scandalizing Christ's little ones.

What really scandalizes, however, needs careful appraisal, for
scandal may equally be caused by silence where Catholics are
rightly expected to speak out as by the expression of views
regarded by some as too liberal or too critical. There may be
greater danger in restrictive censorship than in trust to the
orthodoxy of Catholic theologians and thinkers and to the good
sense of reviewers. An atmosphere can be created which inhibits
that free play of theological discussion by which alone theological and cultural insights are developed and perfected to the
great advantage of the Church of God. The example of the condemnation of certain works of St Thomas Aquinas by some local
authorities is instructive; had those condemnations prevailed,
the loss to religion would have been incalculable. Today
Catholics inevitably hear and read in newspapers, periodicals,
on radio and television, things which in earlier times would
have upset them, but which today leave their faith solid and
unmoved. Hence the danger of scandal assumes quite different
aspects than it used to do.

A comparison may help: in modern cities and roads there
is need of traffic regulations in order to secure free flow of
vehicles and to avoid accidents. Those who use the roads may
judge that traffic regulations in certain cities or districts could
be improved, but pending their improvement through
representation to competent authority, the regulations must be
obeyed for the sake of free movement in safety. The comparison
fails in some respects, but holds in general. The prudential guidance given by the Church is designed to secure at once the safety
of the essential Christian message and the due liberty of members
of the Church. It should not be forgotten that the central
authority has repeatedly intervened against local arbitrary
action, and has repeatedly, even in modern times, protected
authors and leaders against charges of unorthodoxy made
locally with more zeal than discretion.

This *prudential guidance,* however, has a wider scope than
I have so far mentioned. During the nearly two thousand years

of its existence, the Church has had to deal with many diverse peoples, with different civil laws, customs, languages and ways of thinking; and even today the Church includes in its membership representatives of almost every nation on the earth. It was and is a formidable task to maintain essential unity and yet secure the diversity needed so that the whole Church may be enriched by each of the diverse elements in it. Over the centuries the Church has shown an astonishing flexibility in prudential guidance. The large number of Rites and liturgical languages, the different methods of appointing bishops and ruling dioceses, the enormous variety of religious orders and congregations, the multitudinous institutions for charitable purposes of all kinds, the diverse "movements" which have arisen in the Church and have been wisely encouraged, the high intellectual and spiritual quality of those who have been attracted to the Catholic Church and have served it so nobly—all this is evidence that the authorities of the Church, though certainly not perfect, yet over the centuries have had breadth of view and liberal outlooks. Equitable judgement should be based not merely on conditions in our own day and place, but upon some general survey of the history of the Church throughout the centuries; judgement, also, should compare the Church as a human institution with other human institutions: is there any other institution which for so long has stood for the supra-racial and supra-national unity of men, and, in essential unity, for the just diversity of individuals and of nations?

This is not meant in any boastful or complacent spirit. I am acutely aware that the Church has numbered sinners in its membership, and that even in its highest places, arrogance, worldliness, spiritual blindness, simony and a multitude of sins have been found. Yet I plead that the temporary should not be confused with the permanent, the accidental with the substantial, the local with the universal. The authority of the Catholic Church is unmistakably demanding. To follow the Church's teaching about marriage, for instance, may sometimes demand nothing less than heroic virtue and even the spirit of the martyr. But Christ himself was obedient even to death upon

a cross, and Catholic, and indeed Christian, obedience must
be judged in the light of Christ's example and teaching; and
must be judged by the standard of eternity and not merely by
the transitory and the temporal.

(c) *Free theological discussion* is wider and more radical than
many outside the Church are aware. It is true that for a period
there was nervousness and anxiety about the application of certain "critical" methods in study of Scripture; but it is also true
that some advocates of those "critical" views went to extremes
which serious scholars now reject and the propagation of these
extremist views both shook, or even destroyed, the faith of many
and brought suspicion on methods in themselves legitimate. The
Encyclical *Divino Affiante Spiritu* of Pius XII in 1943 did
much to lessen suspicions and to give new impetus to serene
and deep investigation into all aspects of the Scriptures. Catholic
scholars, naturally, may, and do, disagree, in courtesy, among
themselves, for there is no "party line" which all must follow.
There have been passing and limited flurries of anxiety lest some
Catholic biblical scholars may by incautious pronouncements
disturb the faith of the simple; but these flurries need not be
taken too tragically, for in the main biblical scholarship among
Catholics is sound, forward-looking and in friendly touch with
other biblical scholars both Jewish and separated Christians.

Freedom of theological views and investigation has always
been traditional in the Church, though the post-Reformation
controversial writings unhappily tended to make this freedom
less evident and conspicuous. Of old there were the divergent
"schools" of Alexandria and Antioch; from the thirteenth century onwards the Thomist, Scotist and Nominalist "schools" or
tendencies persisted and still persist, and sometimes rouse
acrimonious differences of opinion. Greater approval has been
given to the main lines of the "Thomist synthesis", but the
followers of Scotus still maintain a College at Rome and here,
too, there is no rigid "party line". Catholic theologians have
indeed been accused of excessive "rationalism" or of too great
reliance upon logic; this charge, however, involves no charge
of lack of liberty, and is sometimes made by those who, to the

way of thinking of many, unduly depreciate the worth and
capacity of human reason. There is, however, development
proceeding among Catholic theologians, with more attention to
historical and pastoral theology and to the interdependence of
philosophical outlooks and theological expression. Thoughtful
Catholics are by no means complacent about Catholic intellectual effort and achievement, and there have been very frank
self-criticisms, perhaps especially in the English-speaking world.
The criticisms, however, have not centred upon the question
of freedom, but rather upon dispersal of effort and upon a
certain inertia and lack of vigour; and it is noteworthy that
the critics do not complain of too much but of too little
centralization.

A NEW ERA

In conclusion, the message of the Church has always been a
message of freedom, especially of inner freedom, of freedom
from all within men which hinders them giving themselves to
the great ideals of truth, justice, love and the service of the
neighbour and of God. The unity of the Church is a unity which
protects freedom and brings power from God to know "the
truth which makes us free" (John 8:32) to curb self-centred
pride and to remain firm in humble service to mankind. The
reception of the most holy Eucharist is at once a protestation
of desire to follow the self-dedication of Christ for the whole of
mankind, and a means, divinely given, to fulfil that desire in
deeds. Loyal obedience of faith, to the religious authority which
God has established, is no slavish service but a glad self-giving
to the cause of human unity and a token of belief in God's action
in the world.

This does not mean that all is perfect or that ideals will be
attained either easily or quickly. Members of the Church bear
the burden of mortal flesh and blood, and the Church is ever
marked by the cross of humiliation and suffering.

Let me repeat: we live in a new era, an era full of dangers,
full of opportunities. Old ways of thinking are being revised.

New horizons are opening. Christians are seeking unity, and seeking it not for their sakes, but for the sake of their fellow-men all over the world. To those who are not Christians or not Catholics, aspects of Christianity and of Catholicism may seem strange and unacceptable; and yet we can appeal with confidence, as did Pope John XXIII, to all men of good will to work with us in human brotherhood towards the goal of the true unity of mankind.

9

The Scandal of Christian Divisions

SOME FACTS ABOUT DIVISIONS

NOT LONG AGO A YOUNG JAPANESE CHRISTIAN wrote:

> My father is a member of the Holiness Church, my mother is a Methodist; my brother is an Episcopalian, my wife is a Baptist, and I am a Congregationalist. Why are there such divisions in the family of God?[1]

This question of that young Japanese will strike the mind and heart more acutely after a very superficial glance at the Christians in the world. There are some 900 million Christians, who form about 32 per cent of the entire human family; but they are divided as follows: about 500 million, or 52 per cent of the Christians, are Roman Catholics; about 250 million, or 27.8 per cent, can be called "Protestants" and belong to Churches or communities which originated from the Reformation of the sixteenth century; and 150 million, or 16.7 per cent are "Orthodox", or "Eastern" Christians separated both from the Roman Catholics and from the Protestants. The "Orthodox" in turn are divided into two main groups; one consists of seven groups, separated from the Church in the fifth, sixth and seventh centuries, and divided among themselves (these include some of the Armenians, the Copts in Egypt, the Church

[1] Quoted by James E. Wagner from William Axling's *This is Japan*. "The Compulsions of a Church Unionist", in Robert McAfee Brown and David H. Scott, *The Challenge to Reunion*, New York, 1963, p. 28.

in Ethiopia and the "Syrian" Church in India); the other consists of the main body of the Orthodox who became separated from Rome from the eleventh century onwards and form some thirteen "autocephalous" churches, legally independent of one another but otherwise united in doctrine and general ethos.

The "Protestants" who broke from Rome in the sixteenth century, include six main groups, Anglicans, Baptists, Congregationalists, Lutherans, Methodists and Presbyterians (or the "Reformed"). To these may be added the Disciples of Christ. These main groups, however, are divided into smaller groups, independent of one another as regards administration and to a greater or lesser degree as regards doctrine or doctrinal emphasis and customs; there are, also, a number of churches quite different from the seven main groups, so that in the United States there are about 250 Protestant denominations.[1] Some of these last, however, have an exceedingly small number of adherents. More than three quarters of all the Protestants in the United States are to be found in the fourteen largest denominations with membership of a million or more, while at the other extreme, almost 200 of the 250 Protestant denominations are so small in membership as to constitute, all combined, only about 5 per cent of American Protestants.[2] Accordingly, 95 per cent of American Protestants belong to 27 different

[1] In 1957 Dr Frank Mead calculated that there were 266 distinct denominations or sects in the United States; cf. *Handbook of Denominations in the United States* (1957), New York, 1957, pp. 216-224. Benson Y. Landis's *Yearbook of American Churches*, for 1961, gives 254 bodies which reported their statistics, p. 257.

[2] Cf. the article of James E. Wagner, cited in note 1, p. 136. The term "denomination", or the more usual term on the continent of Europe, "confession", is a very general term indicating only lines, more or less broad, of church affiliation or allegiance. An American Baptist, for instance, may belong to the Northern or to the Southern Baptist Convention, a Lutheran may belong to the Missouri Synod or to the American Lutheran Church. In "congregationalist" theory, which is followed by Congregationalists, Baptists and the Disciples of Christ, each local congregation is strictly a complete church, owing nothing but charity to other local churches; in practice, however, unions or associations of local congregations into "conventions" or "synods" much modify the theory of local congregational autonomy.

allegiances, and the remaining 5 per cent are divided into 200 different allegiances.

In other parts of the world the "pluralism" of Christianity is similar to that in the United States. The *World Christian Handbook* for 1962 enumerates forty-two "Protestant" bodies in Great Britain, twenty-eight in Germany (fifty-one, if members of five unions are counted separately), and twenty-seven in France, though here, too, the impression of "pluralism" and disunity is lessened by the fact that a few churches contain the far greater numbers.

THE EFFECT ON NON-CHRISTIANS

But it is outside America and Europe that "the scandal of Christian divisions" is most striking. It is difficult even to attempt to classify the agencies engaged in efforts to bring Christianity to non-Christian peoples. In general, the same divisions exist in "missionary" countries as exist in America and Europe, but the divisions are accentuated by three factors. First, many "mission boards" or agencies are independent of churches; secondly, a number of the smaller groups are most active in "missions" and may carry an influence greater than their numbers would suggest; and, thirdly, many if not most missionary agencies are national and carry to non-Christian lands both their independence and the tone, if not the interpretation, of Christianity associated with their national history and ethos. Thus in India there are some 229 "missionary agencies" at work, in Japan, 179, in the Union of South Africa, 71, in the Congo, 44 and in Tanganyika, 41. Even granted very considerable charity and "comity" among Protestant missionaries, granted geographical separation and granted the immense amount of devoted work and medical and educational help, nevertheless the divisions among Christians remain both a grave obstacle to the acceptance of Christianity by non-Christians and a scandal in themselves.

It is our Protestant brothers who have given most forcible and eloquent testimony to this fact: "To ask the world," says

Professor Robert McAfee Brown, "to unite in a common humanity centred in Jesus Christ is flabby advice when those making the request are not even able to unite among themselves".[1]

"How can the Church," says Dr James E. Wagner, "speak to the world of peace and brotherhood while she herself presents to them the spectacle of disunity ?"[2]

Dr Lesslie Newbigin, a Bishop of the Church of South India, puts it concretely :

> The missionary cannot evade the question: "What body are you asking me to join?"

and, Dr Newbigin goes on to say, that question involves the whole problem of the broken unity of Christians, a problem which may be forgotten in a western city, but which cannot be evaded "if you stand in the streets of a great Asian city to preach the Gospel".[3] And, inevitably, Asians and Africans ask why differences, divisions, rivalries and antagonisms should be introduced from Europe and America and perpetuated in their countries, where they are not only irrelevant but can be an element disturbing the harmony of the citizens.

Speaking of co-operation in the Near East, Pope John XXIII said sadly in 1958 that "the agonizing problem of the shattered unity of the heritage of Christ always stands in the way to upset and impede the work of solving weighty difficulties and doubts".[4]

These practical difficulties only reveal the intrinsic evil of any division or disunity among Christians. Disunity contradicts the fundamental concept of Christianity. It disowns the prayer which Christ offered up to his Father the night before he died, that his followers should be united even as he and his Father are united. Christ came to bring men the unifying and liberating

[1] "Whence and Whither", in *The Challenge to Reunion*, New York, 1963, p. 9.
[2] *Ibid.* p. 19.
[3] J. E. Lesslie Newbigin, *Is Christ Divided?*, Grand Rapids, Michigan, 1961, p. 13.
[4] *Acta Apostolicae Sedis* 51 (1959), pp. 9-10.

force of the truth of God; disunity brings confusion about that truth. Christ came to bring the force of his mysterious presence and action in the mysteries or sacraments; disunity in belief about sacraments closes hearts and souls to the release of Christ's power in these mysterious ways. Christ came to enable men to proclaim his authentic message and continue his directives for human life; disunity obscures the message and confuses the directives. Christ came to unite men with his obedience to his Father; disunity strikes at the very roots of the obedience of faith, for it leads to doubt whether it may not be merely men, and not God, who invite obedience. Christ meant the unity of his followers to be the sign to the world that God had sent him; disunity clouds the clearness of that sign.

Familiarity with the fact of Christian divisions may, indeed, bring about a certain acquiescence; but even from a merely human point of view it is distressing to see the disagreements among those who sincerely profess, and so largely carry out, such noble and charitable ideals. But to the committed Christian the divisions are a humiliation, a grief and a stimulus; a humiliation, because a reproach, even from worldly people, must fall upon all Christians; a grief, because he is divided from his brothers whom he sincerely loves in Christ and the division is almost like a quarrel in his own family; and a stimulus, because the Spirit of God, the Spirit of charity, works within his heart, because new hopes are dawning and because the difficulties are a challenge.

IS THE DIVISION COMPLETE?

Christians, of course, are well aware of their membership in the great human family and their share in human brotherhood. But there is a bond—tenuous though it may sometimes seem, and forgotten as it not seldom is—between Christians which goes beyond the bond of the natural ties which link all men. To some extent this bond of Christianity arises from a common history and a common cultural heritage; this must be frankly admitted and its implications faced, since it causes doubts and hesitations in the world of Asian and African resurgence.

The bond, however, between Christians rises above historical and cultural association. In fact there have been Christians of non-European stock in Asia and Latin America for more than three centuries and in modern Africa for more than a century; and most Christians, basically, appreciate that anything approaching national or racial pride is contrary to the fundamental concept of Christianity. Faith in Christ is not a human attainment, it is the unmerited, unearned, gift of God, offered to all races and all nations and all "cultures". A Christian is not made by descent from his parents. A Christian is made by a new birth "of water and the Holy Spirit", and so is made a "new creature", "a new man".

Nothing could be stronger than Christ's denunciations against those who thought themselves privileged because of birth or wealth or superior knowledge : "I tell you, many will come from East and West and sit at table with Abraham, Isaac and Jacob in the kingdom of heaven, while the sons of the kingdom will be thrown into the outer darkness" (Matt. 8 : 11); "It shall be more tolerable in the day of judgement for Tyre and Sidon than for you" (Matt. 11 : 22)—words which apply to any Christians who take pride in the merely natural "heritage" of a Christian civilization and thus confuse the gift of God with the attainments of race or nation. Christian brotherhood rests upon faith in the fact that God has accepted us and through the new birth of baptism made us sharers in the sonship of his own natural divine Son. This was the reason why Pope John XXIII could "turn to those separated from us and call them brothers", using the words of St Augustine : "Then only will they cease to be our brothers, when they cease to say 'Our Father'."[1]

That prayer, the "Our Father", contains much of the common Christian conviction about life : man's dependence on God, the need to do God's will, and especially, perhaps, the need to be forgiven, the need to forgive, and God's protection in

[1] *A.A.S.* 51 (1959), p. 515.

trial. Almost all Christians, too, believe what is expressed in the brief summary called "the Apostles' Creed"; they accept, at least as an ideal, the teaching of Christ, summed up in "the Sermon on the Mount". All these things are implied, indeed, by baptism into Christ, as is manifest by the practice of almost all Christian groups of reciting the "Our Father" and the Apostles' Creed during the ceremony of baptism. And, in spite of all the sins and defects of Christians, in spite of the apparent bellicosity of nations which should have been truly and not merely nominally Christian, it would be hard to find any Christian church which did not feel the obligation to extend practical charity to fellow men; all over the world there are hospitals, clinics, educational and beneficent institutions of all kinds built and for long supported by the spontaneous gifts, and often the personal self-giving service, of Christians. If there have been many merely nominal Christians, who by their conduct brought dishonour on the Christian name, there have been, too, a multitude of Christian saints and heroes and simple unassuming people, who by uprightness, faithfulness and perseverance in self-forgetting labour for others, brought blessings on the Christian name.

All these things, and most especially the precious gift of baptism, which joins the baptized to Christ in his mystical body, unite Christians. It is true—and must be admitted with deep grief—that there have been periods when these principles and facts of unity seemed to be forgotten amid the bitterness and resentments which followed breaches among Christians. But in these last decades, Christians seem almost to be wakening, as if from a long and heavy sleep, and to be realizing how much there is that unites them in spite of their divisions.

CATHOLICS, ORTHODOX, ANGLICANS, PROTESTANTS

Even looking at the different Christian groups in more detail, there is much in common between the Eastern Orthodox and Roman Catholics : belief in Tradition, in the regular and full Apostolic succession of bishops and the teaching authority of bishops, in the divine efficacy of the seven mysteries or sacraments, and especially in the Holy Eucharist, the centre of religious life, a true sacrifice of reconciliation. There is, also, common belief that the first seven general Councils declared the true Christian faith, and a common veneration of the martyrs and saints, especially of St Mary, the mother of God, who is all pure and is now in heaven with her divine Son, and a special esteem for the monastic life. Many, though by no means all, Anglicans share these beliefs.

With regard to those who are generally called Protestants, beyond what I listed above as common to all Christians, it is more difficult to select specific matters of agreement. Generalizations about "Protestants" are admittedly hazardous for the word may be taken as including at the one extreme "high church" groups or movements (which now exist in many "Protestant" churches) and at the other extreme, various small "evangelical" bodies such as, for example, the Plymouth Brethren and the "Church of the Illumination". But I venture to refer to the very general veneration for the word of God contained in Scripture, devotion to the Person of Christ, a sense of the initiative and grace of God in all man's religious life, and, among the faithful generally, a sincere and deep piety, manifested in their moving hymns. In the last two centuries, their efforts to bring what many call "the glorious gospel of the blessed God" to non-Christians has been impressive, as have their translations of the Scriptures into many languages. All Christians are indebted to the scriptural insights and learning of so many eminent Protestant scholars. Moreover, the Christian faith of many Protestants has withstood the fire of persecution, for they have faced gaol and even death rather than be unfaithful to Christ. There can be no doubt that all this goodness is the fruit of their union with Christ through the grace of baptism and of the action of the Spirit of God in them. Anyone, therefore, who loves Christ and his Church will recognize, with joy and gratefulness to Christ, so much that is good and noble in these our brethren, separated from us.

THE UNITIVE MOVEMENT AMONG CHRISTIANS

In the last fifty years a change has been developing among the majority of Christian bodies, a change comparable to those of the "Reformation" of the sixteenth century; and just as the changes in the beginning of the sixteenth century were complex, affected the national, literary and cultural life of Europe, and were, by action and reaction, felt in the whole Christian world, so too, the changes developing through "the unitive movement", often called "the ecumenical movement", among Christians are complex, affect very many aspects of Christian thinking and living and are felt both in Christianity itself and in Christianity's impact on the world.[1]

At the root of this movement is the common conviction that existing Christian divisions are contrary to Christ's will, and a scandal to the world, and consequently must be eliminated in the complete union of all Christians. There are many factors which have helped to bring about this grief at divisions and a sense of compulsion towards unity: time and a changing world have softened the sharp outlines of the original causes of division; rapidity of travel and of communication together with increased migration or mobility of population tended to draw churches out of isolation; general modern developments favouring centralizations and standardizations had their effect on the organization of churches; deeper and more independent research into Scripture and early Christian sources led away from the nineteenth century "liberalism" and individualism, and towards more esteem for orthodoxy; the history of the

[1] The literature on the subject is immense. Bibliographies will be found in Ruth Rouse and Stephen Charles Neill, *A History of the Ecumenical Movement, 1517-1948*, London, 1954; H. R. T. Brandreth, *Unity and Reunion. A Bibliography*, second ed. with supplement, London, 1948; N. Goodall, *The Ecumenical Movement*, London, 1961; B. Leeming, *The Churches and the Church*, second ed., London, 1963; R. M. Brown and D. H. Scott, *Challenge to Reunion, The Blake Proposals under Scrutiny*, New York, 1963. Much useful bibliographical material will also be found in E. L. B. Fry and A. H. Armstrong, *Rediscovering Eastern Christendom*, London, 1963.

Christian Church began to be written with a greater sense of its complexity and with greater impartiality; awareness that Christians are becoming a dwindling minority in the world increased the conviction of the need for a united Christian witness. Within all this, and above all this can be recognized the influence of the Spirit of God, as the Holy Office did not hesitate to declare in 1949.[1]

Speaking generally—for here it is not necessary to enter into details—the movement is first conciliar, or consultative. Churches of "congregationalist" polity, which hold that the local congregation is itself a complete church, more and more became united into "Conventions" which managed things like theological colleges, missions at home and abroad, the building of new places of worship, publications, and the provision of chaplains in the armed forces, in hospitals and factories. The major "denominations" drew together in international association and of recent years more importance is attaching to the Lutheran World Federation, the Anglican Communion, the Presbyterian World Alliance, the Methodist World Conference and similar world councils of Baptists, Congregationalists, Disciples of Christ and Pentecostalists.

In different countries, various Christian bodies united together for consultation about common interests; such are the British Council of Churches and the American National Council of Churches. Missionary bodies in different countries formed "conferences" or "councils" to discuss matters of common interest,[2] and in 1920, largely as a result of the great World Missionary Conference at Edinburgh in 1910, a large number of these national missionary councils united to form the International Missionary Council, whose main purpose was to try to co-ordinate missionary activities, to stimulate thinking about

---

[1] *A.A.S.* 42 (1950), pp. 140-143.

[2] These national conferences or councils of missionary bodies include the missionary agencies of churches, and interdenominational missionary agencies such as the London Missionary Society and the Mission to Lepers, and, also, agencies less directly concerned with missionary work, such as the Society for the Promotion of Christian Knowledge, the United Society for Christian Literature, and Bible Societies.

missionary questions and to exchange information. It publishes the useful *International Review of Missions*, and has held large international conferences.[1]

Together with these conciliar movements, two other organizations arose in the second decade of the twentieth century : the *Faith and Order* Conferences and the *Life and Work* Conferences. The first of these, as its name indicates, was concerned to resolve the differences between Christians as regards their doctrinal tenets and the ministry; large conferences were held in Lausanne in 1927 and in Edinburgh in 1937. The Life and Work movement was concerned with the application of Christian principles in matters affecting international, social and economic order; and it held large conferences in Stockholm, 1925, and in Oxford, 1937.

THE WORLD COUNCIL OF CHURCHES

In 1948 the Faith and Order and the Life and Work movements, in association with the International Missionary Council, amalgamated and formed the World Council of Churches, whose membership now includes some 203 churches. In 1961 the International Missionary Council was fully integrated into the structure of the World Council.

All these associations are purely consultative and disclaim any authority over their constituent members. The various *reports* of the World Council of Churches are usually submitted to the member churches for their consideration. About 75 per cent of the non-Roman Catholic Christians in the world belong to churches which are members of the World Council; but of the Protestant missionaries perhaps only half belong to agencies associated with the World Council, and it has been said that 75 per cent of the Protestant missionaries in Latin America have no connection with the World Council or its Division for Evangelism.

---

[1] Jerusalem, 1921, Madras, 1938, Whitby, Canada, 1947, Willingen, Germany, 1952 and in Ghana, 1957/8.

THE SCANDAL OF CHRISTIAN DIVISIONS 147

The Basis of the World Council of Churches in 1961 was expanded to read as follows:

> The World Council of Churches is a fellowship of churches which confess the Lord Jesus Christ as God and Saviour according to the Scriptures and therefore seek to fulfil together their common calling to the glory of the one God, Father, Son and Holy Spirit.

In 1961, also, a definition of the goal of the movement, drawn up by the Faith and Order Commission, was commended to the churches for study and appropriate action. The text is as follows:

> We believe that the unity which is both God's will and his gift to his Church is being made visible as all in each place who are baptized into Jesus Christ and confess him as Lord and Saviour are brought by the Holy Spirit into one fully committed fellowship, holding the one apostolic faith, preaching the one Gospel, breaking the one bread, joining in common prayer, and having a corporate life reaching out in witness and service to all, and who at the same time are united with the whole Christian fellowship in all places and all ages in such wise that ministry and members are accepted by all, and that all can act and speak together as occasion requires for the tasks to which God calls his people.
>
> It is for such unity that we believe we must pray and work.

The *Report* goes on to say that this description of unity leaves many questions still to be answered, as indeed it does, notably how the "one apostolic faith" is to be determined, what doctrines of the Eucharist and of the Ministry are to be held and by what agency all are to speak together to the world. Nevertheless, this description of the Church represents a definite advance, brings many scattered ideas to a focus and can serve admirably as a clear basis for discussion. The *Report* adds that the achievement of unity "will involve nothing less than a death and resurrection of many forms of church life as we have known them. We believe that nothing less costly can finally suffice."[1]

From the beginning of these movements prayer has been recognized as the first essential in efforts at unity, and the need of prayer has been more frequently and more zealously urged, as time and experience show the intractable nature of the causes of division. Many, if not all, Christians feel that these fervent prayers have been answered in the new climate of charity among Christians and in the devoted and self-sacrificing efforts of so many to attain the unity which Christ wills; and yet they realize, too, the need of the interior guidance of the Spirit of God, so that human opinion may never be confused with God's truth, nor compromise with charity, but that through energy, patience and dependence upon God a solid and a lasting union in Christ may at last be established.

Alongside these conciliar movements have gone actual re-unions of diverse Christian groups, some merely the amalgamation of bodies of the same general denominational allegiance, which were organizationally separated, and others, unions of bodies from different denominational tradition. Of these last, the Church of South India was formed in 1947 by Anglicans, Congregationalists, Methodists and Presbyterians; and the United Church of Christ, in the United States, by Lutherans, Reformed (of Calvinist tradition) and Congregationalists. Definite plans for other such reunions are proposed, notably in the United States, of the Methodists, Presbyterians, Protestant Episcopalians and the United Church of Christ, and in England of the Anglicans and the Methodists.

A considerable number of Christians, however, take no part in this ecumenical movement, and, indeed, view it with various suspicions, as, for instance, that the World Council of Churches aims at becoming a "super-church", or that its attitude is weak as regards "Romanism", "Modernism" and "Communism". Some of these suspicions are shared by certain members of churches which belong to the World Council, mostly by those called "evangelicals".

---

[1] *New Delhi Report*, pp. 116-117.

ATTITUDE TO ROMAN CATHOLICS

The leaders of the World Council have steadily "kept the door open" to any possible contacts with the Catholic Church; and of recent years Catholic "observers" have been present at several of its meetings and assemblies and have been treated with the utmost frankness and friendliness. Personal friendships have grown up between many of the Staff of the W.C.C. and many Roman Catholics, a fact which has increased sympathy and understanding. The present official attitude is best summed up in the following statement of the General Secretary of the W.C.C., Dr W. A. Visser 't Hooft, to the Central Committee, in August 1962, about Vatican Council II :

(1)   We must follow the Council in the realization that much is at stake for the cause which we serve. We should accompany it with our prayers, seek to be fully informed about its work, do nothing which can make the task of the Council fathers more difficult, do everything that can encourage them in the accomplishment of the task of renewal of their church.

(2)   It should be made clear to the W.C.C. constituence that there is no question of any negotiations about organizational links and of course even less of the W.C.C. acting in any way for any or all of its member churches in this connection.

(3)   Hopes should be fostered of "dialogue" not only between individuals and in books, of which there are many, but between the R.C. Church on the one hand the W.C.C. and its member churches on the other. Dialogue, in the words of Father Congar, means "to take seriously the questions which we address to each other". It does not mean "surrender of principle or conviction, or indifference to truth, but caring for the others, listening to them, desiring real communication and mutual enrichment".

(4)   We are specially concerned about the action which the Council will or will not take with regard to questions which involve relationships of the churches, such as religious liberty, mixed marriages, prayer for unity and more generally to the question of the nature and limits of the Church. We must

honestly say that even within the membership of the W.C.C. we have not yet drawn all the consequences from our relationship as churches engaged in ongoing dialogue, and we must not ask from the Roman Catholic Church what we have not yet realized ourselves. Nevertheless, the hope is expressed that "the Roman Catholic Church will demonstrate its concern for other Christians and enter into a living dialogue with them".

From all this it is plain that Christians are well aware of the scandal to the world of their divisions and are striving seriously, and with some success, to overcome them and attain the fulness of unity which is the will of Christ. The spirit of charity is already great and is a significant ground for hope. Dr William J. Philbin, Bishop of Down and Connor, Eire, well says: "A drastic re-thinking of the attitude of Christians towards one another is the most extraordinary religious phenomenon of recent years. It's almost as if it remained for our age to realize acutely how anti-Christian is ill-feeling towards anyone who is endeavouring to follow Christ."[1]

WHAT DIVIDES US?

The division between the Eastern Orthodox and Western Christians has lasted for over nine hundred years; that between Catholics and Protestants for over four hundred. During those long centuries there grew up whole mountains of ignorance of one another, of misunderstandings, resentments, and rivalries, magnified and intensified by controversial writings and by memories of ill-treatment and persecution. Too often religion and politics became intertwined, and this fact has left an aftermath of antagonisms and suspicions, sometimes amounting to psychological complexes almost impossible to dispel, and this among some Christians of all allegiances.

It would be profitless to attempt any review of the sad history of the causes and growth of these sad divisions. Even to list the differences in doctrine can be misleading since the doctrines

---

[1] *Praying for Unity*, ed. Michael Hurley, Dublin, 1963, p. 11.

themselves carry overtones of historical associations; much Protestant feeling towards "Rome" is one example of this, and much Scottish feeling about bishops is another. Moreover, doctrines do not stand as pure disembodied truths, but are applied in actual religious life and, being interwoven with language, customs, music, literature, and sometimes even dress, become "group attitudes", with strong loyalty to the "religious heritage" of the group. Property is sometimes, or even often, held on explicit or implicit doctrinal conditions, and the trustees of that property feel obliged in conscience to administer the property according to the exact terms of the trust. Thus religious doctrines become embedded in an "institution" heavily resistant to change, even when the doctrines have lost their relevance or have been modified by new insights. All this is very manifest where a religion is "established" in a State; but it holds, also, wherever property is held for religious purposes.[1] In short, a religious body is also a sociological entity; and this to a considerable extent explains the slowness with which reunions of Protestant churches seem to proceed.

SPECIFIC DIFFERENCES

To come, however, to specific matters, both the Orthodox and all Protestants deny that the primacy and infallibility of the Bishop of Rome is part of the essential Christian message, while Catholics believe that it is. The Orthodox, indeed, with some Anglicans and others, might agree that the Bishop of Rome is Patriarch of the West, and might allow him a certain "primacy of honour". Other factors, too, have tended to soften the acerbities of older Orthodox and Protestant objections. Realization that according to Catholic teaching an Ecumenical Council has supreme power in the church (Canon 228); a

---

[1] William Stringfellow's *Law, Polity and the Reunion of the Church*, Faith and Order Commission Paper No. 32, 1961, is illuminating about the relation of the law of the different States in the United States upon the reunion or mergers of different denominations and upon factional disputes within a church. Mr. Stringfellow holds that the civil courts tend to favour "a conservation of the divisions of the past", p. 25.

growing appreciation that the infallibility has a more restricted scope than was sometimes imagined; the final settlement of the question of the temporal power of the Pope; studies like that of Dr Cullmann of the position of St Peter, as shown in the New Testament; the personalities of Pius XII and of John XXIII; the growth of conciliar movements among both Orthodox and Protestants, together with wider and deeper views of the unity and the continuity of the Church, the question of authority rising in the background—all this has put "the papal claims" into a somewhat new setting. Nevertheless, the primacy and infallibility of the Bishop of Rome remain still a deep chasm of division.

It is more difficult to make precise other differences between the Orthodox and the Catholics. It has been suggested that the differences lie in "the very nature of their theological thinking; in the very soil out of which their dogmatic, liturgical and canonical developments arise, in the very style of their religious life".[1] There is much truth in this, partly because the history of the East and the West was different, the West having to deal with different races than the East, and having to meet distortions of the Christian message which left the East unaffected. At the same time, both Orthodox and Roman Catholics agree that unity in the orthodox faith leaves room for a wide variety of theological thinking, of liturgical and canonical development, and of "style" of religious life. The Orthodox, however, would deny the right of the Latin Church to settle any strict dogma save in a Council in which they took part and hence would deny the binding force of any definitions since the second Council of Nicea in 787, even though they might agree with the substance of the doctrines so defined. Many Orthodox, however, object, on grounds both of procedure and of doctrine, to the addition in the Creed . . . "and in the Holy Ghost who proceeds from the Father", of the words "and from the Son", an addition retained by practically all the Protestants who use this

[1] Cited by Fr Georges Florovsky from an unpublished paper of L. A. Zander, "The Ethos of the Orthodox Church", in *Orthodoxy, A Faith and Order Dialogue*, Geneva, 1960, p. 68.

"Nicene" creed.[1] The Orthodox object, also, to the definitions of the Immaculate Conception of the Mother of God and of her Assumption, though the substance of these doctrines is contianed in the Orthodox Tradition and in the devotion of their faithful.

As regards Protestants, it is extremely difficult to give any adequate account of their differences from the Orthodox and the Catholics on the one hand, and their differences among themselves on the other. The "Confessions of Faith" of the sixteenth and seventeenth centuries[2] are no longer regarded as binding by many, if not most, denominations today, although there are some who cling to them even to the letter. Older books, even classic ones like Moehler's *Symbolism*, published in 1832, though still valuable, can be misleading about more modern times; and even the most recent books inevitably fail in some respects to reflect the complexities of the present situation.[3] To give even a superficial judgement of the impact of a form of Christianity upon the mind, the emotions and upon the life of its adherents, attention must be paid not only to what is held, but also to the emphasis given to certain elements and the relative unimportance attributed to others, manifest sometimes by the mere fact of omission. Thus, for instance the continuity of the Church throughout history has been a matter which had

[1] The doctrine of the procession of the Holy Ghost also from the Son is strenuously defended by Professor Karl Barth, *The Doctrine of the Word of God* (Prolegomena to Church Dogmatics, Vol. I, Part I). Translation by S. T. Thomson, Edinburgh, imp. 3, pp. 550 ff. Professor Barth holds strongly that the question of the procession also from the Son is not a mere matter of language, nor a mere *theologumenon*, but affects the correctness of the Christian apprehension of God and the very meaning of God's revelation.

[2] For instance the Augsburg Confession of 1530 (Lutheran), the Confessio Gallicana of 1559 (Calvinist), the Thirty-Nine Articles of the Church of England, 1571, the Westminster Confession of 1643 (Presbyterian), the Savoy Declaration of 1658 (Congregationalist), the Confession of 1646 (Baptist).

[3] For modern bibliographies on the subject, cf. n. 1, p. 144 above. For an introductory survey, cf. E. Molland, *Christendom. The Christian Churches throughout the World: their Doctrine, Constitutional Forms and Ways of Worship*, London, 1959.

little or no interest for many of the older Protestants, especially those of the "sect-type". They tended to leap from the present day straight back to New Testament times, as if nothing of importance had happened in the intervening centuries. Implicit in this omission is a view of the way in which God deals with men and with the Christian Community itself. Of more recent times, however, there has been far greater interest in the whole history of God's dealing with men, and new horizons are opening on the question of "Tradition".[1]

As regards the Orthodox and Roman Catholics[2] on the one hand and Protestants on the other, a very obvious and significant difference lies in attitude toward the first seven "Ecumenical Councils" of the Christian Church, Orthodox and Catholics regarding them as having final binding force, Protestants, with conspicuous exceptions, feeling free to doubt or to reject them. The differing attitude, for instance, to the seventh Council, Nicea II in 787, regarding the use of ikons, or images and pictures of Christ and the saints, revealed a deep

[1] In his sermon proposing a union of Methodists, Presbyterians, Protestant Episcopalians and the United Church of Christ, preached in San Francisco, Dec. 4, 1960, Dr Eugene Carson Blake, a Presbyterian, said: "The reunited Church must accept the principle of continuing reformation under the Word of God by the guidance of the Holy Spirit. A few years ago I would have felt that here was an issue on which no possible agreement could be reached. The Reformation Churches have traditionally found the authority for faith and life in the Scriptures alone. So long as the wording *sola scriptura* is required, no bridge can be made between catholic and evangelical. But it is now clear in ecumenical conversations that Protestants generally have come to recognize the right place of tradition, just as Catholics have generally become aware of the rightness of judging all tradition by the Scriptures as interpreted to the Church by the Holy Spirit." The sermon is reprinted in Brown and Scott, *The Challenge to Reunion*, New York, 1963, pp. 271-283.

[2] It should be noted that the word "catholic" is claimed by many. When in 1947 a group of Anglicans produced a book entitled *Catholicity*, a group of "Protestants" answered with a book entitled *The Catholicity of Protestantism*, ed. R. N. Flew and R. E. Davies, London, 1950. Some Roman Catholics dislike that designation, as implying they are only a category, or branch, in the universal Church. Others however like it, as indicating their association with Rome, of which they are proud. Thus the very titles used have theological overtones, as, obviously, has also the word "church". Such words, however, can, and indeed in practice, must, be used without doctrinal implications.

cleavage of conviction as regards the symbolic element in religion. The Orthodox and Catholics, for instance, make more use of vestments, ceremonies, incense, gesture and movement in their worship, whereas the Protestants tend towards greater simplicity and even austerity in worship, though congregational singing is usual.

Orthodox and Catholics make comparatively frequent use of "the sign of the Cross", that is, the moving of the hand to head, breast and shoulders to indicate the lines of a cross, together with an invocation of Father, Son and Holy Ghost, a practice used only by the "catholic" wing of Protestants. The church buildings erected by Catholics and Orthodox seem over-decorated and even tawdry to Protestants, while places of worship built by Protestants seem unduly bare and bleak to Orthodox and Catholics. Thus difference in acceptance of the "seven councils" not only illustrates a difference in determining Christian truth, whether by Scripture alone or by Scripture and Tradition together, but is very conspicuously manifested in practice.

As regards sacraments, or "the mysteries", Protestants in the main hold only two, Baptism and the Eucharist, whereas Orthodox and Catholics hold seven, regarding Confirmation, Marriage, Penance, Orders and the Anointing of the sick as in the same essential category as Baptism and the Eucharist, that is, as means by which the Spirit of God acts upon the souls of men. This difference shows itself in marriage, where Orthodox and Catholics give greater canonical and social significance to a ceremony in church than Protestants theoretically need to do, and in many cases actually do. The difference also shows itself in questions relating to the ministry, Orthodox and Catholics holding that episcopacy is part of the fundamental and essential constitution of the Church, that decisions about doctrine ultimately rest with the body of bishops, that this power of episcopal decision secures the continuity of the church in faith and sacramental order, and that a bishop is the ordinary minister of ordination. Protestants of presbyterian and congre-gationalist polity generally doubt or deny this "catholic" concept of episocpacy, while others who maintain episcopacy in practice give differing interpretations of the office of a bishop, some regarding it merely as the most suitable form of Church management, others accepting the whole ".catholic" position about episcopacy, and others holding various intermediate positions. In plans for reunion among denominations the question of episcopacy and of episcopal ordination looms large; several denominations of presbyterian and congregationalist polity are inclining to acceptance of episcopacy, provided no adverse reflections are made about their previous, non-episcopally ordained, ministry. Great developments here are in process. As regards forgiveness of sins, Protestants traditionally have denied the absolute need of individual confession to a bishop or a priest, while the Orthodox and Catholics have maintained it; but here, too, developments are in process and generalizations are hazardous. The same, likewise, is true of the doctrine of the Eucharist; there is a liturgical movement among very many separated brethren of almost all denominations and it has doctrinal repercussions.

Sometimes both Catholics and Orthodox are distressed and troubled when they become aware that there are those among our Protestant brethren who doubt or deny that Christ is truly God; but they recognize that such doubts or denials are not representative or characteristic and rejoice in the firmness of the World Council of Churches in making its Basis an unequivocal confession of Christ as God and Saviour, and of the doctrine of the Trinity.

Probably the issue of authority on the Church is the most radical difference between Roman Catholics and all other Christians. Catholics believe that acceptance of a loving, beloved living authority is the means revealed in Christ by which the essential message of Christ is protected from adulteration. They believe that this authority is a defence of human and Christian liberty against tyranny, an abiding safeguard amid the vicissitudes of history and the mutability of human opinion. It can permit and protect reasonable variations in matters accessory while maintaining unity in essentials. This Catholic position is, of course, denied both by the Orthodox and by Protestants. But both the affirmation and the denial now take place in an atmosphere of Christian charity which seems the dawn of a new era.

It is a significant fact that the secular press, radio and television throughout the world generally gives a favourable account of the efforts of Christians to unite among themselves. This is manifest in the coverage and comment about the meetings of the World Council of Churches and of the second Vatican Council. Such a sympathetic outlook may be merely a matter of courtesy as of general good feeling. One may also think, however, that these organs of publicity reflect a recognition that Christianity is a force in the world which upholds those spiritual values on which human freedom, human progress and human happiness ultimately depend; and that the more Christians are united the better they will be able to spread appreciation of those values, and to help on the cause of world peace and the harmonious development of mankind.

THE CHRISTIAN VIEW OF DIVISIONS

For Christians, their disunity is a cause of pain, humiliation and even, sometimes, of a temptation to depression or despair. The obstacles seem almost insuperable. But there is no reason for either depression or despair. God stands sure, and his providence guides and directs human affairs, even through human liberty, in ways that the human mind cannot fathom. Christian divisions are an evil, due not only to the sinfulness of men but also to "the world rulers of this present darkness, the spiritual hosts of wickedness in the heavenly places". (Eph. 6 : 12). The struggle for Christian charity and Christian unity is a manifestation of the cosmic struggle of "the god of this world" against God and against "his Christ". (cf. Luke 22 :53; John 14 :29; 2 Cor. 4 :4; Ps. 2 :2)

But God permits evil only because his all-powerful goodness can turn that permission of evil to a greater good. And God's plan, revealed in Christ, was not to overcome evil by the sole exercise of his own omnipotent spiritual power, but to overcome it in man and through men. If men succumb and are overcome by the spirit of disorder and sin, there is one Man, Christ the Son of God and Son of Man, who overcomes evil, and overcomes it, not merely by miraculous power, but by accepting all the conditions of human existence, by showing in his own human life that no pride can overcome humility and no hate can overcome love, and by giving to men a union with his humility and love so that they too can share in his victory on the Cross over the power of hate and pride and sin. And Christ's Church, which he wills to be his mystical body, is, like him, subjected to all the conditions of human life and to the vicissitudes of human history, keeping always its identity of being his body but yet often wounded, disfigured and sharing the shame of his Cross. Unlike Christ, however, the Church suffers from the sins and disloyalties of its own members.

And yet the words of Christ are still true : "In the world you will have affliction. But take courage, I have overcome the world" (John 16 :33). "The reason the Son of God appeared was to destroy the works of the devil" (1 John 3 :8). As he conquered by suffering, humiliation and death, so, too, must his Church.

What is the ultimate purpose of this mystery of the Cross, of the sufferings and the humiliations? St Paul answers : "For the foolish things of the world has God chosen, that he may confound the wise; and the weak things of the world he has chosen that he may confound the strong ... so that no flesh should glory in his sight and that he that glories may glory in the Lord." (1 Cor. 1 :27, 29, 31)

"But we hold this treasure in earthen vessels, to show that the transcendent power belongs to God and not to us.

"We are afflicted in every way, but we are not crushed; perplexed, but not driven to despair; persecuted, but not forsaken; cast down but not ruined; always carrying in our body the dying of Jesus, so that the life of Jesus may also be made manifest in our mortal frame." (2 Cor. 4 : 7-10).

Is not this why Christ allows the weeds to continue to grow

among the wheat (Matt. 13 : 29), the bad fish to be in the net along with the good (Matt. 13 : 47), and why he calls his Church "a little flock" (Luke 12 : 32) trusting utterly in God? The Church is like the yeast in the dough to be leavened, that is, in humanity until it is permeated by the spirit of God and raised to the dignity and glory which God plans for it.

10

The Council and Christian Unity

A MIRACLE

THREE DAYS AFTER THE OPENING OF THE FIRST Session of the Second Vatican Council, on October 13th, 1962, Pope John XXIII received the "Delegated Observers", about forty in number, who represented the great majority of Christian bodies separated from Rome. That evening, speaking to some journalist friends, I said : "It's a miracle, a real miracle." I had been, it is true, much moved by the meeting between the Observers and the Pope, who was seated, not on the usual throne, but in an armchair among them and spoke with a touching simplicity and open-heartedness; but my exclamation about a miracle included the whole experience we had had during the two years' activity of the Secretariat for Christian Unity.

Not long afterwards, Dr Oscar Cullmann, a Lutheran theologian and an observer, spoke as follows in a press conference :

> I subscribe entirely to what Cardinal Bea has already told you about our presence here : it is a miracle. Each morning as I watch us take our places—and they are places of honour, facing the Cardinals—then the Secretary of the Council, when Mass is over, pronounces the *Exeant Omnes* ... , and we can remain in our places, I am amazed more and more at how we really form part of the Council, and in making Cardinal Bea's word "miracle" my own, I give special thought to what past Councils meant to Christians who were not Catholics. I do not know if all laymen fully appreciate what our presence means in that light.

Probably Dr Cullmann had in mind the Councils of Trent (1534-1543) and Vatican I (1869-1870), when relations between Catholics and Protestants were certainly antagonistic, to put it mildly. The sad history of the nine long centuries which followed the separation of East and West, and the four centuries which followed the Reformation, make afflicting reading : fratricidal wars, bitter persecution, hatred, calumnies, prejudices, resentments, animosities handed down from father to son, and nourished by new and fresh sources of discord and misunderstandings.[1] The invitations to send observers, and their acceptance, on so solemn an occasion was a sign that the walls of division are beginning to crumble and that breaches in them have been made. There have been only twenty Ecumenical Councils in the long history of the Church, not more than once a century, and the presence at this twenty-first Council of representatives of so many separated bodies was in many respects unique. The World Council of Churches had indeed set a partial precedent by inviting "observers" from Churches which are not members of the World Council; the World Council, however, is not a church but a council of churches.

[1] Merely for the sake of examples, in the seventeenth century some Protestants could say: "There is no other head of the church but the Lord Jesus Christ, nor can the Pope of Rome in any sense be the head thereof; but is that antichrist, that man of sin, and son of perdition, that exalteth himself in the church against Christ and all that is called God." Some Catholic controversialists were no less vehement and virulent, saying, for instance, that "the fiends of hell begot Lutherans, Zwinglians, Calvinists and their churches are synagogues of Satan" . . The Reformers were said to be "detestable blasphemers, impudent liars, wicked libertines, slaves of the devil". Andrew Willet in his *Tetrastylon Papisticum*, London, 1593, collected a considerable number of "intemperate raylings, with shameful slanders and untruthes" from Catholic controversialists. As late as 1954, Dr Oliver Tomkins, now Anglican Bishop of Bristol, wrote: "Some Churches hold that the Church of Rome has so far departed from the truth of the Gospel that no other attitude can be taken up towards it than that of resolute and uncompromising opposition. Such contacts as the ecumenical movement has had with the Roman Catholic Church have exposed it to criticism from some of the more strongly Evangelical bodies, and have been among the reasons advanced by them for not joining the World Council of Churches." *History of the Ecumenical Movement*, London, 1954, p. 686. Among Catholics, too, what may be called a "war-psychology" or its aftermath, was not wholly extinct.

Individual Christian bodies occasionally invite a very limited number of "observers", usually of similar outlook, to their Assemblies, Synods or Conferences. Vatican Council II is a Council of the Roman Catholic Church, to discuss its own affairs and its own renewal. Dr Cullmann remarked that the presence of the Observers was a mark of trust :

> I want to underline the importance of this mutual trust, which in regard to us is translated into terms of being allowed to share all secrets, and to trace the very varied currents of thought in Catholicism. We must only hope that this trust will be passed on to the laity on both sides.

Indeed I can say that there was not only mutual trust : there was a conviction that we met in the deep faith of being still and always brothers in Christ, in spite of all the divisions and differences, and we met not merely with external courtesy, but in a spirit of prayer, charity and the frankness which can be used between brothers. The award of the Balzan Peace Prize for 1963 to Pope John XXIII was a recognition that the invitation to the Observers was a notable contribution to the cause of fraternity among men and peoples. It was a concrete sign that even centuries of mutual dislike, prejudice and resentments can be overcome in sincere if as yet incomplete reconciliation and as such it had implications for all human relationships.

NO IMMEDIATE UNION

After a short period of misunderstanding, it became generally recognized that the purpose of the Council is not to discuss any immediate union of all Christians, but to prepare the way for it by long-term planning. Unhappily the conditions are not yet ripe for a Council with representatives of different branches of the Christian faith to deal with union; the evidence for that is multiple and, sad to say, convincing. Nevertheless, the welcome given to this second Vatican Council was unexpectedly cordial. The majority of Christian bodies of different allegiance, through their leaders, asked for prayers that the Spirit of God might guide and inspire the members of the Council. To mention only some—for any list would run the risk of being incomplete—such appeals for prayers were made by the leaders of the Orthodox and other Eastern Churches, the Anglicans, Baptists, Congregationalists, Evangelical Christians, Lutherans, Methodists, Presbyterians, Reformed, Old Catholics, and by the World Council of Churches; and the appeals were made all over the world, in Africa, Australia, India and Japan, just as in the United States, Canada, and in Europe: Austria, France, Germany, Great Britain, Holland, Switzerland. Lord Fisher of Lambeth, former Archbishop of Canterbury, in Grace Cathedral, San Francisco, said:

> No council of the Church of Rome has ever met so surrounded by the prayers of other Churches, prayers in no sense against them—but for them and with them.

This prayer is regarded by Christians as of great and fundamental importance. Unity is a gift of God, not the result of mere human efforts or contrivances; the Spirit of God enlightens minds, inspires generous ideals and resolves; guides coincidences of events which we call "providential" and prepares men to be able to receive God's gifts. Christ gave an explicit assurance:

> Truly, I say to you, if two of you agree on earth about anything they shall ask, it shall be done for them by my Father who is in heaven; for where two or three are gathered together in my name, there am I in the midst of them. (Matt. 18:19-20)

This common prayer of Christians for the Council shows, too, that Christians already feel themselves to be united in a real way and to belong together. These prayers, and the general interest and good will shown towards the Council was noted by Pope John XXIII, who in his Christmas broadcast of 1962 spoke as follows:

> The Council was the occasion of an unplanned, and almost unexpected, disclosure of a certain reaching out toward unity; —or, perhaps it would be better to say, of an impulse towards

brotherhood, first sensed, then recognized and finally welcomed : towards that brotherhood in fact meant by the words of the Creed "one, holy, catholic and apostolic Church", which seeks not domination over men but service to men,—that brotherhood designed and willed by Christ, which meets the instinctive aspirations of mankind, even though its pattern and the way of its realization are not fully grasped.

Pope John went on to say that the heart-felt yearning for the unity willed by Christ is almost unique in the twenty centuries of the Christian era :

> Our contemporaries through the Council have become more feelingly aware of the religious problem, and there is an approach towards appreciation of the meaning of "the one flock and the one shepherd"—an approach as yet timorous and apprehensive because of doubts which we are able to imagine and which we desire, also, to understand so that by the grace of God, they may be dispelled.[1]

THE INFLUENCE OF THE DELEGATED OBSERVERS

The presence of the "Delegated Observers" had a notable effect upon the Council. The forty or so of them were, numerically speaking, almost a drop in the ocean of the 2,500 Council Fathers. Yet more than one bishop declared, and publicly, that the presence of the Delegated Observers had profoundly influenced the climate of the Council. Their presence, before the eyes of the Council Fathers, was concrete, almost tangible, evidence of the great problem of the divisions among Christians; and the Fathers were very conscious of this and showed it. Both in formulating doctrine and in discussing discipline and customs voices were repeatedly heard warning that no door should be closed whose opening might offer prospects of contacts with separated brethren. And they were not lifted in vain.

It should be noted, however, that the presence of the Delegates Observers was in no sense a weakening of the Roman

[1] *Acta Apostolicae Sedis* 55 (1963), p. 17.

Catholic conception of the Church; just as it should be noted that their presence did not imply recognition or acceptance of that conception by the bodies represented, or any weakening of their own position. Moreover, the Delegated Observers had no commission whatever to "negotiate" about union.[1] They were, as the name "observer" indicates, present to inform themselves of the proceedings and their significance and to report back to the bodies who delegated them. They could and did sometimes make known to the Roman Secretariat the beliefs and attitudes of the bodies to which they belonged. But this was done in an informal way and did not commit anyone save themselves. Nor did the mutual courtesy and even friendliness which was noteworthy in the relations between many "observers" and many prominent Roman Catholics imply that differences were of small consequence.

Nevertheless the presence of the Delegated Observers was of great significance. The Delegated Observers met once a week with members of the Secretariat for Unity, and expressed their ideas and their criticisms with the most complete freedom. As Dr Cullmann said, "the fact that it was possible to hold such open and such brotherly discussions, and at the fringe of the Council at that, must be considered a very positive element, and deserves a special mention by any future historian of the Second Vatican Council".

From all this it is clear that there was a true ecumenical spirit at the Council. This became known to a wider public as time went on. But of greater importance is the fact that the Bishops themselves have carried their impressions with them throughout the world, to their own dioceses and flocks. The same is true of the Delegated Observers, several of whom have expressed themselves in the same terms as those used by Dr Lukas Vischer, of the World Council of Churches: "It is true,

[1] The word "negotiate" in discussions of reunion of divided Christian bodies does not imply that doctrine is subject to "negotiation"; but it is rightly used of non-doctrinal matters, such as new delimitations of parishes or districts, distribution of man-power, co-ordination of missionary efforts and similar matters.

we have not overcome the difficulties which exist. Our separation has not suddenly disappeared. . . . We still have a long way
to go together. We do not yet know what the outcome will
be. But one thing is certain : the weeks that we have spent at the
Council have shown very clearly the desire to take this path
together, and this fills us with gratitude and hope."

THE NEW SECRETARIAT FOR UNITY

The establishment of the Secretariat for the Promotion of Christian Unity, and the enhanced status given to it during the
Council, is of definite significance. Hitherto, the Secretariat has
arranged contacts with separated brethren, and the invitation
to send Delegated Observers; and it has prepared and presented to the organs of the Council *Schemata* about various
questions which arise in relation with separated brethren. But
the importance of the Secretariat will be even greater after the
Council; its work during these last three years has been blessed
by God's goodness. But this is only a beginning, a promising
beginning, indeed, but yet no more than a beginning. There is
much still to be done. In the efforts towards unity, there is urgent
need—not of uniformity—but of prudent co-ordination, assistance, support and direction. There is need to receive and furnish
information, to promote the exchange of experiences, to en-
large contacts. And perhaps the most urgent task of all is the
spreading of the ecumenical apostolate among Catholics by
carrying it into every diocese, every parish, to every social group
or profession, into the life, no matter how humble it is, of each
one of the faithful.

The Secretariat, for its part, is already making preparations
for the task. At the end of the first session of the Council there
was announced the establishment—under a single president and
a single secretary—of two distinct sections: one for the
separated Eastern Christians of various rites, the other for those
which arose out of the Reform in the sixteenth century. The
two sections are now fairly well organized. These are all reasons
for making a proper comparison between the institution of the

Secretariat and the decision taken by the Holy See in the seventeenth century to establish the Congregation of Propaganda, that is, for the Missions. The basis of this comparison naturally does not lie in the fact that non-Catholic Christians are regarded in the same way as non-Christians—for certainly they are not —but only in the fact that the institution of the Secretariat shows how the Church is more vividly aware of its permanent responsibility towards Christians separated from the Apostolic See and has felt the need to establish a permanent organ to foster good relations with them, in a spirit of understanding, sympathy and respect. The Secretariat is an authoritative channel of communication, and a means of helping in all possible co-operation towards the realization of full unity.

POPE JOHN XXIII AND POPE PAUL VI

It is not too much to say that the world recognized true greatness in the humanity of Pope John XXIII. During his short Pontificate he had an astonishing influence on people of all kinds; his illness and death was felt almost like the illness and death of a father. And in the grief at his passing inevitably rose the anxious question: "What would become of the work he had outlined and begun, which stood in so much need of consolidation and development?"

Relief, then, was great when his successor Paul VI, within twenty-four hours of his election, announced to the whole world that he regarded the work of Pope John XXIII as his inheritance and intended to make its continuance the programme of his Pontificate: the Council, the reform of Canon Law, social and international justice in freedom, peace among nations, and the unity of Christians.[1]

[1] Cf. *Urbi et Orbi*, *A.A.S.* 55 (1963), p. 571. Before his election as Pope, Cardinal Montini had been quoted as saying that Pope John XXIII had "outlined certain paths which will be wise not only to remember but to follow. Can we turn aside from the path he opened so boldly to future religious history, that of the universality of the Catholic faith and of Roman ecumenism?"

In his address at the beginning of the second Session of the Council,

We open our arms, he said, to all who glory in the name of Christ, and call them by the sweet name of brothers; they will find in us unfailing good will and understanding; and we should like them to know that they will find in the Roman Church their own home, where the rich treasures of their history and their cultural and spiritual heritage will be enhanced and adorned with new splendour.[1]

In his coronation address, June 23rd, 1963, he spoke thus of Pope John and his work for unity :

In this matter we inherit the legacy of our unforgettable Pope John XXIII. Moved by the very breath of the Spirit he raised immense hopes and we regard it as a duty and an honour to endeavour not to disappoint them.[2]

In his address to the Delegated Observers on October 17th, 1963, Pope Paul VI said :

Thank you for having accepted our invitation, thank you for having come; thank you for your presence at the sessions of the Council. Be assured of our respect, of our esteem and of our desire to form with you, in Our Lord, the best possible relations. Our attitude does not hide any snare—nor does it yield to the intention of concealing the difficulties for a complete and definitive understanding; it does not fear the delicacy of discussion nor the pain of waiting. Good faith and charity is the basis which we offer to your presence here; the esteem we have for you personally and for the institutions and the Christian values you represent, makes it easy for us to take up with you the great dialogue, the duration of which no one today can determine because of the existence of doctrinal divergences which have not yet been resolved; and the confidence in Our Lord Jesus Christ, to whom we are all linked through

Pope Paul VI spoke in most moving terms of Pope John and said that his personal decision to call a Council sprang from divine inspiration, as did his pastoral outlook and his vision of the Church's call to speak to the modern world in language it can understand. Cf. *Osservatore Romano*, 30 Sept.-1 Oct., 1963, p. 2.

[1] *Ibid.* p. 574.
[2] *Osservatore Romano*, 1-2 July, 1963, p. 2.

faith and baptism, fills the heart with a sweet and powerful hope.[1]

In his opening of the second session of the Council, September 29th, 1963, he turned to address the Delegated Observers :

We speak now to the representatives of the Christian communities separated from the Catholic Church, who have been sent to take part as observers in these solemn meetings. We greet them from our heart. We thank them for their participation. We transmit to them our message—as an affectionate father and brother—to the venerable Christian communities they represent. Our voice trembles and our heart beats the faster both because of the inexpressible consolation and fair hope that their presence stirs up within us, as well as because of the deep grief we feel at the prolonged separation.

"FORGIVE US OUR TRESPASSES"

If we are in any way to blame for that separation, we humbly beg God's forgiveness, and ask forgiveness too, of our brethren if they feel themselves to have been injured by us. For our part, we willingly forgive the injuries which the Catholic Church has suffered, and forget the grief endured during the long history of dissension and separation. May the heavenly Father deign to hear our prayers and grant us true brotherly peace.[2]

Pope Paul reverted to this theme of forgiveness in his address to the Delegated Observers on October 17th :

"In what direction does our thought instinctively turn when there is question of giving a precise significance to the encounter—which is taking place, as you can see, in the highest quarters and at the level of highest responsibility—of the Catholic Church with the other Christian confessions? Thoughts might be tempted to turn to the past. That would mean getting lost in the labyrinths of history, and, undoubtedly, would reopen wounds which are not completely healed.

[1] *A.A.S.* 55 (1963), pp. 878-879.
[2] *Ibid.* p. 853.

"In our address of September 29, we ventured to give the first place to Christian forgiveness, mutual if possible. 'Veniam damus petimusque vicissim' (We grant pardon and we ask it in turn : Horace). Our spirits need this tranquillity if they are to enter into friendly relations, serene conversations. First of all, because it is Christian : 'So if, says the Lord, you are offering your gift at the altar, and remember that your brother has something against you, leave your gift there before the altar and go, first be reconciled to your brother and then come and offer your gift' (Matt. 5 : 23-24). And then, it is the better method for us : to look not towards the past but to the present and, above all, the future. Others can and ought to pursue their studies of history; we now prefer to focus our attention, not on what has been, but on what ought to be. New things must come into existence, a dream must be made real. May we be permitted to borrow the words of St Paul : 'Forgetting what lies behind and straining forward to what lies ahead, I press on toward the goal for the prize which God calls us to receive, in Christ Jesus' (Phil. 3 : 3-14). Hope is our guide, prayer our strength, charity our method, all at the service of the divine truth which is our faith and our salvation."[1]

UNITY WITHOUT UNIFORMITY

Another affirmation of great importance was made by Pope Paul VI in his inaugural address at the second session of the Council : unity in faith, in sacraments and in guidance is fully compatible with

a large variety of languages, of ritual forms, of historical traditions, of local prerogatives, of spiritual currents, of legitimate institutions and preferred activities. That which must be preserved is our faith which comes from God and constitutes our most precious treasure.[2]

[1] *A.A.S.* 55 (1963), pp. 879-880.
[2] *Ibid.* p. 852.

He had referred explicitly to the Eastern Orthodox in his coronation address :

> The Church—is it necessary to repeat this, after so many and such explicit statements of our Predecessors?—has a matchless enrichment in the variety of languages and of Rites in which heaven is approached. The Eastern communities, who inherit and live such ancient and noble traditions, are in our eyes worthy of honour, of esteem and of confidence.[1]

In August, 1963, speaking of the visit to Moscow of Mgr Charrière, Bishop of Fribourg and Geneva, to congratulate the Patriarch Alexis on his fiftieth episcopal jubilee, Pope Paul said :

> The object of that visit was to carry the homage of the Catholic hierarchy to the great Eastern Churches; to make plain that there is among us no thought of rivalry or prestige, far less of pride or ambition; no desire to perpetuate discords or divergencies.... Anything of that kind seems today quite out of date, whatever may have been conditions in the past.
>
> I also venture to make my own the heart-felt and spontaneously generous call of my predecessors, especially of John XXIII : Let our voice turn into a shout of angels saying : Come ! Let the barriers which separate us fall, let us discuss the points of doctrine which divide us and which are still the object of controversy. Let us seek to make our creed a common one, render articulate and join together our hierarchical union ! We want neither to absorb nor to oppress this great flowering of Eastern Churches, but we would like to see them reinstated upon the one tree of Christian unity, and this our cry also becomes our prayer. We pray because, though it may be too much to expect in our age, coming ages at least may see the unity restored of those who are still real Christians, especially unity with these most venerable and saintly Eastern Churches.
>
> What is lacking? Is it perhaps that we Catholics are without sufficient understanding? Do we perhaps not fully comprehend the great religious traditions of the East? Are they, on their part, aware of our feelings, of the legitimate way in

[1] *A.A.S.* 55 (1963), p. 622.

which our traditions have developed and have been enriched by truth which must be acknowledged by those who believe in Christ? I cannot tell. I only know that the gospel of today, as we Latins and Romans read it, contains a remarkable word, one of the very rare words—three, I think, there were—which the evangelists have preserved in the original language used by Christ. This word is "effeta" which means "open". The Lord gave power of hearing and power of speech to him who was deaf and dumb, and who, in the interpretation of the Fathers, represents mankind. We are all a little deaf, we are all a little dumb. May the Lord enable us to hear the voices of history, the voices of the chosen spirits, his own voice, the echo of the gospel, always our law and power, since it is the word of God.[1]

THE ATTITUDE OF POPE PAUL VI

Pope Paul, likewise, stressed what Christians have in common. In his opening address to the second session of the Council, he said he hoped the Observers would make known to their respective Christian communities "our attitude" towards reconciliation with separated brethren, and he then went on :

"May our voice also reach those other venerable Christian communities separated from us, which did not accept the invitation freely extended to them to attend the Council if they wished. We believe that the Catholic attitude is well enough known, but it may be useful to state it again.

"We speak to separated brethren in friendliness and complete sincerity. There are no snares, no hidden desire of temporal interests. We owe our faith, which we honestly believe to be divine, the most open and firm attachment. Nevertheless we are convinced that this is no obstacle to the longed-for agreement between us and separated brethren; the matter concerns divine truth and this is a principle of unity not of difference or separation. In any case we refuse to make our faith a cause of contention with separated brethren.

"Next, we hold in justified reverence the religious heritage

---

[1] *Osservatore Romano*, 19-20 August, 1963, p. 1.

received of old and shared in common, which our separated
brethren have preserved and in some of its elements have
excellently developed. We give glad approval to the efforts of
those who are working to bring into right knowledge and right
honour the real treasures of truth and holiness possessed by our
separated brethren, thereby to improve our mutual relations.
In turn, we are confident that separated brethren will share
our feeling, and will seek to have deeper knowledge of our
doctrine and to see how naturally and coherently it grows from
the original revelation. We are confident, too, that they will
try to know more about our history and our religious life.

"Finally, we wish to say that we are aware of the massive
obstacles still blocking the way to the union we yearn for; but
this awareness leads us humbly to put our trust in God. We shall
continue to pray. We shall try to give better proof of our efforts
to lead truly Christian lives and to practise brotherly charity.
And should future events fail to meet our hopes and expectations, we shall remember the heartening words of Christ:
'What is impossible with men, is possible with God'." (Luke
18 : 27)[1]

POSSIBILITIES OPEN TO THE COUNCIL

In his opening address to the second session of the Council
Pope Paul VI summarized the purposes of the Council under
four heads: a better knowledge of the Church's nature, the
renewal of the Church, the unity of Christians and the dialogue
with the contemporary world. It is clear that all these are inter-
connected, perhaps especially the last two, for it is obvious that
one of the greatest motives for seeking Christian unity is that
"the world may believe that thou hast sent me". (John 12 :21;
cf. above, chapter 8)

Regarding the first matter, better and deeper knowledge of
the Church's true nature, Pope Paul VI said:

It is twenty centuries since the Church was founded. During

[1] *A.A.S* 55 (1963), pp. 853-854.

these centuries the Catholic Church has increased greatly. So, too, have other religious communities which bear the name of Christ and are called Churches. Is it then surprising that, after so long an experience, there is still need of a more accurate statement about the true, profound and full nature of the Church which Christ founded and the Apostles began to build? Let no one think it surprising. For the Church is a mystery. It is a unique reality penetrated by the presence of God. Such being the nature of the Church, there is always room and need for new and deeper investigations into it. Human thought moves forward. Man advances from empirically observed fact to scientific truth; from one truth by dialectic he infers another, and, confronted by reality, which gives him an initial certitude, but which is full of complexity, he bends his mind now to one of its aspects, now to another. It is thus that thought evolves. The course of its evolution can be traced in history.

The time has now come, we believe, when the truth regarding the Church of Christ demands closer examination, deeper reflection and better expression.[1]

He said, also, that the theological doctrine of the Church

opens possibilities of magnificent developments which deserve the attentive consideration of our separated brethren also, and which, we ardently hope, may make the path towards common agreement easier.[2]

The *Schema* on the Church was discussed at great length, and, after many modifications had been suggested, was referred back to the Theological Commission for further revision. Much of the discussion turned upon the function of the episcopate and its relation to Peter. Pope Paul VI had said that he hoped for much from the discussions and decision on this head:

For us personally it will provide doctrinal and practical standards by which our apostolic office, endowed though it is by Christ with the fulness and sufficiency of power, may receive

[1] *A.A.S.* 55 (1963), p. 848.
[2] *Ibid*. p. 849.

more help and support, in ways to be determined, from a more effective and responsible collaboration with our beloved and venerable Brothers in the Episcopate.[1]

Concrete suggestions turned upon the questions of regional or national conferences of bishops and of the possibility of something in the nature of an episcopal senate to assist the Pope and the Curia. Many bishops insisted upon the principle of "collegiality", which seems to mean not only that all the bishops together, with the Pope, have supreme responsibility for the Church, but also that each bishop, by virtue of his office, should feel responsible for the spread of the faith all over the world, and should co-operate with other dioceses in all possible fields. Final decision, however, was postponed to the next Session in 1964.

The renewal of the Church most manifestly affects its relations with separated brethren, though that is only an incidental to the holiness which is the essential of renewal. Pope Paul spoke as follows :

The Council is evidence of a determination to bring about a rejuvenation both of the interior forces of the Church and of the regulations by which her canonical structure and liturgical forms are governed. The Council, that is, is striving to enhance in the Church that beauty of perfection and holiness which imitation of Christ and mystical union with Him in the Holy Spirit can alone confer.

Yes, the Council aims at renewal. Note well, however, that in saying and desiring that, we do not imply that the Catholic Church of today can be accused of substantial infidelity to the mind of her divine Founder. Rather it is the deeper realization of her substantial faithfulness that fills her with gratitude and humility and inspires her with the courage to correct those imperfections which are due to human weakness. The reform at which the Council aims is not, therefore, a turning upside down of the Church's present way of life or a breaking with what is essential and worthy of veneration in her tradition, but it is rather an honouring of tradition by stripping it of what is

[1] *Ibid* pp. 849-850.

unworthy or defective so that it may be rendered firm and fruitful.[1]

He then went on :

> May the living Church be conformed to the living Christ. If faith and charity are the principles of her life, it is clear that no pains must be spared to make faith strong and joyful and to render Christian instruction and teaching methods more effective for the attaining of this vital end. The first requirement of this reform will certainly be a more diligent study and a more intensive proclamation of the word of God. Upon this foundation an education of charity will be built up, for we must give the place of honour to charity and strive to construct the *Ecclesia Caritatis* (Church of charity) if we would have a Church capable of renewing herself and renewing the world around her : there indeed is a tremendous undertaking. Charity must be fostered because it is the chief and root of the other Christian virtues : humility, poverty, religion, the spirit of sacrifice, fearless truth, love of justice, and every other force by which the new man acts.[2]

Two concrete matters give proof of this desire for renewal. The Decree on the Liturgy simplifies the worship of God and envisages a far greater use of vernacular languages, in place of the Latin which has been customary. This Decree was approved by the Council, but its application in many points depends upon the decisions of episcopal conferences in different regions. The other matter was Pope Paul's announcement to the Curia, that is, the Departments with their officials who assist the Pope, that he wished for changes and invited their collaboration in bringing them about. In particular, the Pope envisaged some decentralization, a development of ecumenical concern and a greater internationalization in the Curia.

THE SCHEMA ON ECUMENISM

About the unity of Christians, a *Schema* was drawn up by the

[1] *Ibid.* p. 851.
[2] *Ibid.*

Secretariat for the Promotion of Christian Unity in collaboration with the theological commission and that for the Eastern Churches. The text of the *Schema* has not yet been made public, but from what has been published about it I can repeat that it contained five sections, one on the general principles of Catholic ecumenism, a second on its practical applications, a third on the Orthodox and the communities stemming from the Reformation of the sixteenth century and after; a fourth on the relation of Christians and Jews; and a fifth on religious liberty.

During the discussions, although many of the Fathers of the Council gave warm and convinced approval to the general approach and outlook of the *Schema*—which in fact broke no new ground, but only summed up the general Catholic attitude, as it has been approved by Pope John XXIII and by Paul VI —certain doubts were expressed.

It was said that the emphasis upon the elements which unite Christians was too pervasive and forceful, while the divisive elements were given less prominence; and Catholic truths were not asserted vigorously enough. This feeling, however, failed to take account of the scope of the *Schema* and its purpose. The *Schema* is only one of the many documents which the Council will produce, and the *Schema* presupposes the declarations of the Council about the nature of the Church, the primacy and infallibility, the unicity of the Church, etc., and falls into place beside them. The *Schema* was not meant to be and, indeed, could not be, a whole treatise on the Church. Nor is the *Schema* addressed to separated brethren, as if to commend Catholicism to them or as if to give them guidance; it was directed to Catholics, who are already convinced of the truth of their faith, who are aware of the rejection of much Catholic teaching by non-Catholics, but who may not be so well aware of the true Christian elements, and of the gifts of the Holy Spirit existing among them, doubtless as part of the grace of their baptism. Nothing more was said, on this aspect, than has been said by many of the Popes, notably by Leo XIII, Pius XI, John XXIII and the present Holy Father, and that has been said by very many Catholic theologians whose writings have won highest approval.

FEARS ABOUT "INDIFFERENTISM"

Fears were also expressed lest "the ecumenical outlook" might tend to "indifferentism", or to a false "eirenicism" and thus might lessen firmness and confidence in the faith among the faithful, and encourage the idea that all forms of Christianity are equally acceptable. These fears are not, of course, wholly unfounded, as the Schema itself makes plain by the safeguards it commends to obviate danger of "indifferentism"; there have been some instances in which enthusiasm outran discretion, perhaps especially in cases where speakers or writers were not fully informed about the complexities of the situation.

Dr Stephen Neill, an Anglican Bishop, has said :

> One often has the impression that Roman Catholic friends are hardly aware of the chasm in matters of faith that separates them from those with whom they long to be united.[1]

But the admitted dangers, which can easily be exaggerated, are in any case no reason for a withdrawal which would involve even greater dangers, especially the danger of an appearance of reluctance to accept loyally and confidently the clear directions of the Holy See. As early as 1949, the Holy Office issued an *Instruction* on the subject, which ends with the following clear statement :

> This excellent work of "reunion" of all Christians in the one true Faith and in the Church should daily assume a more significant place within the Church's universal pastoral care, and every Catholic should pray ever more earnestly to God for this object. It will prove a great help if the faithful are suitably instructed, for example, by pastoral letters, about these questions and the steps being taken, together with the Church's instructions on this matter and the reasons underlying them.

[1] *Men of Unity*, Ch. 13. "John XXIII and a Roman Council", p. 177.

All, especially priests and religious, should be encouraged to take an ardent interest and do everything in their power, by prayer and sacrifice, to work for the success of this cause. Finally, all should be reminded that nothing will contribute more towards preparing the way for our separated brethren to embrace the Faith and enter the Church than the living by Catholics of edifying lives in accord with their Faith.[1]

THE BEST SAFEGUARD

It is the duty of the bishops to foster and encourage this work, as it is their office to preach the Gospel and to be shepherds to their flocks. The best safeguard against possible dangers is that the bishops themselves take the lead in this admirable and necessary work. The Secretariat for Unity, which acts in the name of the Holy See, can lay down general principles and norms, and these in fact will be set forth in an *Ecumenical Directory* which is in preparation. But the application of these norms depends upon the bishops, since conditions differ in different countries, relations with separated brethren may differ greatly, and only those who actually live in these conditions can estimate and judge. Regional or national Conferences, or Committees, appointed by the bishops could prove a useful means of co-operation with the Roman Secretariat in guiding and co-ordinating the movement.

In this way danger of any false ecumenism or "eirenicism", feared by some, can be removed, and "dialogue" with separated brethren initiated by reliable and suitable people, theologically competent. Such can far better be chosen by local bishops than by any Roman organ; and all danger of "indifferentism" avoided. It should be added that separated brethren have no wish to be presented with any diluted or attenuated kind of Catholic doctrine, and, also, that many of them are very well informed about Catholic doctrine, and are fully able to make a true estimate of anything like an undue "eirenicism".

The Catholic faithful who live in close contact with non-

[1] *A.A.S.* 42 (1950), pp. 146-147.

Catholics should be and can be instructed about the ecumenical movement. Indeed such solid instruction, given either in classes for religious doctrine, or in sermons and conferences by sensible and reliable people, can be a definite help to increase knowledge and love of the faith.

An article in the Anglican *Church Times* for December 13th, 1963, unsigned, but evidently written by someone with accurate knowledge, contains the following observation, about the *Schema* on Ecumenism :

> The general spiritual principles underlying the Schema are a model for all Christians. One section reads :
> "Let all the faithful bear in mind that they will the better promote and even practise union among Christians, the purer and more evangelical life they strive to lead. For the more deeply united in communion with the Father, the Word and the Spirit they are, the more deeply and easily will they be able to increase their mutual brotherhood.
> "Therefore let them all know that no small impediment to separated brethren is found in that tepidity and sinful life of those who are honoured with the name of Catholic, whereas, on the other hand, holiness in the faithful gives open testimony to the fulness of the inheritance which they claim to enjoy in the Church."

II

Towards Christian Unity

THE VISIT OF POPE PAUL VI TO JERUSALEM WAS both unprecedented and symbolic. It was a gesture which proclaimed that, in the work of the renewal of the Church, of the dialogue with separated brethren and with the contemporary world, it is Christ whom all must seek, Christ who is the origin of our religion, the greatest of all lovers of mankind, and the source of all the blessings we hope from God. The Pope's pilgrimage was the occasion of his receiving the visits of three Patriarchs of Orthodox Churches, Athenagoras of Constantinople, the Ecumenical Patriarch, the Patriarch Benedict of Jerusalem, the Armenian Orthodox Patriarch Yeghishe Derderian of Jerusalem. In returning their visits, the Pope followed a protocol which has had no precedents for centuries. In this procedure Pope Paul VI showed himself a true "servant of the servants of God", imitating Christ who did not think it beneath his dignity to visit his friends and even to eat with them. In this too, the Pope's pilgrimage to Jerusalem was symbolic.

This meeting of the Pope with the Ecumenical Patriarch and the other Patriarchs has been called, in some newspapers, "a summit meeting". In a sense it is such; and it would be poor-spirited to set bounds to the great effects which God may produce through such meetings. And yet Pope Paul himself said to the "Delegated Observers" on September 29, 1963 : "We are aware that serious and complicated questions remain to be studied, treated and resolved. We would wish that this could

181

be done immediately, on account of the love of Christ that 'urges us on'. But we also realize that these problems require many conditions before satisfactory solutions can be reached, conditions which as yet do not exist. Hence we are not afraid to await patiently the blessed hour of perfect reconciliation."[1]

What then are these conditions which require time and patience?

Apart from the doctrinal differences, of which I spoke a little in chapter 9 (cf. pp. 150-157), there are "non-doctrinal factors" whose great practical importance should be neither exaggerated nor attenuated.

MUTUAL SUSPICIONS

Among the non-doctrinal factors are the mutual suspicions among some, if not many, Catholics, Orthodox, Anglicans and Protestants. Some of our separated brethren suspect that "Rome" seeks to dominate over all others and impose its rule, from unworthy motives such as love of power, prestige and even money. It is painful to say this, but I feel obliged to say it out of love of truth and love of the Church of Christ and of the cause of unity. The fact of these suspicions has recently been noted by two of the "Delegated Observers", Professor Robert McAfee Brown of Stanford University, California, a Presbyterian, and by Professor José Migues-Bonino, of Buenos Aires, a Methodist, both of whom have been noteworthy for their efforts to improve relations with the Catholic Church, and both of whom have written nobly in efforts to dispel the suspicion. Both, however, say the suspicion exists. Professor Brown, interviewed on television by the British Broadcasting Corporation, said that some of his Protestant friends had asked him whether the new "ecumenical" attitude of Rome was not "a soft sell", that is, merely a new way of "getting round" Protestants. Professor Bonino put it even more bluntly. While admitting that "the spirit of renewal in the Catholic

[1] *A.A.S.* 55 (1963), p. 853.

Church has given Latin American Protestants a view of ideas and of attitudes which they did not know existed in Roman Catholicism", nevertheless "there is an impatience among Latin American Protestants for concrete actions during the next few years". "There is an apparent contradiction between the irenic statements and the recent expressions of polemics and suppression. Protestants in Latin America can interpret this at the present only as a two-faced attitude, a change in tactics, a new way of trying to achieve the usual aim—the suppression of Protestantism."[1]

On the other hand, not a few Catholics are suspicious of much that exists among Protestants: some feel that among Protestants there is not only a lack of the unity of faith which is a mark of the Christian Church, but a rejection of all principles on which unity of faith can be secured and maintained, and this causes fear lest closer relations lead to dilution of doctrine and "indifferentism"; others feel that many Protestants have a settled hostility to the Catholic Church, to its stand on moral matters and on education, and—to invert Professor Bonino's words—a resolve "to achieve the usual aim—the suppression of Catholicism".

How widespread are these mutual suspicions, it is not easy to know. They certainly exist among some and the practical question is : how can they be eliminated ?

Obviously, a first step is to spread accurate knowledge and understanding about the convictions and outlooks of others. But this itself presents serious difficulties. Able men in all churches are often occupied with the affairs of their church, with efforts to maintain the faith of their own people (and practical defections from the faith are all too numerous the world over) and with missionary interests, all of which are so urgent and pressing that there is little time and energy left for study of "ecumenical" questions. Add to this that at first sight the obstacles to reconciliation seem so great, so complicated and so pervasive

---

[1] Quoted in *The Ecumenist*, vol. 2, No. 1, Nov.-Dec. 1963, p. 16. I do not know to what recent "polemics and suppression" the Professor refers; but this is irrelevant to my present purpose.

that there is small hope of overcoming them, and hence "ecumenical" activity appears scarcely worth while, or at best an "extra". It must sadly, even ruefully, be admitted, and is admitted by very many ecumenists, that the number of those who are really interested is woefully small, and that "the ecumenical idea" has been accepted only by a few and has not yet made much practical impact even upon the majority of the clergy, especially in certain parts of the world.

What more, then, can be done to remove ignorance and suspicions and to spread knowledge of the true nature of the efforts towards unity?

LEADERSHIP

First of all, much, though not all, depends upon leadership. About this, I think it can be said that the lead given by Pope John XXIII and Pope Paul VI has been matched or even anticipated by the leaders of many separated churches. It would be difficult to name them all, but I cannot fail to mention the Ecumenical Patriarch, Athenagoras; the Patriarch of Moscow, Alexis; the former Archbishop of Canterbury, Geoffrey, Lord Fisher; and the present Archbishop Dr Michael Ramsey; Dr A. C. Craig, former Moderator of the Church of Scotland; Dr Lichtenberger, Presiding Bishop of the Protestant Episcopal Church in the United States; the Most Rev. Fred Pierce Corson, President of the World Methodist Council; Pastor Marc Boegner, President of the Protestant Federation of France; and many prominent personalities of the Evangelical Church in Germany. It is needless to mention the leaders of the World Council of Churches, like Dr William A. Visser 't Hooft, Dr Franklin Fry, Dr Lesslie Newbigin, Dr Eugene Carson Blake, Dr Norman Goodall. These, however, are only a few, for the sending of the "Delegated Observers" to the Vatican Council is evidence of the ecumenical outlook among the leaders of the bodies from which they came. Leadership at the very top has not been lacking; but among some local authorities and leaders, there have been certain hesitations, based, I conjecture, partly upon fears about the integrity of the faith of the ordinary faithful, partly upon the inclination to follow accustomed ways of thinking and acting, and partly upon doubts about the best way to carry general directives into practical effect in local situations.

INTERDEPENDENCIES

Secondly, it must be repeated most urgently that the good estate of the Church, both generally and locally, is inextricably bound up with the Church's renewal, and this in turn with the cause of the unity of Christians and with the dialogue with the contemporary world. This may be illustrated by the admitted fact that interest in "the missions" and generous help to them tend to increase the devotional life and general well-being of a parish. No parish, no diocese, no local grouping of Christians, can live a truly Christian life if it lives for itself alone, as if it were a self-sufficient unit, just as no organ in a body can be healthy except through the health of the whole body.

The deliberations of the Council have shown that all the doctrines of the Church are interdependent : the doctrine of the papacy is linked with that of episcopacy, and this in turn with the priesthood and the laity and the liturgy and methods of teaching catechism. So, too, all the activities of the Church are interdependent : holiness is linked with a sacramental life, with standards of family life, with education and the formation of holy and learned priests, with the apostolate of the laity, with publications and, above all, with the mission of the Church to the whole human race, and this, in turn, with relations with separated brethren. In the chapter on the scandal of divisions[1] some indication was given to show how great an impediment are Christian divisions to the acceptance of faith in Christ by the non-Christian world. It is, as Pope John XXIII so forcefully reminded us, only by love of all mankind that we can bring Christ to all mankind. Pope Paul VI declared that "we must

[1] Cf. pp. 136-159.

give the place of honour to charity and strive to construct the *Ecclesia Caritatis* if we would have a Church capable of renewing herself and renewing the world around her". But how can we have real charity if we exclude our separated brothers from our affection, our interest, our work, our anxieties? How can we give a gift to God, unless we seek first to be reconciled with our brothers?

POPULATION INCREASE

Thirdly, the greatness of the task which confronts the Church in the modern world must be realized. The population of the world increases rapidly. It has been calculated that the population of Latin America, now about 195,000,000, will by the year 2,000 have increased to some 600,000,000, which means an increase of about 400,000,000 in less than forty years. The natural resources of some countries in that area are, likewise, immense, but are in need of technical skills to develop them, and these in turn will bring changes in industry, in social patterns and in mental outlooks. Can Christians not combine to help in such a situation? Even if Christians are not able to attain full reconciliation, it is still possible to co-operate in matters of social welfare for the physical and mental well-being of the people.[1]

What is true of Latin America, is true also almost all over the world. The *Encyclical* of John XXIII on Peace lays foundations on which all men of good will can agree to co-operate.

Fourthly, regarding relations between Christians of different allegiances, I am well aware that conditions differ in different parts of the world. In spite of this, there are certain guiding principles of general validity, and the Secretariat for Unity is codifying them in an *Ecumenical Directory*, which, however,

---

[1] In Latin America particularly, though not exclusively, the document of the W.C.C. on *Christian Witness, Proselytism and Religious Liberty* has application. (cf. Appendix III, pp. 240-251). Unhappily, there are some who claim the name "Protestant", who reject, almost equally, the standpoint of the W.C.C. and of the Roman Catholic church.

can scarcely take final form until the Council has given final approval to the *Schema* on Ecumenism. Meantime, the encouragement given by the *Instruction* of 1949, cited above pp. 178-179, gives not only full approval to work for unity, but affirms that such work is a duty incumbent on all bishops. In particular, it gives explicit approval of dialogue.

WHAT IS DIALOGUE?

Dialogue definitely does not mean an effort to persuade others of the truth of one's own faith; nor does it mean an effort to "convert" the other partner or partners to one's own allegiance. Nor does "dialogue" imply that either partner in any sense surrenders his faith, or regards it as open to change or to modification. Far less does dialogue even remotely suggest that we do not know what the faith is and have to enquire, or to discuss, in order to discover it. In all circumstances, and perhaps especially in dialogue with separated brethren, the purity of doctrine must be sedulously maintained.[1]

During this past year I was informed that a prominent and respected Anglican dignitary had expressed himself as judging that the dogmatic differences between "Rome" and separated brethren were so great as to be insuperable; and that in confirmation of this he cited me as having written : "We would be showing a very misguided love for unity and for our separated brethren if we allowed them to hope that we will not demand of them anything more than the recognition of 'fundamental articles', that we will no longer ask for the acceptance of the dogmatic decrees of the Council of Trent or that we are ready to revise the dogma of the primacy or the infallibility of the Pope." Since he judged these doctrines unacceptable, he concluded, if I am correctly informed, that there is no real hope of reunion. Hence, a reader may well ask : "What good, then, will

---

[1] Cf. my repeated assertions about this in *The Unity of Christians*, London and New York, 1963, pp. 24, 25, 54-55, 68, 81; 108, 116-117, etc.

dialogue do, since both sides begin it with convictions which antecedently rule out any fruitful result?"

Nevertheless, it must be held that dialogue can be most useful and fruitful. First of all, it can help to clear away the non-doctrinal factors with which pure doctrine is not seldom intermingled. Next, it can help on agreement about matters in which Christians, even remaining divided in faith, can co-operate. Many such matters are indicated by Pope John XXIII in his *Encyclical* on Peace; and Christians certainly can, even without unity in faith, co-ordinate their efforts in defence of the general Christian cause and of religious liberty, in works of charity, and in many social areas. For instance, in some countries Christians have taken the initiative in forming a banking institution to lend money at low rates of interest to young married couples.

Next, dialogue can greatly help towards clearing up misunderstandings about the doctrinal tenets of one side or the other, or both. About the doctrine of the real presence, of the Eucharistic sacrifice, and of episcopacy, for instance, dialogue, written and spoken, has already proved fruitful and shows a gradual approach to agreement, both among Protestants of different allegiances, and among Catholics, Orthodox and Protestants. The dialogue often results in more careful examination of customary formulas and sometimes reveals that the meaning is the same, though the manner of expression may be different.

Further, dialogue between Christians can help the "dialogue with the contemporary world". Unhappily, the language traditional among Christians has become largely meaningless to many modern people, instances being words like "atonement", "redemption" and "salvation". Dialogue can help us all to speak more understandably to modern men. Dialogue, too, taken in the wide sense, can give mutual enlightenment about the Christian approach to great non-Christian world religions like Hinduism, Buddhism and Mohammedanism.

Efforts are being made to secure an English version of the Bible which will be acceptable to all English-speaking Christians, and it looks as if these efforts will prove successful.

DIALOGUE ABOUT DOCTRINE

On purely doctrinal matters there is also hope of an approach to agreement through patient and wise dialogue. The dogmas of the Christian Church, and the specific dogmas of the Catholic Church, must always be understood in their historical context, which sometimes throws unexpected light upon them. It has been pointed out as an example, that the Orthodox rejection of the addition of the *Filioque* (that is, that the Holy Spirit proceeds also from the Son), was inspired by fear of false views which reduced the Holy Spirit to the status of a creature made by the Son. The Latin addition was inspired by the fear lest Christ be conceived merely as an adopted son of God, made such by the gift and action of the Holy Spirit. Thus both formulas, understood in this historical context, stress different aspects of the same truth. Closer and more objective study of the historical context in which other doctrinal differences developed may reveal unexpected sources of agreement.

It should, too, be appreciated that doctrinal formulas do not exhaust the truth. The Councils of Nicea in 325 and of Ephesus in 431 defined the divinity of Christ, but these definitions did not express the full doctrine of the Incarnation, since the Council of Chalcedon in 451 had to define the full humanity of Christ. The same holds for the Catholic doctrine about the Church; the Councils of Trent and of Vatican I laid stress, because of existing conditions, on the juridical and institutional elements in the Church. Later, Pius XII, in his Encyclical on the mystical body, revealed other equally important elements in the Church, and, as Pope Paul VI said, the present Vatican Council is in process of enlarging the Church's awareness of itself as a mystery, and this "has the possibility of magnificent developments" which may make the path towards common agreement easier.[1] What is true about the doctrine of the Church is true also of other doctrines, notably of sacramental doctrine. Dr W. A. Visser 't Hooft remarks that "sometimes representative spokesmen of Roman Catholic ecumenism give the

[1] Cf. the actual words, cited in Chapter 10, pp. 173-174.

impression that all that is needed for the success of such dialogue
is a different way of formulating the same positions". Such an
impression ought not to be given and is mistaken. Pope Paul
VI affirms that development of doctrine is in process; and he
affirmed, too, that "the reform at which the Council aims is not
a turning upside down of the Church's present way of life or a
breaking with what is essential and worthy of veneration in her
tradition, but it is rather an honouring of tradition by stripping
it of what is unworthy or defective so that it may be rendered
firm and fruitful".[1] To affirm real development in understanding and a willingness to strip away what is unworthy or defective is surely much more than mere different "formulation of
the same positions".

In turn, our separated brethren are looking more closely into
the historical context in which their specific doctrines developed
and into the relation of the doctrines one to another. Thus, for
instance, some Presbyterians and Congregationalists are beginning to conclude that episcopacy is not contrary to their fundamental convictions. Deeper investigation into the unity of
Christ's Church is leading many of our separated brethren to
appreciate more fully the unity of the Church throughout
history and the means by which that continuity is secured.

Hence, even where at first sight doctrines may seem irrecon-
cilable dialogue may reveal principles of agreement. When
doctrines are seen, not in isolation, but in a total vision of Christ's
revelation and action, they appear different and their import
and impact upon life is different. As has often been repeated,
dialogue is not a monologue, and Catholics can and do rejoice
to be able to learn from separated brethren. Catholic biblical
scholars owe an inestimable debt to Protestant scholarship; and
Catholic theology owes an infinite debt to Eastern Fathers and
theologians. Eastern insights about "a Eucharistic ecclesiology"
can be a welcome enrichment to all other Christians.[2] Thus,

[1] Cf. above, pp. 175-176.
[2] Here I may refer to my address at the opening of the academic year
at the University of Fribourg, Switzerland, November 15, 1961, re-
published in *The Unity of Christians*, Ch. 7, "How University Research and
Teaching Can Further Christian Unity", London, 1963, pp. 94-110.

Christian bodies at present divided from one another, can exercise a reconciling role with regard to one another, as the Orthodox can commend Tradition and liturgical prayer, Anglicans episcopacy, Protestants the importance of a biblical theology, and Roman Catholics tradition in theology and the need of firm authority.

Consequently, it is a pleasure to agree with the Central Committee of the World Council of Churches, which, in August 1963, expressed a desire for dialogue with Roman Catholics which should face "the profound dogmatic differences in a spirit of love and humility". The Report went on :

"The dialogue of which we speak rests upon the one foundation of God's revelation of Himself in Jesus Christ. It is a dialogue between churches who recognize one another as confessing the same Lord, sharing the same baptism, and participating in a common calling to the glory of the one God—Father, Son and Holy Spirit. It aims at deeper understanding, mutual enrichment and the renewal of the life of the churches. It is for this kind of dialogue that we long, for we have begun to taste its fruitfulness within our own fellowship."[1]

WHO ARE COMPETENT?

A difficulty about such dialogue with learned men among separated brethren may be felt by some on grounds of lack of sufficient theological competency and sufficient time; for many of the clergy are already almost overburdened with urgent pastoral or teaching tasks and are unable to find time for study and reading. The difficulty, however, is not insoluble. Dialogue need not be restricted to theology proper, for most useful conversations can take place about methods and problems in pastoral duties, about devotional matters and about methods of preaching and of instructing young people and the faithful generally. Nor need dialogue be carried on only between theo-

[1] *Ecumenical Review*, XVI, No. 1, Oct. 1963, p. 108.

logians of the highest grade or only between Professors; it is not a trial or test of intellectual or theological attainments, but a meeting of brothers who are glad to know one another and to be known to one another as they actually are. If ignorance is revealed, it is revealed among friends, and its revelation can be a stimulus to find time for enquiry or reading. What is most needed is sincere humility and charity, and patient trust in the power of God, especially when hopes sink low.

I add that such dialogue can be a very definite stimulus to the deeper theological knowledge which a more educated laity is seeking, and a stimulus, also, to better teaching of religion in our secondary schools and colleges.

PREREQUIREMENTS TO DIALOGUE

What, then, is to be thought of the mutual suspicions which were mentioned in the beginning of this chapter? Is it true that Catholics aim at the suppression of Protestantism, and Protestants at the suppression of Catholicism?

As regards the Catholic attitude towards Protestants, the reader should turn back to chapter 2, pp. 19 and 20, and to chapter 7, on religious liberty. The document on *Christian Witness, Proselytism and Religious Liberty,* printed in Appendix III, has won wide approval from respected Catholic theologians, and observance of its provisions would be a definite help. It is said, however, that some of the smaller Protestant sects do not accept the provisions of that document, but in countries predominantly Catholic are offensively aggressive. Catholic reaction may well have been unduly belligerent. However, Latin America, which Professor Bonino seems to have in mind, is a very large area; conditions differ greatly from country to country in Latin America, and reports sent abroad are not always reliable. A change, however, is in process. The Rev. Jorge Mejia, editor of the Catholic publication *Criterio,* of Buenos Aires, writes as follows:

"A new generation of priests and ministers, imbued with respect for each other as Christians, have been able, here and

there, to undertake some common tasks such as urging the celebration of Easter and Christmas and advising matrimonial re-
unions. Moreover, and this is of great significance, important
contacts now exist among the Catholic, the Inter-denomi-
national and the Lutheran theological faculties of the Buenos
Aires area, whose influence—at least in the case of Protestants
—is felt throughout Latin America.

"But it is the Vatican Council alone that has been able to
break the ice definitely. And a deep crack has been opened in it.
In this respect, the attitude of John XXIII was of utmost importance. His personal attitude in receiving bishops and ministers
from other churches, his creation of the Secretariat for the
Promotion of Christian Unity and the subsequent invitation of
non-Catholic observers to the Council—one of whom is a Latin
American, the Director of the Evangelical faculty of Theology
in Buenos Aires—are responsible for this thaw.

"All things considered, one feels that the atmosphere is beginning to change. And the change affects both Catholics and
Protestants. While Catholics are ceasing to be belligerent and
defensive simply by trying to be Christian, Protestants, too, are
modifying their attitude. Signs of this rebirth are already in
evidence throughout the South American continent. And this is
true not only at the level of the faculties of theology, but among
pastors of souls and the laity as well."[1]

SUPPRESSION?

These remarks about Latin America are almost a diversion from
this main question : are there substantial grounds for the
suspicion of some Protestants and of some Catholics that each
wants to suppress the other ? I answer, after serious reflection
and considerable consultation, that there is no real ground for
these suspicions, whatever may have been the case in the past,
and whatever may be the attitude of some few individuals or
comparatively small groups. The vast majority of Christians

[1] *The Ecumenist*, 2, No. 1, Nov.-Dec. 1963, pp. 5-6.

not only do not think in terms of "suppression", but most sincerely regret the persecutions of the past and are deeply convinced that any compulsion in religious matters is radically anti-Christian, and, indeed, anti-religious and an offence to the God-given dignity of man.

It is true that Catholics would like all their separated brethren to agree with them in unity of faith, of sacramental life and of authoritative guidance; but they are—if I may say so—intelligent enough to understand that this agreement would be useless and even evil unless it sprang from sincere conviction. Catholics do not want to impose the Pope upon Protestants; they would like Protestants to want the Pope of their own free choice and out of sincere conviction. In turn, Protestants, Anglicans and Orthodox would doubtless like Catholics to modify their convictions about the authority and infallibility of the Pope, and about a number of other matters; but they, too, are—again if I may say so—intelligent enough to understand that such agreement with them would be useless and evil unless it sprang from sincere conviction. They would, I imagine, like the Pope himself freely and from sincere conviction to declare that he is not infallible, and to accept the position of an equal with perhaps some honourable precedence. On all sides there is agreement that faith must be free.

Such a general statement of agreement about the essential freedom of the assent of faith does not at once dissolve all the suspicions. Many Orthodox, Anglicans and Protestants may still remain wary lest "Rome" seeks, and may gain, unless they beware, a position of dominance. Many Catholics may still remain wary of Protestant liberalism in doctrine and of some Protestant and Orthodox prepossessions against Catholicism.

Such suspicions cannot be dissipated by words or arguments. They can only be dissipated by deeds and facts, by mutual knowledge, by the renewal of all churches and by prayer. By the mercy of God, all this is coming about. The World Council of Churches is a fact, as is its conspicuous declaration about Christ as God and Saviour, about the Trinity, and as is its definition of the goal of the movement.[1] It is a fact that the World Council and many of its member churches gave a most generous welcome to the Roman Council. The openness of John XXIII was a fact, as was its general welcome by the Catholic body. The Council, and its frankness to the Observers is a fact. The humble asking of forgiveness by Pope Paul VI, and his visit to the Holy Land are deeds and facts. Mutual knowledge is increasing, renewal is going on in many churches (though unevenly) and the spirit of prayer spreads more widely and deeply. I should agree that some facts can be alleged which do not tend to dissipate suspicions. But the balance is swaying in favour of antecedent trust, and this we must attribute, not to ourselves, but to the action of the Spirit of God. Considering past history, I say again that this spirit of mutual trust is a miracle of God.

CAUSES OF OFFENCE?

The Central Committee of the World Council of Churches in its meeting in Rochester, New York, August, 1963, mentioned some matters which it regarded as "cause of offence" :

"There are issues which must be frankly faced if true dialogue is to be possible. They include policies and practices regarding mixed marriages, religious liberty, proselytism, and the rebaptism of converts from other churches. The removal of cause of offence at these points will open the way for brotherly dealing with the more fundamental issues of faith and order which divide us."[2]

This mention of "cause of offence" was, one must suppose, to be taken in conjunction with the statement of the General Secretary of the World Council in August 1962, in which, after mentioning some matters affecting the relationship of the churches, he added, "we must honestly say that even within the membership of the W.C.C. we have not drawn all the consequences from our relationships as churches engaged in ongoing dialogue, and we must not ask from the Roman Catholic

[1] Cf. ch. 9, p. 147.
[2] *Ecumenical Review*, XVI, No. 1, Oct., 1963, p. 108.

Church what we have not yet realized ourselves".[1] Here we must face some of the sad effects of Christian divisions; it is difficult to discuss many matters frankly without seeming to enter into controversy, or at least, into debate. In no controversial spirit, then, but with the frankness which improved relationships permit, I say a word or two about mixed marriages, and "re-baptism" of converts, having, I think already said as much as I can about religious liberty and proselytism.

MIXED MARRIAGES

The legislation of the Catholic Church in its main provisions requires that a Catholic must be married before his parish priest or a duly delegated priest, with two witnesses, and that there be reasonable assurance that the children of the marriage will be brought up in the Catholic faith. Some separated brethren, even independently of the statement of the W.C.C., have expressed their feeling that this legislation does not give due consideration to their conscientious convictions.[2] These feelings have been represented by the Unity Secretariat to the Commissions of the Council, and there is no doubt that the bishops will bring to bear upon the matter pastoral experience gained in all parts of the world and in many different conditions.

Without in any way anticipating the decisions of the Council, or possibly, of the Commission for the revision of canon law, I venture to give here some general reflections.

1. The problems connected with marriages between Catholics and other Christians are, indeed, brought to a focus by the Church's legislation, but they are not made by that legislation and a change in the legislation could not remove the radical cause of the problems. The root of the difficulties lies in our sad divisions. If religious differences are taken seriously, prospective

[1] Cf. Chapter 9, p. 150.
[2] For instance, Professor Peter Brunner, in "Das Geheimnis der Trennung und die Einheit der Kirche", in *Konzil und Evangelium* herausgegeben von Kristen E. Skydsgaard, Göttingen, 1963, pp. 180-181, English edition, *The Papal Council and the Gospel*, Minneapolis, 1961, pp. 170-210.

husband and wife must face the question of what their possible children are to be taught and how the religious division between father and mother is to be explained. The obvious danger, inherent in the position, is that the minds of the children may be confused and that they may lapse into the practical indifferentism of thinking the convictions of both parents are equally good and that the religious differences between them are of no practical significance. No doubt this danger may in some cases be overcome; but the difficulty is great and is felt not only when there is question of a marriage between a Roman Catholic and a member of a Protestant denomination, but also of a marriage between members of different denominations, and, more particularly, between an orthodox and any other non-orthodox Christian.

The marriage question brings to a focus the agony of our divisions. There is no ultimate solution save in the unity of Christians, and the sadness and affliction so often attending the "mixed marriage" question must be an added stimulus to us all to pray more and work harder for unity.

2. I have heard it said, and have no reason to doubt it, that in some if not many countries all Christian churches suffer most, as regards the marriage question, from the too frequent acceptance by their members of a purely secular view of marriage. The Church ceremony is rejected or omitted in favour of a purely civil marriage, and in a way which indicates an unreligious view of marriage and a lack of interest in the religious education of children.

Attention to this more serious problem should not be lessened by too much interest in the question of mixed marriages, serious as this latter may be.

3. Central to the Catholic position is the belief that it is a revealed doctrine that consummated Christian marriage can never be dissolved. The Church feels bound to this doctrine by loyalty to Christ himself, and feels, moreover, that in this stand she renders a service to Christian standards and to society in general—and this in spite of her stand being very different from

that of many civil governments and being unacceptable to many modern people.

The increase in divorce in a number of countries leads many in the Church to feel more strongly that prospective husband and wife should understand the serious obligations they are undertaking in marriage and should undertake them only by responsible decision made in full freedom. Moreover, marriage is not merely a personal matter, since it affects society, as civil laws amply prove; nor is it merely a secular, or civil, matter, since it is an image of the love of Christ for the Church (Eph. ch. 5) and brings increase to the new people of God.

4. The regulations made by the Catholic Church about the manner of contracting marriage apply only to those who have been baptized as Roman Catholics, or have been received into the communion of the Church. It holds even if only one of the parties was baptized as a Catholic, but does not apply to the marriages of those who have never been in communion with the Church.

These regulations were not made in view of the unhappy divisions among Christians, but were made to remedy the troubles caused by what were called "clandestine marriages". These were marriages celebrated outside the Church, with greater or less secrecy, and were what may be called "hole-and-corner" marriages or, as they sometimes were called, "hedge marriages". Such marriages had certainly been forbidden as early as the eleventh century and repeatedly afterwards, for the obvious reason that, as the Sarum Manual put it: "In secret marriages it often happens that one of the parties alters his mind, and sends the other away destitute of all evidence and powerless to obtain remedy for the wrong." Since, however, such marriages were admitted to be true marriages, even though made in defiance of the Church's prohibition, no adequate remedy seemed possible to the Council of Trent except to declare that the Church would accept as evidence of a true marriage only the witness of the parish priest of one of the parties and of two other witnesses, without which the marriage would be held as void. This was the effect of the canonical regulation called *Tametsi* issued by the Council of Trent in 1563, but not promulgated in those districts where Protestantism was predominant. Thus, in Great Britain, Hungary, Scandinavia, Prussia, Saxony and certain other countries and districts the old law held good.

Experience, however, showed that these provisions of canon law were not satisfactory. It was confusing that what was regarded as sufficient in one country to form the indissoluble bond should be wholly insufficient in another. In 1908 St Pius X, by the decree *Ne Temere*, applied the Tridentine law to all who are baptized in the Catholic Church (except in Germany), and the Code of Canon Law of 1917, with minor modifications, applied the *Ne Temere* universally.

Thus, the Church's legislation was designed to correct an abuse existing among Catholics and had no application to separated brethren, except incidentally through "mixed marriages".

5. Many Catholics feel convinced that the question of mixed marriages cannot be fruitfully discussed apart from its place in the whole context of Christian marriage.

It is an unhappy fact that our separated Anglican and Protestant brethren have no concordant answer to the question : "What are the Christian standards which must apply to the marriage of Christians?" Very very many of our separated brethren give in their own family life a most admirable example. Yet it remains true that it is difficult to find among them a clear and agreed doctrine regarding marriage : is marriage merely a personal matter? is it merely a civil matter? does it carry the obligation of absolute indissolubility? is it a sacrament? is its relation to the Church of Christ merely optional? To such questions our separated brethren give no common answer, and it is a sad but undeniable fact that some clergymen among them judge it right to admit to the marriage ceremony in church those who have been divorced by the civil courts, although others exclude divorced persons from the church ceremony. There is, I sincerely regret to say, considerable diversity among our separated brethren regarding the standards of Christian marriage.

The Catholic Church feels unable to divest itself of responsibility for the spiritual welfare of its members, and therefore unable to approve of them making a marriage contract which binds them indissolubly to a partner who does not feel bound in the same way. Hence it is that the Catholic Church is obliged to ask explanations and promises of those who do not accept the Catholic faith, when they marry Catholics; and this is the reason for the provisions of Canon Law about precautions. However, as conditions differ in different countries, and as ideas about marriage differ among different groups of our separated brethren, the Council might decide that norms might differ in different countries or regions, as they once used to do.

But the solution to the problem does not depend merely on the good will of the Church, but goes back to matters more radical and essential. It would greatly help towards a solution of this agonizing problem if our separated brethren would explain for us their general convictions about Christian marriage. There could then be fruitful conferences together about the matter and even if perfect agreement were not reached, at least there would be far greater understanding and mutual sympathy.[1]

[1] The Lambeth Conferences, notably those of 1948 and 1958, contain much that is valuable in itself about Christian standards in marriage, with which Catholics cordially agree. There must be, however, disagreement about the admission of divorce for adultery, cf. the *Lambeth Conference* of 1948, pp. 98 and 104-105, and about some things said about "family planning" in the *Conference* of 1958. The Committee Report on the Church's Discipline in Marriage, of the 1948 *Conference*, has a section on mixed marriages which reads as follows:

"In regard to marriage between an Anglican and a member of another Communion, it is important to remember that the religious education and spiritual training of their children by word and example is a paramount duty of parents and should never be neglected nor left entirely to others. It sometimes happens that, as a condition of marriage, one of the partners is required to sign a declaration that children of the marriage will be brought up in the practice of a religious system in which he or she does not believe. To give such an undertaking is a sin as it is an abrogation of a primary duty of parents to their children. Young Church people must be taught to seek their future partners

RE-BAPTISM ?

There seems confusion, in the statement of the Central Committee, between conditional baptism and re-baptism. Conditional baptism is a ceremony in which the formula is used "If you are not baptized, I baptize you in the name of the Father and of the Son and of the Holy Spirit". Such conditional baptism is very generally administered privately to converts, mainly for two reasons, first, as a precaution and to avoid all possible future scruples, secondly, in order readily to have an authentic document attesting that the person is undoubtedly baptized. But not all converts are conditionally baptized; for where the minister of the baptism is known, and the fact duly attested, a profession of faith is all that is required. There have been many such cases. But it not infrequently happens that people baptized as infants do not know where or by whom the sacrament was conferred; it happens, also, unhappily, that sometimes converts, because of the objections which may be made, do not desire to make known their reconciliation to the Catholic Church until it is "over and done with", as we say. In times past an application for attestation of baptism might have been refused or neglected, because of disapproval of the "going over to Rome". Thus conditional baptism casts no aspersions on baptisms administered by non-Roman Catholics; but it avoids all possible future doubts, saves trouble and provides immediately the certificate needed for confirmation, marriage or orders.

The Catholic Church generally presumes that baptism administered with water and the trinitarian form is valid. The usc of the correct essential rite is taken as implying the intention to do what the Church of Christ does; and since the time of the Donatist controversy it has been accepted Catholic doctrine that

among those with whom they can be at one in this vital respect. Otherwise they imperil their own and each other's religious life, make complete union impossible and put a great stumbling-block in the way of their children. We strongly deprecate such mixed marriages, and we assert that in no circumstances should an Anglican give any undertaking, as a condition of marriage, that the children should be brought up in the practice of another Communion." Part II, p. 102.

heretics and wicked ministers can and do validly and, granted due dispositions in the recipient, fruitfully baptize. Explicit decisions have been given affirming the presumption that baptisms conferred by Pelagians, Zwinglians and Calvinists are valid,[1] and the same explicit decision was given in 1949 regarding baptism conferred by Baptists, Congregationalists, Disciples of Christ, Methodists and Presbyterians.[2] These decisions were given because of doubts expressed by some Catholics; and, since no doubts appear to have been raised about the validity of baptism conferred by Anglicans, Lutherans or the Reformed, the accepted doctrine applies to them, as indeed, it applies to all baptisms conferred with water and the trinitarian formula.

This doctrine has two important consequences. Because of the validity of their baptism the marriages of non-Catholic Christians, granted true consent, are held to be just as truly sacramental and indissoluble as are the marriages of Roman Catholics. And this acknowledgement of the general validity of their baptism is the foundation of the special brotherhood of all Christians, as I have explained at considerable length in *The Unity of Christians*.[3]

STATUS AS CHURCHES

Some prominent separated brethren have felt that the Roman Catholic Church does not give proper recognition to the standing of Anglican and Protestant bodies in their corporate entity. The Rev. Dr Lukas Vischer says : "Many authoritative Roman Catholic statements mention the non-Roman churches and non-Christians in one and the same breath. (I am thinking here also of papal pronouncements such as the Encyclical *Pacem in Terris*.) The profound difference between a non-Roman Christian and a person who does not confess Christ at all is often dis-

---

[1] Cf. *Collectanea S. Congregationis de Propaganda Fidei*, Romae, 1894, n. 659, p. 260.
[2] Cf. *Acta Apostolicae Sedis* 45 (1949), p. 650.
[3] London and New York, 1963, cf. pp. XV, XVI, 30, 32, 39, 55, 56, 121, 201.

regarded; the non-Roman Christians are often simply bracketed together with people belonging to non-Christian religions as 'people of good will' with whom co-operation is possible under certain circumstances".[1] Moreover, Catholics use the word 'church' of the Orthodox, but refuse to use it of Anglican and Protestant bodies, thus implying that the non-Roman churches are merely "a loose fellowship of baptized Christians and have no ecclesiological status as organized bodies".[2]

A word of explanation will, I hope, be helpful. In certain Catholic references to "non-Roman Christians" there is sometimes need, or desire, to include not only the larger Christian denominations, but also groups which the World Council would not admit to membership, or which would not seek such membership—some of the smaller, sect-type, Protestant groups and some of the groups in Africa calling themselves churches, of which there are a multitude. Bodies, also, would be included which claim the name "Christian" but do not call themselves "Churches" but "Missions", "Fellowships", "Unions" or "Societies".

Then, too, the word "church" has different connotations and applications. According to "congregationalist" theory only the local congregation is strictly a church, although "Conventions" of such local congregations are admitted as members of the World Council of Churches. The "Anglican Communion" is not usually called a "church", nor are the world denominational associations, such as the Lutheran World Federation. The World Council of Churches does not claim to be a church, even though it may have some "elements" of a church.

In short, the diverse and multitudinous groupings of our

[1] "Report on Second Vatican Council: *Ecumenical Review*, XVI, No. 1, Oct. 1963, pp. 52-57. Substantially the same observation is made by Professor Peter Brunner about Pius XII's *Mystici Corporis*, "Das Geheimnis der Trennung und die Einheit der Kirche", in *Konzil und Evangelium*, herausgegeben von Kristen E. Skydsgaard, Göttingen, 1962, pp. 199-200, English ed., pp. 109-202. The same feeling is indicated by Dr W. A. Visser 't Hooft in his Report to the Central Committee of the World Council of Churches in August 1963, of *Ecumenical Review, ibid.* p. 97.
[2] Dr. Vischer, *ibid.*

separated brethren are a little bewildering to Catholics, and it is not easy to find language which will include them all without giving offence to any. Some Catholic theologians have thought that the word *communitas* would best indicate the diverse groupings among our separated brethren. Others, however, have felt and feel that in modern times the word "church" is used without theological implications and that it need not be refused to bodies which claim it. The World Council of Churches agrees that member churches need not regard other member churches as "churches in the true and full sense of the word", though they do recognize in them "elements of the true Church". (*Note* Cf. the Declaration at Toronto, 1950, nn. 4 and 5.) The use of the term *communitas* might appear to deny to them any "elements" of the Church in their corporate entity, whereas much of our common Christian heritage has been preserved by them not merely as individuals but as corporate bodies. Further, the word *community* in certain parts of the world may indicate a group having, or claiming, special political status.

Consequently, it was suggested that the terms "churches and ecclesial communities" would best correspond to the reality of the diverse groupings among our separated brethren. It may be hoped that the Council will accept this suggestion.

In substance, however, baptism is universally admitted by Catholics as making a basic distinction between Christians and non-Christians. Here I venture to cite my own words : "We must emphasize the fact that heresy and schism, even when they are formally such, do not completely destroy that membership in the Church of Christ which, as *Mediator Dei* (the Encyclical of Pius XII) and St Paul teach, is created by baptism. Non-Catholic Christians must not, therefore, be put in the same plane as the non-baptized, for they always bear, not only the name of Christ on their foreheads, but his actual image in their souls, deeply and indelibly imprinted there by Baptism."[1] In this statement I was expressing ordinary Catholic teaching.

Catholics most gladly admit "elements" of the true Church

---

[1] *The Unity of Christians*, London and New York, 1963, p. 32.

in "communities" of separated brethren, though, as separated brethren themselves hold, these "elements" may be more or less significant in the diverse Christian communities. The reader is invited to turn back to the chapter on the scandal of divisions, where I listed some of the "elements" of the true Church common to all Christians, pp. 140-2, and common to Catholics and Protestants, pp. 142-3. It may be added that all our separated brethren, to our sorrow, reject the Catholic position, and not a few, like Professor Peter Brunner, hold that the Catholic Church has fallen into various heresies. All would, however, admit "elements" of the true Church in the Roman Catholic Church, though they might differ considerably in estimating exactly what these "elements" are.[1] This surely denies our status as the Church of Christ. In turn, Catholics hold much the same about our separated brethren.

This difference about the doctrine of the Church is one of the matters on which dialogue can bring clarifications, corrections and developments. It cannot be solved antecedently nor made a condition for entering into dialogue, as the World Council itself has explicitly recognized.[2]

I would like, however, to say that we Catholics must recognize with sincere gratitude that it was our separated brethren, Orthodox, Anglican and Protestant, who gave the first impulse to the modern unitive movement and that we have learned much from them, and can learn still more. We differ in many matters, but our mutual charity already makes a cer-

[1] Cf. the article of Professor Brunner, already cited, p. 196, n. 2.
[2] Cf. the famous Declaration made at Toronto by the Central Committee entitled "The Ecclesiological Significance of the World Council of Churches", Part I, No. 3: "The World Council cannot and should not be based on any one conception of the Church. It does not prejudge the ecclesiological problem."; and cf. also, n. 4 and 5, and Part II, nn. 4 and 5. The little volume entitled *The Church*, prepared for the Lund Conference of 1952, published in London, 1951, has a section on the theological assumptions of the World Council of Churches, in which the same statements are made, v.g., n. (2): "The Council assumes that every known view of the nature of the Church has a legitimate place within it, and that it is within the Council that any or all of these views may be brought into living confrontation with each other," p. 54.

tain bridge across the differences, the divisions are growing less, and we are convinced that the Holy Spirit of God has already given proof of his guidance in our efforts and will continue to guide us, step by step, towards the attainment of the perfect unity which Christ wills.

COMMON PROBLEMS

The Central Committee of the World Council of Churches made another statement, in its meeting of August, 1963, with which it is also a pleasure to express hearty agreement :

"The dialogue is not only for our mutual edification. It is also in order that we may bear witness faithfully to Jesus Christ as the one Lord and Saviour of the world. It is in the context of the vast missionary task which faces the Church in our time, in the context of a pastoral concern for all mankind, that the dialogue has to be conducted. One of the indispensable conditions of fruitful dialogue will be an honest examination of the missionary policies and practices of all our churches in order that we may learn not to hinder but rather to help each other to be true witnesses to Christ."[1]

This last suggestion may prove most useful and helpful, although the multiplicity of missionary bodies, both in the Catholic Church and among separated brethren, together with the very different conditions in different parts of the world, would indicate that such dialogue must require considerable preparation, though it might well take place in different regions of the world.

"Pastoral concern for all mankind", however, calls attention to the many important matters mentioned in the *Encyclical* of Pope John XXIII on Peace, about which further investigation and dialogue could be fruitful. The matter of racial relations is acute in more than one country of the world, and there is rising resentment against the assumption of superiority, real or imagined, of the white race. Christians in more than one coun-

---

[1] *Ecumenical Review*, XVI, No. 1, Oct. 1963, p. 108.

try, not only as individuals, but as representatives of their Communities, have made noble, and in some cases costly, protests against policies and practices based upon a denial of the racial equality of men. Sometimes these protests have been made by Catholics and Protestants together; but it is to be desired that all Christians should unite in statements of the common Christtian teaching on this complicated and agitated question.

CHRISTIANS AND JEWS

Pope John XXIII had directed the Unity Secretariat to prepare for the Second Vatican Council a statement on the attitude of Catholics towards Jews. After more than two years of preparation a draft document was prepared, which represents the agreement of a large number of leading Catholic scholars and thinkers of various backgrounds and nationalities.

The document, which forms the fourth chapter of the *Schema* on Ecumenism, is exclusively religious and spiritual in character and purpose, and its perspective is not towards Jews as a race or as a nation, but as the people of the Old Testament. The draft points out that, in God's design, the Church has its roots in the covenant made by God with Abraham and his descendants. All the Christian faithful were included in the call of Abraham and are children of Abraham according to faith (cf. Gal. 3 :7); the Church, though a new creation in Christ, can never forget that it is the continuation of that people with whom in ancient times God mercifully made the Old Covenant.

It is the belief of the Church that Christ, who is our peace (cf. Eph. 2 :14) had the same love for Jews and Gentiles, and made both to be one, and by that union of both into one body (cf. Eph 2 :17) announced to the whole world reconciliation in Christ. It would, then, be unchristian to use injurious language of that chosen people, even though in great part they do not accept Christ. In spite of that, as St Paul declares, they remain dear to God because of the Fathers and the gifts God gave them (cf. Rom. 11 :28). Christ died to atone for the sins of the whole world (cf. Luke 23 :34; Acts. 3 :17; 1 Cor. 2 :8); and the death of Christ, regarded historically, was certainly not brought about by all the Jews then living, and far less by the Jewish people of today.

The draft, without discussing the various causes of anti-semitism, declares that the events narrated in the Bible, and in particular, the account of the crucifixion of Christ, are no justification whatever for disdain or hatred or persecution of Jews. The draft admonishes preachers and catechists always to bear this in mind in the accounts they give of the life and the death of Christ, and to make clear that Jesus Christ himself, according to the flesh, his Virgin Mother and all the Apostles were Jews by birth.

The draft refers to the heritage which the Church and the Synagogue have in common, and expresses the hope that mutual understanding and esteem may be fostered and increased. It ends with a very forthright declaration that Catholics, who must condemn ill-treatment of any men, have special reason to deplore and condemn hatred and persecution of Jews, whether in the past or in our own day.

In a Press release about the draft, the Secretariat said that there was no reason to fear that the draft in any way modifies the traditional interpretation of the New Testament; and expressed, also, its confidence that the draft would meet the approval of many Islamic leaders, since they are well aware of the value of a statement on the religious heritage which is shared by all those who revere Abraham and the prophets of the Old Testament.[1]

The Press release from the Secretariat added, also, that the draft document has no bearing whatever on relations between the Vatican and the State of Israel; and has no relevance to any political groups, or even religious groups, which exist among Jews. The draft is neither pro-Zionist nor anti-Zionist, such matters being quite outside its scope. Consequently, no political use can rightly be made of it.

From the reaction of some of the Delegated Observers there

[1] Cf. the *Press Release* of the Arab Information Centre of the League of Arab States, New York, July 3, 1963.

is every confidence that our separated brethren will agree with the draft on Christian and Jewish relations, a fact which will give evidence of increasing Christian understanding and mutual help.

EXPECT MORE MIRACLES

In this chapter I have been frank, but not, I hope, depressing. The change of atmosphere, which is really a change of spirit, is, I repeat, nothing less than miraculous. God has blessed us all and we have every reason to hope that he will continue to bless us. Unity is his will, and must be his doing, not ours. We must, then, advance without fear. Mistakes and upsets there may be. But nothing must shake our confidence, for it rests upon the all-powerful goodness of God.

12

A Two-fold or a Single Unity?

MORE HAS BEEN SAID THROUGHOUT THIS BOOK about a unity within the human family than of the unity of the human family; that is, more has been said about the unity of Christians than of the unity of mankind as such. Yet we began with a search for the unity of all men, whatever their nationality, race, culture or even religion.[1] We looked to unity on the purely human level, a unity based on possession of the same human nature, which makes men truly brothers, with intelligence and free will, all, in fact, existing under the fatherly care of the Supreme Being, God. We looked to the principles which unite men as men, whatever their religious beliefs.[2]

Then we turned to the question of the unity of Christians, which is a specifically religious unity, based upon belief that God became a man and through his God-manhood designed to unite men in a more sublime kind of unity through a divine gift to men.[3]

Now a reader may well ask : "What is the connection between these two unities, between the unity of mankind (apart from or even independent of any religious belief), and the unity of Christians in the Church ?" We have seen that some relations do in fact exist. On the one hand, the Church has sincere concern for the unity of men on the purely human level, and one evidence

[1] Cf. Chapter 1.
[2] Cf. Chapters 1, 3, 4.
[3] Cf. Chapters 6, 7.

of this is the purpose of the Second Vatican Council[1] and the Encyclicals of Pope John XXIII, especially *Pacem in Terris*.[2] On the other hand, whoever loves humanity and seeks the good of humanity, of whatever faith he may be, cannot reasonably be indifferent to the impact of Christians on the world in general, and to Christian efforts to secure social justice and peace. The resources, intellectual and spiritual, and indirectly even material, which Christians can deploy to promote human unity, the contributions they are in fact making towards it, and even the sad divisions which exist among Christians—all these have too much weight to be ignored. Christians are about a third of the human family, the ideological influence of Christians is probably greater than their numbers, and hence it is of interest to all mankind how that influence is exerted. Thus there do exist certain factual connections between the two unities, that of mankind as a whole and that of Christians.

Nevertheless, a basic question still remains: are there two unities to be regarded as permanently different and divided, admitting and encouraging mutual collaboration, but still remaining separate, or are they to be considered as converging lines, having a dynamic tendency to meet together? This is to ask whether the natural principles and forces which unite men in a common nature stand, as many think, independent of the religious problem. It is to ask whether the great world religions —Animism, Confucianism, Hinduism, Buddhism, Judaism, Christianity, Mohammedanism—are to continue until the end of time, having at the most tolerance toward each other; or whether there is, by God's planning and mysterious designs, a dynamic of history which tends towards an ultimate merging between the natural and the religious unity of the human family?

TWO CLEARLY DEFINED UNITIES

First, a clear distinction must be recognized between the two

[1] Cf. Chapter 5.
[2] Cf. Chapter 4.

unities, such as was indicated in Chapter 6.[1] What is the basic distinction between these two unities? The answer cannot be that the one is "civil", the other "religious", however plausible this might appear at first sight. Unity in the "civil" or "secular" order, as the early chapters of this book indicated, depends ultimately upon God, the source of right reason and of all order, even though this may not be recognized by everyone. Furthermore, many men play their part in civil society through religious motives; and it remains to be proved that any civil society can subsist in justice and freedom and mutual good will when all religious motives have been excluded.

For this reason, the distinction between "the sacred and the profane" or "the civil and the religious" is inadequate. Many, if not all, religions have seen the whole universe as it were lit up with some divine light which excludes nothing from its illumination and its influence. It is true, of course, that civil governments have no specifically religious function, just as religious societies have no specific function in civil or secular affairs. But the natural unity of mankind cuts across any unity made merely by civil governments, and is based on principles which rise above nationality, race and the historical development of peoples. All religions hold convictions about the meaning of human life and about human destiny; and even the effort to exclude the influence of those convictions has very deep effects upon the unity of mankind.

The difference, rather, lies in this, that the one unity derives from, and is based upon, the inherent characteristics of men as men, upon what we call "natural" principles or "the order of creation", while the other is based upon an order which derives from God's free gift, from his will that men should share in the intimacies of the divine life itself, a share brought to men by the "enfleshment" of the Son of God himself. This is called a "supernatural" unity, because, though in a sense intelligent beings are "open" to any communication from God, nevertheless the actual share of the inner divine life is something beyond any definite natural aspirations of men. It is a unity based upon

[1] Pp. 90-96, above.

what is called "the order of redemption", understanding the word "redemption" as not merely freedom from the compulsions of sin but as including all the gifts which Christ gives.

The first unity, the natural one, is based on a common possession of intelligence and free will, and upon their derivation from the ultimate Intelligence and Freedom, God. Men are all equal in their common nature, which is not changed by race or by personal decisions; and since men are all made as finite reflections of the Infinite, it follows that the Infinite finds something of infinity in men, and cares for them in sincere love made manifest in the share given in the ultimate Infinity by that very possession of intelligence and freedom. Men, in turn, feel that they are all radically the same in nature and that consequently their reciprocal relations must be governed by the law of truth and of justice, and by mutual respect for one another's freedom, in equally mutual good will. This ground of unity can be, and often is, accepted even though its ultimate derivation from God is denied. Men who do not believe in God, may and do still accept the need of fair-mindedness, equity and natural benevolence based upon "our common humanity".

The other unity, that of "the new people of God" gathered in the Church of Christ, is based not only upon a new revelation of God's intimate nature, but also upon a new communication of God's very being to men. The revelation that God is not only one, but is also Father, Son and Holy Spirit is indeed mysterious, but it gives new glimpses into the nature of ultimate reality, which is not a mere undifferentiated unity, not some absolute self-enclosed lonely "God" above and beyond and remote from the world, but is a self-communication, a complete and utter sharing, an unlimited self-giving, whose inmost nature is revealed by and in the self-giving of Christ upon the Cross. It was God who was crucified. This fact is basic to the whole new order brought by Christ. The mystery of God is the mystery of love.

Christ brought to men not only the assurance that truly God is love, as St John says (cf. 1 John 4 : 8, 16), but brought also the power to share in that ultimate reality of God's own self-giving. And to be able to do that, Christ makes man "a new creature", "a new creation", a brother of Christ through the Spirit of sonship within man's being, capable of living a new life in union with the self-giving of Christ. Man's individual personality is not destroyed, but is amplified, expanded, lifted up to new heights, given a share in the very life of Father, Son and Holy Spirit. Christ was both true God and true man : true man, born of a woman, eating, sleeping, rejoicing, sorrowing, weeping, loving children, loving his friends, hurt by rejection of his offer of affection, "in all things like to us, sin excepted" (Heb. 4 : 15). His Godhead in no sense diminished his true humanity. So, too, the Christian when "deified" by baptism, is still truly a man, even more truly himself, and the bonds which link him with Christ link him also to the whole of mankind just as Christ by his manhood was linked with the whole of mankind.

This conviction of the gift of God giving a new kind of life is fundamental to Christianity, and to the new kind of unity upon which Christianity is based. It does not mean, of course, that each and every Christian preserves the divine life given him in baptism, for men always remain free and able by sin to reject God's gift. It does mean, however, that the Christian concept of the unity which God wills for men is based upon the Incarnation of the Son of God and the gift of divine life which he gives.

THE CHURCH AND PURELY HUMAN UNITY

From what has been explained about the specific basis of Church unity, important consequences follow regarding the attitude of the Church to purely human unity : for the Church, as it is a society—which is also perfectly human—feels itself intimately linked with all mankind, and co-operates in the achieving of unity for mankind. Those who are baptized, although they are "deified", are still wholly men in every respect and for every purpose, in no way different in this from Christ the God-man, and thus they live and feel as all other men. It has been said of Christ that, although being "equal with God", "(he) emptied himself and took upon him the form of a servant, being born in the likeness of men" (Phil. 2 :6-7). Consequently, he was capable of sharing our weaknesses, and was tempted in all points as we are, yet remaining sinless (cf. Heb. 4 :15); for sin is not, as it were, a quality of humanity or essential to it, but is a negation of man's nobility. In the same way, the man who has been baptized is and remains a member of the human family, and as such, and by virtue of his human nature, he feels himself to be everyone's brother, on the human level, and leaves to God judgement about their interior spiritual state;[1] and, on this human level, he forms together with all of these one single family. Thus both individuals who have been baptized and the Church co-operate, and must actively co-operate, for the achievement of the unity of mankind even on the purely

[1] Besides baptism of water there is what is called "baptism of desire", consisting in a willingness to do what God wants. The Church is the ordinary means established by God to bring men to happiness both in this world and in the next. But, at the same time, as Pope Pius IX said, we must hold for certain that "those who are ignorant of the true religion have no fault in the eyes of God, if that ignorance is invincible". Pius IX then went on to say "Who will ever dare to claim to determine the limits of ignorance according to the character and variety of peoples, regions, mentalities and countless other circumstances?" Nothing is more certain than that God condemns no one save because of his own deliberate fault. Pope Alexander VIII in 1690 condemned the assertion that "pagans, Jews, heretics and suchlike people have not sufficient grace", Denzinger, *Enchiridion Symbolorum*, 1928 edn., 1295; and Clement XI condemned the statement that "outside the Church no grace is given", Denzinger, 1379. Pius XI, speaking of atheists and referring to Romans 1 : 20, where St Paul uses the words "inexcusable" of the atheists of his day, said: "The distinctions between excusability and inexcusability are among the most difficult for even the greatest minds to apprehend. God alone, who is Truth, the whole Truth, who calls all creatures to a knowledge of the truth, and gives them the means of finding it, God alone surely sees these distinctions, even if the Apostle Paul spoke of inexcusability". *Osservatore Romano*, 31 January, 1938. Thus the Christian conviction, based upon the clear teaching of Scripture, that God gives the wondrous gifts of grace through actual baptism, implies no judgement about what God's goodness may give to those who in good faith do not receive the actual sacrament. Natural human solidarity and brotherhood remain, even in the case of baptized sinners, and in the case of the unbaptized. It is about this that I am speaking here.

human level. Thus there is not, nor can there be, any conflict between this purely human unity and specific Church unity: the Church recognizes with sober equity of judgement the good that is in all men, even when they do not believe in its message. It gladly acknowledges the dignity and the nobility in all men, and their inalienable rights as men, and endeavours to protect and to foster this dignity and nobility and to maintain men's rights.

This is why Pope John XXIII, whose memory is blessed, addressed himself, in the *Encyclical* on Peace, "to all men of good will" and felt that he could and should speak of them as "his brothers", whatever their nation or race or religious faith. This is, likewise, the basis of the Church's teaching on social problems and of its interest in the general welfare of mankind; it is the reason why Pope Paul VI said that one of the main purposes of the Council is to enter into dialogue with the contemporary world. There are no opportunist motives here. Christians do not lose their humanity, but on the contrary become more human, and, being such, are more aware of their obligation to work for justice and charity in the whole human family. Pope John XXIII was an outstanding example. He was a great churchman and a great humanist; the one because of the other, for the Church is meant to serve mankind, even as the Founder of the Church served mankind (Matt. 20:26-28).

It is sad, but yet a fact, that some surprise was expressed when Pope John XXIII addressed his *Encyclical* on Peace "to all men of good will" without distinction of faith. Did this surprise spring from the idea that the Church must be interested only in "supernatural" things, in life after death, and need not trouble about life in this world? Or did it spring from the idea that the Church's unity must be a self-enclosed, almost an exclusive unity, protecting itself against a hostile world and believing that the natural and the supernatural are radically opposed, and that the unity of the Church stands independent of the unity of mankind? If it were so, the surprise sprang from forgetfulness of the example of Christ, the Church's Founder and model. He came, certainly, to give eternal life (John 17:2);

but not on this account did he scorn care for men's earthly and temporal life, using for this purpose even his power to work miracles—to feed men and women when they were hungry, and to cure them and restore them, even from death. And this he did not just once and again but many times. St John witnesses this in the epilogue to his Gospel: "And there are also many other things which Jesus did, the which, if they should be written every one, I suppose that even the world itself could not contain the books that should be written" (John 21 : 25). And the people said of him in admiration : "He hath done all things well : he maketh both the deaf to hear, and the dumb to speak" (Mark 7 : 37). St Peter, summarizing the life of Jesus, in one of his speeches, said simply that he "went about doing good, and healing all that were oppressed of the devil" (Acts 10 : 38). And why all this? The reply is to be found in the words which Jesus uttered before one such miracle, namely, before the miracle of the loaves and fishes : "I have compassion on the multitude, because they have now been with me three days, and have nothing to eat" (Mark 8 : 2). St Matthew, after having described how he went about every town and village, teaching in the synagogues and "healing every sickness and every disease among the people", adds : "When he saw the multitudes, he was moved with compassion on them, because they fainted and were scattered abroad, as sheep having no shepherd" (Matt. 9 : 35-36). In other words, Jesus loved men as such, and helped them whenever he was able.

As Christ conceived his task and his mission, so too the Church is meant to conceive its task and mission. When the Apostles sought the first place—the place of honour and power, —Christ's reproof is as gentle as it is penetrating : "Whosoever will be chief among you, let him be your servant : even as the Son of man came not to be ministered to, but to minister, and to give his life a ransom for the multitude" (Matt. 20 : 27-28). To affirm the obligation of serving in this way clearly does not deny, nor tend to deny, the divine mission of the Church, just as Christ did not, with these words, deny his divine mission; but it does stress that this very mission and the authority it

implies is at the service of the good of mankind—to the point of sacrifice of life. The Church essentially is at the service of mankind, as was Christ.

TOWARDS UNITY IN CHRIST

The Church, then, must devote its energetic attention towards achieving the purely human form of unity among men. But the Church knows that, although this is essential, yet it is not all, and not even the principal thing; for the Church is conscious that Christ brought the inestimable gift of divine, eternal life to man, and hence the possibility of an infinitely superior unity among men, a unity infinitely superior in being achieved in God and in Christ, on the foundation of the implanting in man of the life of grace, which makes man the adoptive son of God, sharing in God's very nature and hence sharing God's Spirit. And as the Church is the continuer of Christ's work, it desires that all men may share in this divine gift, in this divine grandeur, and so achieve—on the basis of and by virtue of this life—a higher unity, that of all men in Christ; bringing about the fulfilment of the prayer offered by Jesus to his Father at the Last Supper: "... (I) pray ... for them also who shall believe in me through their (the Apostles') word; that they all may be one; as thou, Father, art in me, and I in thee, that they also may be one in us: that the world may believe that thou hast sent me" (John 17 : 20-21).

At this point, however, more than one reader may well express a fear : is not all this a disguised kind of racialism on the religious level? Does this not really mean that the white man's religion proclaims itself to be superior to every other, with the consequent aim of extending it, as one of its own higher conquests, over every race—if it does not even go so far as to impose it?

At the present time, when, happily, mankind is showing itself ever readier to acknowledge the complete equality and brotherhood of all peoples, without distinction of nationality, race and culture, this fear is most understandable, and deserves

the most serious consideration. In answer, it might be pointed out that in other spheres, even in the sphere of culture, men do not refuse the inventions, the techniques and the intellectual achievements of other nations or races, simply because they come from a race different from themselves. But to this it may be urged that in the sphere of religion the case is different. Religion touches the most intimate point of man's dignity, namely, his most personal relations with the Ultimate, and hence these relations should really be the expression of each individual's personal spiritual yearnings, and the aspiration and religious expression of each people or race.

In answer, it could be pointed out that Christianity is not Western and European in its origin, but Eastern and Asiatic, and, more precisely, Semitic. This, however, is not the main point. The fundamental answer is this: Christianity, and the gifts which Christ brought to the world, are not in any sense the invention or the conquest or even the possession of any man or any one people, whether white, black or yellow. It is simply a free gift of God's infinite mercy. God does, indeed, use men and is served by men to bring this gift to others. But these men do no more than transmit a gift which is not theirs, but God's. This gift is for them, too—neither more nor less than for others—an undeserved gift from God. And the greatest of these messengers are perfectly aware of their own unworthiness before this message and gift. That great Apostle, St Paul, says very firmly : "This is a faithful saying, and worthy of all acceptation, that Christ Jesus came into the world to save sinners, of whom I am the foremost" (1 Tim. 1 : 15). Jesus himself admonished the Apostles : "When ye shall have done all those things which are commanded you, say, We are unprofitable servants : we have done that which was our duty to do" (Luke 17 : 10). The very greatness of the gift must induce a sense of unworthiness and of sincere humility.

THE MYSTERY OF GOD'S PROVIDENCE

The way in which God chose to communicate these gifts to

men is indeed mysterious. But the mystery involved in it is impacted in the whole mystery of divine providence, and, indeed, in the whole mystery of human life. No man can understand why God permits the evils which he does permit; no human mind can see the whole course of human history and see the mysterious connection of events from the beginning of time even to the end of time. St Paul, faced with the difficulty of "justifying the ways of God to men", honestly confessed his inability :

O the depth of the riches and wisdom and knowledge of God ! How unsearchable are his judgements and how inscrutable are his ways !

For who has known the mind of the Lord,
    or who has been his counsellor?
Or who has given a gift to him
    that he might be repaid?

For from him and through him and to him are all things. To him be glory forever. Amen. (Rom. 11 :33-36)

In spite, however, of this ultimate mystery, some things are clear. Men are intelligent and men are free. If it is God who gives them intelligence and freedom, then it is reasonable that his guidance of the world and his plans for the world should be based upon that gift to men of intelligence and freedom, and it follows that he wills that through intelligence and freedom they should love him and their fellow men and serve in freedom the cause of justice, truth and charity. Moreover, men are interdependent on the natural level, dependent upon their ancestors since they live in a world in so many ways conditioned by the ideas, the institutions and the almost unrealized psychological and communal inheritances from the past; men are likewise dependent on other men for knowledge, instruction, and the ordered society in which they live. It is not then strange that God should give his greater gift of a share in his own intimate life by ways in accordance with man's intelligence and freedom, and in accordance with human interdependence. The life of Christ is the proof of this for he was born of a human mother belonging to a particular race of men, he lived in particular historical conditions and he chose other men to bear his message and his gifts to the rest of mankind.

And yet this does not say all. Very early in Christian history, faced with the question, "Why did not Christ come sooner?", many Christian thinkers gave the answer : "Because God wished to prepare the human race for so great an event. Christ came when God's providence had made the human race capable and ready to receive so great a blessing." The Letter to the Hebrews begins by the assertion that "in many and various ways God spoke of old to our fathers by the prophets" (Heb. 1:1). The words "in many and various ways" should be pondered. In the course of human development, even from prehistoric times, the religious instinct has found an outlet in many forms : the history of religion shows that there was most strange intermingling of "magic" and religion, much that modern man would call "superstitious" and degraded distortions of religion; there has been polytheism, the worship of the powers of nature personified; and there has been and still are the great world religions of a more elevated kind such as Confucianism, Buddhism, Hinduism, Mazedism, Judaism and Mohammedanism. In all of these, and even in the most degraded of primitive religions, is it possible to recognize, amid much that is unacceptable, traces or elements of the "many and various ways" in which God has revealed himself, and to find in those traces and elements of truth, a providential preparation for the ultimate revelation of God in which all that is good and true in other religions found their fulfilment and their completion?

Not that Christianity is a kind of amalgam, or "syncretistic" combination of all religions; St Paul and the earliest Christians were fierce in their denunciations of those features of the religions of their day which degraded mankind by irrational beliefs and filled them with superstitious fears. Many of the non-Jewish religions made even the gods subject to blind fate; and against all this St Paul proclaimed the glorious liberty of the sons of God, based upon the conviction that man's reason can find accord with the ultimate Reason which is God. This is why Christianity is radically optimistic. It holds that the universe is not irrational or the outcome of the struggle between two principles equally ultimate, matter and spirit, good and evil. It holds that all things are the offspring of a supreme Intelligence and a supreme Goodness, that evil is permitted only for a greater good and that man through union with God can overcome all the forces of unreason and disintegration : "all things work together unto good for those who love God" (Rom. 8 : 28).

It can be granted that Christians, in their zeal for the liberation of man, may have sometimes been too vehement and unmeasured in their condemnation of all non-Christian religions; yet it still remains true that Christianity has within it the fulfilment of all the religious yearnings of mankind, and contains, either explicitly expressed or latent in unrealized implications, all the truths which other religions have grasped. To show this in detail needs exact and exhaustive study of all the great world religions; and this is in process. The approach of Christians to other world religions is not one of denial and negation, but of sympathy in our common humanity and of endeavour to show how the true and good elements in all religions find their place and their fulfilment and completion in the faith brought to men by the Word of God made flesh, which "enlightens every man who comes into the world".[1]

UNIVERSALISM

The basic truth of Christianity is universalistic : it is the gift of a special share in the nature of God. Who could doubt that God knows man's nature well enough to make his gift sufficiently malleable and flexible to be adapted and made suitable to any type of man, whatever his race, nationality or type of culture or civilization? And, given that this gift truly means participation (without destroying man's personality) in the Supreme Being's very nature, in the nature of him who created all these

---

[1] The literature is immense on the approach of Christianity to other religions; in general the approach is based upon agreements and not upon oppositions.

men in his own image and likeness—how is it possible to doubt
that this gift is equally suitable to all men of every race?

It may be admitted that from the sixteenth century onward
the great impulse to expand Christianity followed the era of
European discovery of other lands and of European national-
istic expansion; and it may be admitted that "missionaries"
sometimes carried with them ideas and outlooks which failed to
make sufficient distinction between the essential Christian message and the "civilization" in which it had developed. "Missionaries" may not always have had due understanding of the
culture of the people to whom they went. There were, however,
many like de Nobili in India and Ricci in China, of whom this
was not true; and the missionaries on the whole were a force of
restraint upon the too often rapacious domination of governments and of traders. Moreover, the missionaries, if not
perfect, did bring self-sacrificing service for the health,
education and peace of the peoples to whom they went, and
did spread a larger and more penetrating ideal of human
brotherhood of justice, truth and freedom.

Today Cardinals and Bishops from all parts of the world
take their place in the councils of the Church on an equal foot-
ing irrespective of race or nationality; and the variety of languages and of rites used in divine worship is concrete evidence
of a flexibliity in principle which can find larger and wider
application in the future.

There is, then, no reason of nationality, of race, or of historic
culture which antecedently should prevent calm consideration
of what the Church offers in the name of God. There is a prior
assurance and guarantee, inherent in the offer itself, against any
imposition. Christ invited, and did not try to compel; and the
Church, following Christ, insists that faith must be free. The
great Augustine only expressed the common Christian conviction when he insisted that faith is essentially a free act, and, in
more recent times Pius XII only reminded men of this truth:
faith is not faith if it is not free.[1]

To what, then, does Christ through the Church invite?

[1] Cf. *A.A.S.* 35 (1943), p. 243

Christ, in the famous parable of the Good Shepherd made a contrast between himself and all self-seeking teachers or leaders. He seeks not to receive, but to give :

> I am come that they (men) may have life, and have it more abundantly (John 10 :10).

And elsewhere he explains the meaning of this "life" which he has brought. In his prayer, addressed, after the Last Supper, in his capacity as High Priest, to the Father, he said :

> And this is life eternal, that they might know thee the only true God, and Jesus Christ, whom thou hast sent (John 17 :3).

His mission is therefore to spread knowledge of the Father, of the truth, as he declared before Pilate :

> For this end I was born, and for this I came into the world, to bear witness to the truth. Every one that is of the truth hears my voice (John 18 :37).

It is in this sense that he proclaimed solemnly :

> I am the light of the world : he that followeth me will not walk in darkness, but will have the light of life (John 8 :12).

Referring to his function as the guide of men to their heavenly Father, he said again :

> I am the way, the truth, and the life : no man comes to the Father, but by me (John 14 :6).

What man does not desire all these things (even if he refers to them under another name)—life, truth, certainty, light, the right way to attain the goal, the true goal, of life itself ?

Agnosticism and scepticism, though they may pretend to a superior intellectualism, leave the heart cold, give no basis for confident and persevering action, offer no solution to the tragedies of life. Ultimately they despair of all human values and lead only to a self-seeking, or pleasure-seeking, which is at once a denial of the deepest of human aspirations and an invitation to the rule of those who can gain control of the most powerful weapons of brute—or atomic—force.

But besides truth and real life, Christ offers mankind *freedom* —liberty from the compulsions of sin and true inner independence and freedom, in which is man's true worth and dignity. So many religions have offered release from the yoke of sin, from the oppressing sense of guilt, real or imagined; oriental religions are haunted by the hope of escape from the pervasiveness of sin. Modern psychologists are aware of the afflictions caused by the guilt of sin. Christ knew the hearts of men, knew "what is in man", and told the learned men of Jerusalem:

You shall know the truth and the truth shall make you free,

explaining that the deepest and truest freedom is freedom from sin (John 8:31 ff.).

WIDE HORIZONS

St Paul writes to the Romans: "But now being made free from sin, and become servants to God, you have your return in holiness, and its end, everlasting life. For the wages of sin is death; but the free gift of God is eternal life through Jesus Christ out Lord" (Rom. 6:22-23). And to the Galatians he writes: "For, brethren, you have been called to liberty; only use not liberty for an occasion to the flesh, but by love be servants of one another" (Gal. 5:13). This liberation opens wide horizons and such great opportunities, that Jesus could exhort his followers: "Be therefore perfect, even as your Father in heaven is perfect" (Matt. 5:48). And in order that those who accept this sublime aim and are "hungry and thirsty" for justice —that is, for the perfect fulfilment of the will of God and hence for perfect holiness—may not be discouraged, he solemnly reassures them: "Blessed are those who hunger and thirst for justice: for they shall be filled" (Matt. 5:6). And the supreme perfection of God, to be imitated first of all, is charity: "Be therefore followers of God," St Paul writes to the Ephesians, "as beloved children; and walk in love, as Christ also has loved us, and has given himself up for us, a fragrant offering and sacrifice to God" (Eph. 5:1-2). The torturing demon of sin can only be cast out by the Spirit of God who comes into the very hearts of men bringing his strength of all-embracing love.

And lastly, that which Christ offers in addition is an ineffable relationship of friendship and love with God himself. Jesus assures the Apostles, at the Last Supper : "If a man love me, he will keep my words : and my Father will love him, and we will come unto him, and make our abode with him" (John 14 :23). And in the so-called "Book of Consolation", that marvellous Book of Revelation, this same thought is expressed in the image of a feast : "Behold" says Christ to the soul, "I stand at the door, and knock : if any man hear my voice, and open the door, I will come in to him, and will sup with him, and he with me" (Rev. 3 :20). Christ offers and promises who-ever believes in him divine and therefore sweet intimacy with God. This intimacy with God may, indeed, be felt sometimes by what is called "sensible devotion", which affects the feel-ings; it can be experienced in different kinds of liftings up of the spirit, even to the mystical visions or interior movements of "the fine point of the soul". But essentially it is a matter of faith, not of sight or even experience, save in the wider meaning of "experience". It may be called the gift of peace : "Peace I leave with you, my peace I give to you, not as the world gives do I give to you. Let not your hearts be troubled, nor let them be afraid" (John 14 :27). This peace of Christ does not, of course, free a man from sorrow, or affliction or desolation, but beneath all the sorrows, afflictions and desolation the fact of faith stands sure : "It is good for me to cleave to the Lord" . . ."I know him in whom I have trusted" (Ps. 72 :28; 2 Tim. 1 :12). The believer is not exempt from trials and anxieties; but he is free from that gnawing doubt about the ultimate and especially about death and what comes after, which the unbeliever may deny but which not seldom he feels.

The believer has faith that "the sufferings of the present time are not worth comparing with the glory that shall be revealed in us" (Rom. 8 :16). The words of Christ that "he who would save his life must lose it and he who loses his life for my sake shall find it", are true not only for salvation after death, but are true in this life, also. Self-surrender, in union with the self-surrender of Christ, is a gift of God, even in this life, and it brings that peace which "passes all understanding" (Phil. 4 : 7).

THE CHURCH AND THE CONTEMPORARY WORLD

The *Encyclical* of Pope John XXIII on Peace won very general approval among men of all nations, races and religions; just as did the United Nations Universal Declaration of Human Rights. One may then ask whether any other than the outlook of the Church can in the last analysis offer an adequate justification for those documents. I say "in the last analysis", because it is possible to agree about the substance of those documents, even though there is disagreement about their ultimate justification—which, however, need be no cause for anything save calm reflection and reasonable "dialogue".

Hence, in a spirit of calm reflection, I refer briefly to some general alternative to the Christian analysis and outlook.

Is economic determinism adequate? The very words in which it is enunciated deny freedom; and under promise of a Utopia, it generally results in a comparatively small group of the "chosen" dictating, often with brutal force, to the mass of the people; human beings are "expendable" and the end justifies all means. Can a "scientific humanism" ultimately justify man's freedom? Too often its "brave new world" becomes a world in which science may control the very sources of life and the basic thinking of men, making men automatons or robots—and this in the name of humanity. Can men have an indeterminate hope in a power of "evolution" inevitably making things better and better? Wars and the threats of atomic war have dispelled these hopes and left a mood too near to bleak despair. Can religions of "renunciation" defend those documents? Too often, they assume that all life and all reason is an illusion, or that existence itself is an evil, and they have no intellectual power of resistance to tyranny. They carry within themselves no insistent urge towards that conquest of natural powers which alone can provide food for the rapidly increasing population of the world. Can belief in the one omnipotent God, whose will is inscrutable and unalterable, defend the equality of men and give satisfactory reasons for tolerance and for control of the aggressive pride of men ?

HAS THE CHURCH FAILED?

What, then, of the Church? The Church of Christ, even after twenty long centuries, has won no more than one third of mankind, and this third is torn by the scandal of divisions. Is the Church, then, a failure? Before thinking so, God's plan must be pondered. God wills that the Church should be subject to the law of growth and evolution, in both its human and its organic aspects; that it should have to struggle humbly and laboriously against the sin within its own bosom, against the world and "the prince of this world" (John 14 : 30). Christ willed that the life of the Church, like his own life, should bear the mark of the cross, that is, of humiliation and suffering, failures and defeats, and that its triumph should come not merely through the defeats but even by means of these defeats. It was in this way that he wished the Church to be preserved from the temptation to pride and to place its hopes in itself, and in human means, forces or events, and to learn always to look with humble trust to God alone for support.

The Church is well aware that this is the will of its Founder and Lord. "Remember," Jesus said to his Apostles, "the word that I said unto you, the servant is not greater than his Lord. If they have persecuted me, they will also persecute you." And again : "In the world ye shall have tribulation : but be of good cheer; I have overcome the world" (John 15 : 20; 16 : 33). The Church is afflicted but never discouraged. It remains unshakeable with its faith in Jesus' promise : "Lo, I am with you always, even unto the end of the world" (Matt. 28 : 20); and that other promise, "the gates of hell shall not prevail" against the Church (Matt. 16 : 18). The Church understands that the present time is merely one of transition. The true and authentic future of the Church is the consummate perfection which awaits it at the end of time, the eternal glory towards which it is moving with all the unshakeable certainty which faith gives it. But in this time of transition, like Christ in his time of transition through his mortal life, the Church must continue its mission to bring life and freedom and truth and justice and charity to men. It is a share in the life, the freedom, the truth, the justice and the charity of God himself. Even more, it is the Church's mission to bring men a share in the humility of God, the humility of obedience unto death, and even death on a cross (Phil. 2 : 8). Granted all the sins and deficiencies in the Church, is there any other institution which can show such love for men, can give such cogent reasons for sincere concern for the great human family and can offer such founded hopes for peace and true brotherhood among men? Is there any other system of thought which can satisfy the mind and give adequate motives to the mass of men for a life in justice and freedom and charity? Is there a real alternative to the Church?

THE ULTIMATE CONSUMMATION

When St Paul, in his address to the Athenian philosophers, spoke of the resurrection from the dead, "some mocked, but others said 'We will hear you again about this' " (Acts 17 :32). And yet belief in the resurrection after death is a crucial belief underlying the Church's "humanitarianism", and explains the Church's reverence and care for the body as well as for the soul of man. It is a revelation of the nature of God, who approves and loves the whole material creation and wants man, the noblest in that creation, to be everlasting. It means that human love of other human beings, of husband and wife, parents and children and friends, is not bound down only to their temporary terrestrial existence, but can be timeless and unqualified: in heaven we know our own and love them in the glory of their bodily immortality. It means that man's spiritual horizons are not bounded by death but are open to limitless personal and bodily existence. It means that the death-principle rules only for a time but is conquered in the end : "then shall be brought to pass the saying that is written : 'Death is swallowed up in victory' " (1 Cor. 15 :54). The Christian martyrs did not fear to die, for they knew that death is not the end.

And the whole material creation is to share, somehow, in this splendour and felicity : St Paul assures us on this point : "For the earnest expectation of the creature waits for the (glorious) manifestation of the sons of God. For the creature was made subject to vanity, not willingly, but by reason of him who has subjected the same in hope. Because the creature itself also shall be delivered from the bondage of corruption into the glorious liberty of the children of God" (Rom. 8 :19-21). St Peter declares : "Nevertheless we, according to his promise, look for new heavens and a new earth, wherein dwelleth righteousness" (2 Peter 3 :13). And the great seer of Patmos writes : "And I saw a new heaven and a new earth : for the first heaven and the first earth were passed away; and there was no more sea. And I John saw the holy city, new Jerusalem (the Church glorified) coming down from God out of heaven, prepared as a bride adorned for her husband. And I heard a great voice out of heaven saying, Behold, the tabernacle of God is with men, and he will dwell with them, and they shall be his people, and God himself shall be with them, and be their God. And God shall wipe away all tears from their eyes; and there shall be no more death, neither sorrow, nor crying, neither shall there be any more pain; for the former things are passed away. And he that sat upon the throne said : Behold, I make all things new" (Apoc. 21 :1-5).

Is all this merely the dream of poets and visionaries too good to be true? He knows little of God's omnipotence and goodness who thinks so. His vision of reality is narrowed, his thinking is dulled and his love for humanity is the more limited. The resurrection is indeed a mystery of faith; but is it more mysterious than life itself, is it more mysterious than the mystery of love?

THE VISION OF THE PROPHETS

Where there is no vision, the people perish. From great dreams, from the great vision of the prophets, great realities are effected. The prophet Isaiah wrote: "And it shall come to pass in the last days, that the mountain of the Lord's house shall be established as in the highest of the mountains, and shall be exalted above the hills; and all nations shall flow to it. And many people shall come and say, Come, let us go up to the mountain of the Lord, to the house of the God of Jacob; and he will teach us his ways, and we will walk in his paths. For out of Zion shall go forth the law, and the word of the Lord from Jerusalem. And he shall judge between the nations, and shall decide for many people: and they shall beat their swords into ploughshares, and their spears into pruning hooks: nation shall not lift up sword against nation, neither shall they learn war any more. O house of Jacob, come, let us walk in the light of the Lord" (Isaiah 2:2-5).

Is this prophecy meant to apply only as an allegory, or only as an expression of a hope which reality inevitably proves to be an illusion? To think so will tend to make it a mere illusion, will tend to produce faith in material swords and spears—which is the greatest of illusions—and to lessen faith in the sword of the Word of God, which is the greatest of realities. Not by bread alone does man live. It is the spiritual forces in God's world which alone can bring the unity in freedom of men on which peace ultimately depends.

No Christian is a true Christian unless he feels his responsibility for the whole of the human family and is moved by sincere love for it. It is *his* family and all men are his brothers. So felt that son of a small farmer, Pope John XXIII, and he expressed the heart and mind of mankind. The Christian knows that Christ is not only "the Prince of Peace" (Isaiah 9:6) but is "our peace" (Eph. 2:14), the peace of the whole of mankind, for he is its Saviour and its peace through time and eternity.

Appendix I

UNIVERSAL DECLARATION
OF HUMAN RIGHTS[1]

Preamble

Whereas recognition of the inherent dignity and of the equal and inalienable rights of all members of the human family is the foundation of freedom, justice and peace in the world,

Whereas disregard and contempt for human rights have resulted in barbarous acts which have outraged the conscience of mankind, and the advent of a world in which human beings shall enjoy freedom of speech and belief and freedom from fear and want has been proclaimed as the highest aspiration of the common people,

Whereas it is essential, if man is not to be compelled to have recourse, as a last resort, to rebellion against tyranny and oppression, that human rights should be protected by the rule of law,

Whereas it is essential to promote the development of friendly relations between nations,

Whereas the peoples of the United Nations have in the Charter reaffirmed their faith in fundamental human rights, in the dignity and worth of the human person and in the equal rights of men and women and have determined to promote social progress and better standards of life in larger freedom,

Whereas Member States have pledged themselves to achieve, in co-operation with the United Nations, the promotion of universal respect for and observance of human rights and fundamental freedoms,

[1] See page 42, the statement of Pope John about this document.

Whereas a common understanding of these rights and freedoms is of the greatest importance for the full realization of this pledge.

Now therefore

THE GENERAL ASSEMBLY proclaims

This Universal Declaration of Human Rights as a common standard of achievement for all peoples and all nations, to the end that every individual and every organ of society, keeping this Declaration constantly in mind, shall strive by teaching and education to promote respect for these rights and freedoms and by progressive measures, national and international, to secure their universal and effective recognition and observance, both among the peoples of Member States themselves and among the peoples of territories under their jurisdiction.

Article 1. All human beings are born free and equal in dignity and rights. They are endowed with reason and conscience and should act towards one another in a spirit of brotherhood.

Article 2. Everyone is entitled to all the rights and freedoms set forth in this Declaration, without distinction of any kind, such as race, colour, sex, language, religion, political or other opinion, national or social origin, property, birth or other status. Furthermore, no distinction shall be made on the basis of the political jurisdictional or international status of the country or territory to which a person belongs, whether it be independent, trust, non-self-governing or under any other limitation of sovereignty.

Article 3. Everyone has the right to life, liberty and security of person.

Article 4. No one shall be held in slavery or servitude; slavery and the slave trade shall be prohibited in all their forms.

Article 5. No one shall be subjected to torture or to cruel, inhuman or degrading treatment or punishment.

Article 6. Everyone has the right to recognition everywhere as a person before the law.

Article 7. All are equal before the law and are entitled without any discrimination to equal protection of the law. All are en-

titled to equal protection against any discrimination in violation
of this Declaration and against any incitement to such discrimination.

Article 8. Everyone has the right to an effective remedy by the
competent national tribunals for acts violating the fundamental
rights granted him by the constitution or by law.

Article 9. No one shall be subjected to arbitrary arrest, detention
or exile.

Article 10. Everyone is entitled in full equality to a fair and
public hearing by an independent and impartial tribunal, in the
determination of his rights and obligations and of any criminal
charge against him.

Article 11. (1) Everyone charged with a penal offence has the
right to be presumed innocent until proved guilty according to
law in a public trial at which he has had all the guarantees necessary for his defence.
(2) No one shall be held guilty of any penal offence on account
of any act or omission which did not constitute a penal offence,
under national or international law, at the time when it was committed. Nor shall a heavier penalty be imposed than the one that
was applicable at the time the penal offence was committed.

Article 12. No one shall be subjected to arbitrary interference
with his privacy, family, home or correspondence, nor to attacks
upon his honour and reputation. Everyone has the right to the
protection of the law against such interference or attacks.

Article 13. (1) Everyone has the right to freedom of movement
and residence within the borders of each state.
(2) Everyone has the right to leave any country, including his
own, and to return to his country.

Article 14. (1) Everyone has the right to seek and to enjoy in
other countries asylum from persecution.
(2) This right may not be invoked in the case of prosecutions
genuinely arising from non-political crimes or from acts contrary
to the purposes and principles of the United Nations.

Article 15. (1) Everyone has the right to a nationality.

(2) No one shall be arbitrarily deprived of his nationality nor denied the right to change his nationality.

Article 16. (1) Men and women of full age, without any limitation due to race, nationality or religion, have the right to marry and to found a family. They are entitled to equal rights as to marriage, during marriage and at its dissolution.
(2) Marriage shall be entered into only with the free and full consent of the intending spouses.
(3) The family is the natural and fundamental group unit of society and is entitled to protection by society and the State.

Article 17. (1) Everyone has the right to own property alone as well as in association with others.
(2) No one shall be arbitrarily deprived of his property.

Article 18. Everyone has the right to freedom of thought, conscience and religion; this right includes freedom to change his religion or belief, and freedom, either alone or in community with others and in public or private, to manifest his religion or belief in teaching, practice, worship and observance.

Article 19. Everyone has the right to freedom of opinion and expression; this right includes freedom to hold opinions without interference and to seek, receive and impart information and ideas through any media and regardless of frontiers.

Article 20. (1) Everyone has the right to freedom of peaceful assembly and association.
(2) No one may be compelled to belong to an association.

Article 21. (1) Everyone has the right to take part in the government of his country, directly or through freely chosen representatives.
(2) Everyone has the right of equal access to public service in his country.
(3) The will of the people shall be the basis of the authority of government; this will shall be expressed in periodic and genuine elections which shall be by universal and equal suffrage and shall be held by secret vote or by equivalent free voting procedures.

Article 22. Everyone, as a member of society, has the right to social security and is entitled to realisation, through national effort and international co-operation and in accordance with the organisation and resources of each State, of the economic, social and cultural rights indispensable for his dignity and the free development of his personality.

Article 23. (1) Everyone has the right to work, to free choice of employment, to just and favourable conditions of work and to protection against unemployment.

(2) Everyone, without any discrimination, has the right to equal pay for equal work.

(3) Everyone who works has the right to just and favourable remuneration ensuring for himself and his family an existence worthy of human dignity, and supplemented, if necessary, by other means of social protection.

(4) Everyone has the right to form and to join trade unions for the protection of his interests.

Article 24. Everyone has the right to rest and leisure, including reasonable limitation of working hours and periodic holidays with pay.

Article 25. (1) Everyone has the right to a standard of living adequate for the health and well-being of himself and of his family, including food, clothing, housing and medical care and necessary social services, and the right to security in the event of unemployment, sickness, disability, widowhood, old age or other lack of livelihood in circumstances beyond his control.

(2) Motherhood and childhood are entitled to special care and assistance. All children, whether born in or out of wedlock, shall enjoy the same social protection.

Article 26. (1) Everyone has the right to education. Education shall be free, at least in the elementary and fundamental stages. Elementary education shall be compulsory. Technical and professional education shall be made generally available and higher education shall be equally accessible to all on the basis of merit.

(2) Education shall be directed to the full development of the human personality and to the strengthening of respect for human rights and fundamental freedoms. It shall promote understanding, tolerance and friendship among all nations, racial or religious groups, and shall further the activities of the United Nations for the maintenance of peace.

(3) Parents have a prior right to choose the kind of education that shall be given to their children.

Article 27. (1) Everyone has the right freely to participate in the cultural life of the community, to enjoy the arts and to share in scientific advancement and its benefits.
(2) Everyone has the right to the protection of the moral and material interests resulting from any scientific, literary or artistic production of which he is the author.

Article 28. Everyone is entitled to a social and international order in which the rights and freedoms set forth in this Declaration can be fully realised.

Article 29. (1) Everyone has duties to the community in which alone the free and full development of his personality is possible.
(2) In the exercise of his rights and freedoms, everyone shall be subject only to such limitations as are determined by law solely for the purpose of securing due recognition and respect for the rights and freedoms of others and of meeting the just requirements of morality, public order and the general welfare in a democratic society.
(3) These rights and freedoms may in no case be exercised contrary to the purposes and principles of the United Nations.

Article 30. Nothing in this Declaration may be interpreted as implying for any State, group or person any right to engage in any activity or to perform any act aimed at the destruction of any of the rights and freedoms set forth herein.

Appendix II

I would like to take this time to say a little prayer for all the people, including myself, involved in this launch operation.

Father, thank you, especially for letting me fly this flight. Thank you for the privilege of being able to be in this position; to be up in this wondrous place seeing all these many startling, wonderful things that you have created.

Help, guide and direct all of us, that we shape our lives to be much better Christians, trying to help one another, and to work with one another, rather than fighting and bickering.

Help us complete this mission successfully. Help us in our future space endeavours that we may show the world that a democracy really can compete and still are able to do things in a big way, and are able to do research, development and can conduct many scientific and very technical programs.

Be with all our families give them guidance and encouragement and let them know every thing will be okay.

We ask in Thy Name. Amen.

Appendix III

REVISED REPORT OF THE COMMISSION ON "CHRISTIAN WITNESS, PROSELYTISM AND RELIGIOUS LIBERTY"[1]

(as adopted by the Central Committee for transmission to the member churches for consideration and comment)

The Central Committee decided at its meeting in Evanston (1954) that, in view of difficulties which had arisen affecting relationships between member churches of the World Council of Churches, a Commission should be appointed for the further study of "Proselytism and Religious Liberty".

This Commission, meeting at Arnoldshain, Germany, in July 1956, prepared a provisional report under the revised title "Christian Witness, Proselytism and Religious Liberty in the Setting of the World Council of Churches". This change in title reflects the recognition that proselytism in its derogatory meaning represents a corruption of Christian witness or evangelism. It also underscores the fact that it is primarily as a problem affecting the relationships of member churches of the World Council of Churches that the study was authorized.

The provisional report of the Commission was amended by a committee of the Central Committee at Galyatetö, Hungary, in August 1956 and approved by the Central Committee for submission to the member churches to set forward our common self-examination on this difficult problem in our relationships with one another and with other churches. The provisional report was published in the *Ecumenical Review* of October, 1956.

When the question of taking further action with regard to the provisional report was raised at the meeting of the Central

---

[1] Reprinted by kind permission of the World Council of Churches; for the document's importance, cf. p. 192.

APPENDIX III 241

Committee at Rhodes in 1959 and considered by a Reference Committee, it was felt that the churches had not given sufficient response to guide the Central Committee. It therefore authorized that the provisional report be transmitted again to the member churches requesting replies by March 1, 1960. It also asked the Commission to consider the advice of the churches and the comments of the Reference Committee and to prepare a statement of policy for submission to the Central Committee in 1960 "for consideration, adoption and recommendation to the Third Assembly, in the hope that such a policy statement would prove acceptable and helpful to the churches in their relationship with one another".

In the meantime, the discussion of the proposed integration of the World Council of Churches and the International Missionary Council had contributed added interest to the study.

This revised report, drafted by the Commission at St Andrews in August, 1960, in the light of a substantial volume of careful responses from a variety of member churches and after further study, is submitted to the Central Committee in accordance with its request.

As our study has proceeded it has become increasingly clear that the poles of our problem are to be found in the right and duty of free Christian witness on the one hand, and in the obligation of an ecumenical fellowship to manifest the visible unity of the Church as the Body of Christ on the other hand. The tension is between the two, and our problem is to deal justly with both in truth and love.

Behind the tension lies the whole ecclesiological problem, which is a major concern in our continuous ecumenical association. The territorial principle is an aspect of that problem. Unsolved problems of faith and order also contribute to the tension.

Consequently, this is a modest and limited report. It attempts not so much to resolve the basic issues as to clarify the nature of the tension and to suggest some guiding principles with regard to the spirit and nature of the relationships within which the churches may best deal with the issues. Specific rules cannot be prescribed for all national and local situations. Churches which live together are therefore encouraged to strive to achieve mutual understanding, earnestly taking into consideration the ecumenical perspective of this report.

While this report is primarily concerned with relations between the member churches of the World Council, we are not unmindful of its implication for our relationships with other churches and religious groups. Our covenant as "churches which accept our Lord Jesus Christ as God and Saviour" to "stay together" in brotherly counsel and mutual aid calls for special self-searching in the way we exercise our freedom of witness. But any light we gain as to our right relations with one another is surely relevant to our relations with other churches.

I. The use of the terms: Christian witness, religious liberty and proselytism

Various meanings have been attached to the terms "witness", "religious liberty", "proselytism". The sense in which we use them in the present discussion needs to be made clear. This is especially true of "proselytism", which today has an almost completely derogatory sense: probably no church and no missionary society involved in the ecumenical movement would wish to call itself a "proselytizing body". It does not seem possible, in practice, to restore the good connotation which the word "proselyte" once carried. Thus, "proselytizing" has come to be set over against true obedience to the Great Commission: "Go therefore and make disciples of all nations, baptizing them in the name of the Father and of the Son and of the Holy Spirit, teaching them to observe all that I have commanded you. . . ." (Matt. 28 :19-20)

For this true obedience the words evangelism, apostolate, soul-winning, witness and others are now in common use. In this report the word "witness" will be employed.

a) *Christian Witness*

Witness in word and deed is the essential mission and responsibility of every Christian and of every church. All disciples stand under the Great Commission of the one Lord.

The purpose of witness is to persuade persons to accept the supreme authority of Christ, to commit themselves to Him, and to render Him loving service in the fellowship of His Church. The witness of Christians to Jesus Christ requires both personal and corporate testimony to the truth as it has been revealed to them, but no human testimony to the truth as it is in Jesus Christ can reflect that truth in its fullness. Even when inwardly compelled to testify against that which appears erroneous in some other religious belief or practice, he who would bear a true witness cannot but be humble and honest. He knows but one weight and one measure, the same for himself as for others.

Such an act of witness seeks a response which contributes to the upbuilding of the fellowship of those who acknowledge the Lordship of Christ. A person enters that fellowship by becoming a member of one of the several existing ecclesiastical communities. Both witness and response must therefore, of present necessity, take place within the existing situation of division in the Church.

This situation gives rise to problems in the relationships between the churches when one church yields to the temptation to seek its own institutional advantage at the cost of real or seeming disadvantage to another. It is a purpose of the World Council of Churches to help the several churches so to carry on their witness as to strengthen one another, and thus by their combined effort in mutual co-operation to spread the Gospel more effectively.

b) *Religious Liberty*

God's truth and love are given in freedom and call for a free response.

God does not coerce men to respond to His love; and the revelation of God in Christ is a revelation that men are not forced to accept. He calls men to make a willing and obedient response to Him in faith, to answer with a free and confident "yes" to the eternal action of His love in which He reveals Himself. This utterly free assent is undermined and destroyed when human coercion enters in. Human coercion denies the respect for every individual person which God's loving action in Christ affirms. The non-coercive method and spirit of Christ is in itself the condemnation of all attempts to force man's religious beliefs or to purchase their allegiance, and for the Christian it is the ground of religious liberty.

Every Christian has the liberty individually or in the corporate body of a church or other group to put his whole existence under the authority of God, to believe, pray, worship and proclaim

Christ, as well as to live in accordance with His will, in the church of his choice according to his own conscience. For such witness and service churches and individuals should have equality before the law.

It also follows that the conscience of persons whose religious faith and convictions differ from our own must be recognized and respected.

The right of all men to freedom of conscience and freedom of religious belief and practice is recognized by law in most countries. The article on religious liberty in the Universal Declaration of Human Rights is consistent with Christian conviction in this matter: "Everyone has the right to freedom of thought, conscience and religion; this right includes the freedom to change his religion or belief, and freedom, either alone or in community with others, and in public or in private, to manifest his religion or belief, in teaching, practice, worship and observance."

Liberty is not absolute, for it must not be exercised in such a way as to impair the Golden Rule (Matt. 7 :12).

c) "Proselytism"

Proselytism is not something absolutely different from witness: it is the corruption of witness. Witness is corrupted when cajolery, bribery, undue pressure or intimidation are used—subtly or openly—to bring about seeming conversion; when we put the success of our church before the honour of Christ; when we commit the dishonesty of comparing the ideal of our own church with the actual achievement of another; when we seek to advance own cause by bearing false witness against another church; when personal or corporate self-seeking replaces love for every individual soul with whom we are concerned. Such corruption of the Christian witness indicates lack of confidence in the power of the Holy Spirit, lack of respect for the nature of man and lack of recognition of the true character of the Gospel. It is very easy to recognize these faults and sins in others; it is necessary to acknowledge that we are all liable to fall into one or the other of them ourselves.

Since the difference between witness and proselytism is a matter of purpose, motive and spirit, as well as of means, objective criteria alone cannot adequately distinguish between the two.

Nevertheless such criteria do exist, and some general objective standards of practice are possible. The fourth section of this report attempts to describe such standards in the hope that a larger measure of mutual understanding can thereby be attained among the churches, thus rendering their common witness for Christ more faithful and more convincing.

II. Background

The issues with which this study is concerned have existed within the ecumenical movement from its very beginning. In 1920 the well-known Encyclical of the Ecumenical Patriarchate with its strong plea for co-operation among the churches asked for a definite cessation of proselytizing activities. When in the same year in Geneva the preliminary meetings of "Faith and Order" and of "Life and Work" took place, the issue was again brought up by the Orthodox representatives. In the larger and smaller ecumenical conferences during the next decades the question was often raised, but no definite action was taken. At the time when the ecclesiological significance of the World Council of Churches was discussed (Toronto 1950), this particular aspect of inter-church relationships was touched upon only very briefly. The Toronto statement says that churches should "refrain from such actions as are incompatible with brotherly relationships" and develops this point in the following manner: "The positive affirmation of each church's faith is to be welcomed, but actions incompatible with brotherly relationships toward other member churches defeat the very purpose for which the Council has been created." It was, however, not said just what is implied in this constructive relationship.

This extremely brief reference to the history of the discussion shows that these issues call for honest and careful consideration by the member churches. Failure to deal with them seriously would leave unnecessary misunderstanding in the relationships between member churches in certain areas.

Behind the issues of "proselytism" and of religious liberty here considered, there lie various historical causes, among which are the following:

1. In the modern age, technological and sociological developments in all parts of our world are changing radically the

previously established patterns of human communities. Because means of communication and of mobility have greatly increased, religious and cultural communities no longer find it possible to remain closed to outside influences, but are increasingly being influenced by ideas and movements from outside. It is only necessary to mention the far-reaching influence of newsprint and literature, radio and films, as well as the presence of foreigners and of foreign influences of all types in most countries. National boundary lines cannot any longer isolate a culture. These pervasive and dynamic influences are such that they could only be thwarted by forcible repression—as by cutting off circulation of newsprint and literature, by jamming radio communication, by forbidding free travel and entry into a country.

2. In recent years, religious and cultural communities find themselves extended far beyond their original national and ethnic borders. Refugee resettlement as well as other forms of migration have led to the extension of Orthodox, Protestant and Roman Catholic communities into new territories.

3. In the area of religious and church relationships the most disturbing situations are found where a particular church has been historically identified with the total life and culture of a country or territory, whether or not as a legally established or "state church", and is confronted by religious movements stemming from outside or appearing as spontaneous movements of renewal threatening its unity from within the territory.

The anxiety and resistance manifested by the church hitherto in sole or dominant occupancy of a territory cannot fairly be ascribed simply to a desire to maintain a privileged monopoly. These may also express a rightful concern for the preservation of the unity and integrity of the church of the nation, and for fidelity to the principle that the church of the territory has a responsibility for the whole human community in which it is set. Indeed we are witnessing, especially in Asia and Africa, vigorous efforts to achieve regional or national church unity. These concerns are often reinforced by nationalist sentiment and the serious desire to preserve the cultural unity of a people.

While it is of the utmost importance that we understand sympathetically these concerns and the real values involved, it is equally important that we recognize the problems they present to religious liberty, and the fact that in other parts of the world

Religious Perspectives

RELIGIOUS PERSPECTIVES REPRESENTS A QUEST
for the rediscovery of man. It constitutes an effort to define
man's search for the essence of being in order that he may have
a knowledge of goals. It is an endeavour to show that there is
no possibility of achieving an understanding of man's total
nature on the basis of phenomena known by the analytical
method alone. It hopes to point to the false antinomy between
revelation and reason, faith and knowledge, grace and nature,
courage and anxiety. Mathematics, physics, philosophy, biology
and religion, in spite of their almost complete independence,
have begun to sense their interrelatedness and to become aware
of that mode of cognition which teaches that "the light is not
without but within me, and I myself am the light".

Modern man is threatened by a world created by himself. He
is faced with the conversion of mind to naturalism, a dogmatic
secularism, and an opposition to a belief in the transcendent.
He begins to see, however, that the universe is given not as one
existing and one perceived but as the unity of subject and
object; that the barrier between them cannot be said to have
been dissolved as the result of recent experience in the physical
sciences, since this barrier has never existed. Confronted with the
question of meaning, he is summoned to rediscover and scrutinize
the immutable and the permanent which constitute the
dynamic, unifying aspect of life as well as the principle of
differentiation; to reconcile identity and diversity, immutability

261

and unrest. He begins to recognize that just as every person descends by his particular path, so he is able to ascend, and this ascent aims at a return to the source of creation, an inward home from which he has become estranged.

It is the hope of RELIGIOUS PERSPECTIVES that the rediscovery of man will point the way to the rediscovery of God. To this end a rediscovery of first principles should constitute part of the quest. These principles, not to be superseded by new discoveries, are not those of historical worlds that come to be and perish. They are to be sought in the heart and spirit of man, and no interpretation of a merely historical or scientific universe can guide the search. RELIGIOUS PERSPECTIVES attempts not only to ask dispassionately what the nature of God is, but also to restore to human life at least the hypothesis of God and the symbols that relate to him. It endeavours to show that man is faced with the metaphysical question of the truth of religion while he encounters the empirical question of its effects on the life of humanity and its meaning for society. Religion is here distinguished from theology and its doctrinal forms and is intended to denote the feelings, aspirations, and acts of men, as they relate to total reality.

RELIGIOUS PERSPECTIVES is nourished by the spiritual and intellectual energy of world thought, by those religious and ethical leaders who are not merely spectators but scholars deeply involved in the critical problems common to all religions. These thinkers recognize that human morality and human ideals thrive only when set in a context of a transcendent attitude toward religion and that by pointing to the ground of identity and the common nature of being in the religious experience of man, the essential nature of religion may be defined. Thus, they are committed to re-evaluate the meaning of everlastingness, an experience which has been lost and which is the content of that *visio Dei* constituting the structure of all religions. It is the many absorbed everlastingly into the ultimate unity, a unity subsuming what Whitehead calls the fluency of God and the everlastingness of passing experience.

These volumes seek to show that the unity of which we speak consists in a certitude emanating from the nature of man who seeks God and the nature of God who seeks man. Such certitude bathes in an intuitive act of cognition, participating in the divine essence and is related to the natural spirituality of intelligence. This is not by any means to say that there is an equivalence of all faiths in the traditional religions of human history. It is, however, to emphasize the distinction between the spiritual and the temporal which all religions acknowledge. For duration of thought is composed of instants superior to time, and is an intuition of the permanence of existence and its metahistorical reality. In fact, the symbol[1] itself found on cover and jacket of each volume of RELIGIOUS PERSPECTIVES is the visible sign or representation of the essence, immediacy, and timelessness of religious experience; the one immutable centre, which may be analogically related to Being in pure act, moving with centrifugal and ecumenical necessity outward into the manifold modes, yet simultaneously, with dynamic centripetal power and with full intentional energy, returning to the source. Through the very diversity of its authors, the Series shows that the basic and poignant concern of every faith is to point to, and overcome, the crisis in our apocalyptic epoch—the crisis of man's separation from man and of man's separation from God—the failure of love. The authors endeavour, moreover, to illustrate the truth that the human heart is able, and even yearns, to go to the very lengths of God; that the darkness and cold, the frozen spiritual misery of recent time, are breaking, cracking, and beginning to move, yielding to efforts to overcome spiritual muteness and moral paralysis. In this way, it is hoped, the immediacy of pain and sorrow, the primacy of tragedy and suffering in human life, may be transmuted into a spiritual and moral triumph.

RELIGIOUS PERSPECTIVES is therefore an effort to explore the *meaning* of God, an exploration which constitutes an aspect of man's intrinsic nature, part of his ontological substance. The

[1] From the original design by Leo Katz.

Series grows out of an abiding concern that in spite of the release of man's creative energy which science has in part accomplished, this very science has overturned man's conception of the essential order of nature. Shrewd as man's calculations have become concerning his means, his choice of ends, which was formerly correlated with belief in God, with absolute criteria of conduct, has become witless. God is not to be treated as an exception to metaphysical principles, invoked to prevent their collapse. He is rather their chief exemplification, the source of all potentiality. The personal reality of freedom and providence, of will and conscience, may demonstrate that "he who knows" commands a depth of consciousness inaccessible to the profane man, and is capable of that transfiguration which prevents the twisting of all good to ignominy. This religious content of experience is not within the province of science to bestow; it corrects the error of treating the scientific account as if it were itself metaphysical or religious; it challenges the tendency to make a religion of science—or a science of religion—a dogmatic act which destroys the moral dynamic of man. Indeed, many men of science are confronted with unexpected implications of their own thought and are beginning to accept, for instance, the trans-spatial and trans-temporal nature of events and of matter itself.

RELIGIOUS PERSPECTIVES attempts to show the fallacy of the apparent irrelevance of God in history. The Series submits that no convincing image of man can arise, in spite of the many ways in which human thought has tried to reach it, without a philosophy of human nature and human freedom which does not exclude God. This image of *Homo cum Deo* implies the highest conceivable freedom, the freedom to step into the very fabric of the universe, a new formula for man's collaboration with the creative process and the only one which is able to protect man from the terror of existence. This image implies further that the mind and conscience are capable of making genuine discriminations and thereby may reconcile the serious tensions between the secular and religious, the profane and sacred. The idea of the sacred lies in what it *is*, timeless existence. By emphasizing timeless existence against reason as a reality, we are liberated, in our communion with the eternal, from the otherwise unbreakable rule of "before and after". Then we are able to admit that all forms, all symbols in religions, by their negation of error and their affirmation of the actuality of truth, make it possible to experience that *knowing* which is above knowledge, and that dynamic passage of the universe to unending unity.

The volumes in this Series seek to challenge the crisis which separates, the crisis born out of a rationalism that has left no spiritual heirs, to make reasonable a religion that binds and to present the numinous reality within the experience of man. In so far as the Series succeeds in this quest, it will direct mankind toward a reality that is eternal and away from a preoccupation with that which is illusory and ephemeral.

For man is now confronted with his burden and his greatness : "He calleth to me, Watchman, what of the night ? Watchman, what of the night ?"[1] Perhaps the anguish in the human soul may be assuaged by the answer, by the *assimilation* of the person in God : "The morning cometh, and also the night : if ye will inquire, inquire ye : return, come."[2]

RUTH NANDA ANSHEN

---

[1] Isaiah 21 : 11.
[2] Isaiah 21 : 12.

Index

267